Cases in Financial Management
Directed Versions

Eugene F. Brigham
and
Louis C. Gapenski
University of Florida

The Dryden Press
Harcourt Brace College Publishers
Fort Worth   Philadelphia   San Diego   New York   Orlando   Austin   San Antonio
Toronto   Montreal   London   Sydney   Tokyo

Address for Editorial Correspondence
The Dryden Press, 301 Commerce Street, Suite 3700, Fort Worth, TX 76102

Address for Orders
The Dryden Press, 6277 Sea Harbor Drive, Orlando, FL 32887
1-800-782-4479, or 1-800-433-0001 (in Florida)

ISBN: 0-03-055024-6

Library of Congress Catalogue Number: 93-70608

Printed in the United States of America

4 5 6 7 8 9 0 1 2 3   0 5 4   9 8 7 6 5 4 3 2 1

The Dryden Press
Harcourt Brace College Publishers

The Dryden Press Series in Finance

Maisel
Real Estate Finance
Second Edition

Martin, Cox, and MacMinn
The Theory of Finance: Evidence and Applications

Mayo
Finance: An Introduction
Fourth Edition

Mayo
Investments: An Introduction
Fourth Edition

Pettijohn
PROFIT+

Reilly
Investment Analysis and Portfolio Management
Fourth Edition

Reilly
Investments
Third Edition

Sears and Trennepohl
Investment Management

Seitz
Capital Budgeting and Long-Term Financing Decisions

Siegel and Siegel
Futures Markets

Smith and Spudeck
Interest Rates: Principles and Applications

Stickney
Financial Statement Analysis: A Strategic Perspective
Second Edition

Turnbull
Option Valuation

Weston and Brigham
Essentials of Managerial Finance
Tenth Edition

Weston and Copeland
Managerial Finance
Ninth Edition

Wood and Wood
Financial Markets

The Harcourt Brace College Outline Series

Baker
Financial Management

Preface

Financial management can be a fascinating, exciting subject, yet students often regard it as being either too mechanical or too theoretical. However, one can overcome this misconception and demonstrate the inherent richness of finance by relating the various topics to practices in the real world. Years ago we found that if we illustrated a point by referring to an actual situation, our students' curiosity intensified, their powers of concentration sharpened, and we were able to impart more knowledge than if we dealt strictly with abstractions or hypothetical situations.

We then began using cases in our courses, primarily Harvard cases, but the experience was not satisfactory, at least not in our intermediate level undergraduate and introductory MBA courses, where we use a combination of lectures and case discussions. To be most effective, we needed a set of cases (1) which deal with the major principles and analytical techniques that are covered in the current mainline texts and which, in consequence, reinforce and illustrate the concepts that are covered in those texts, (2) which contain both numerical and conceptual questions designed to stimulate discussion, (3) which can be worked (generally) in 3 to 5 hours, and (4) which serve to illustrate how computers can be used in financial analysis.

Alternative Versions of the Casebook

Although our cases served our needs well, we and others concluded that we needed somewhat different versions of the cases, and different numbers of cases, in different situations. Accordingly, we have developed several alternatives as discussed below.

Preface

The Directed Casebook. The directed casebook, which is a direct descendent of our original casebook, has been renamed *Cases in Financial Management, Directed Versions*. We use the word "directed" in the title to signify that these cases have end-of-case questions. To create this casebook, we reviewed and screened all the cases we had developed over the years. Overall, after years of use, we have been satisfied with the original cases (at least for some purposes as we explain later), so we decided it would be best not to try to fix something that wasn't broken. Therefore, the changes in the directed casebook are generally minor—we updated, revised, and improved the cases, and we changed some data in almost every case so that student "solution banks" developed for the first casebook could not be easily used with this casebook. However, the general "look and feel" of the 41 cases in the directed casebook is similar to our earlier casebook.

The Nondirected Casebook. Even though we were generally satisfied with the format of the cases in our first casebook, at times we wished we had cases that were less directed. The end-of-case questions provide guidance to students and help keep them on the right track, but these questions have a serious drawback—students do not have to develop a strategy for solving the case, which is perhaps the most important skill in real world problem solving. Therefore, we wanted to have some cases that do not lead students by the hand but, at the same time, do not leave them in such a quandary that they can't get started.

We believed that the solution to our problem lay in a new type of case—one which replaces the end-of-case questions with one or two paragraphs of executive guidance. These cases would require students to develop their own approach to the case solution, but they would be receiving some guidance, just as managers typically receive some guidance from senior executives.

We chose 20 of our most-used cases and recast them into new "nondirected" cases. First, we moved any essential data that appeared in the questions to the body of the case. Then, we replaced the questions with one or two "executive guidance paragraphs." The end result is a set of 20 cases that require students to develop their own approaches to solving the case, but which still provide suffcient guidance to point them in the right direction. This new casebook is titled *Cases in Financial Management, Nondirected Versions*.

The BY REQUEST System. When we first developed the nondirected cases, we thought we would use them in our MBA courses while using the directed cases in our undergraduate courses. Our rationale here was that graduate students would be better able to structure case solutions, and hence require less guidance. However, the advent of the BY REQUEST system has caused us to change our minds. BY REQUEST is a system that permits instructors to create a customized casebook consisting of any number of cases selected from the entire set of 61 directed and nondirected cases.

The BY REQUEST system thus allows instructors to create a casebook that includes a mix of directed and nondirected cases. Now that an easy, cost-effective way exists to use both directed and nondirected cases in a single course, we plan to use both types of cases in our courses. We will start with some directed cases to give students an idea of what a good case solution looks like, and then end the course with some nondirected cases, to give students experience in crafting solution strategies. In that way, we can have the best of both worlds, and our students will gain the most value from the course.

Parallel Cases

Certain key topics such as cost of capital and capital budgeting are essential to any corporate finance course, so we use cases that cover these essential topics every term. To avoid problems with using the same cases in consecutive terms, or in two sections being taught in the same term, we created pairs of cases on several topics. These cases, which we call "parallel cases," are listed below:

Topic	Cases	
Cost of capital	4,	5
Capital structure policy	9,	10
Project cash flow estimation	12,	14
Project risk analysis	13,	15
Dividend policy	19,	20
Lease analysis	25,	26
Financial analysis	35,	36

The case pairs listed here are similar in content, hence they serve as substitutes when preparing a course syllabus. *Do not assign both cases of a pair to a single group of students!*

Use of the Directed Cases

We have used the directed cases primarily in the second-level undergraduate course, although we have also used them in both the introductory and advanced MBA finance courses. In the future, we will likely use a mix of directed and nondirected cases in all of our courses. For both types of cases, we generally require each student to work the case, although we do encourage them to work in groups. Often we have students, in groups of 3 to 4, make presentations, and we and the other students serve as the "Board of Directors," asking questions much as a real board would do. We also require students to write up and hand in a number of the cases, primarily because we feel that they need practice writing but also to ensure that they are working the cases.

We, and others, have found that using cases makes it much easier to motivate our students, majors and nonmajors alike. Students can see the importance of finance in actual business decisions, and, for many students, the cases have transformed finance from a sterile, mechanical, and overly "theoretical" subject into an interesting, pragmatic one. Also, by demonstrating why it is important to master theory, the cases actually cause students to learn more of the abstract, theoretical material than they would otherwise.

Lotus 1-2-3 Models

Lotus 1-2-3 and similar computer spreadsheet programs have become extremely important in all aspects of finance, and especially in financial management. Further, students are becoming increasingly computer literate, and more and more of them know at least the basics of *1-2-3* or a similar spreadsheet program when they come into the course. It is important that those students who have learned something about computers be given the opportunity to hone their skills, and this suggests that they be allowed (or required) to use spreadsheet programs to help analyze cases. If students are not familiar with spreadsheets, it is perhaps even more important that they be exposed to them, because "functional literacy" in finance today means at least some knowledge of spreadsheet analysis. These points motivated us to make *Lotus 1-2-3*, which is the dominant spreadsheet program and which is also compatible with virtually all the other programs, an integral part of the cases, although they can be worked using only a calculator.

As we wrote the cases, we developed well-structured, user-friendly *Lotus* models for most of the cases that analyze the problems presented. These analyses could, of course, be done with a calculator, but the *1-2-3* models are far more efficient, especially if students are expected to perform sensitivity and scenario analyses. The next question was, "Should we provide the models to the students, should we make students do all the *Lotus* programming themselves, or should we provide them with partially completed models?" We experimented with this issue over the approximately three years it took us to write the original casebook, and our conclusions were (1) that it would take our students far too long to do all the modeling, but (2) that if we gave them the completed model, they would simply use it as a black box to generate answers. Thus, the only practical solution was to provide them with partially completed models.

Unfortunately, there is no such thing as an optimal partially completed student model—the optimal amount of completion depends on what the instructor wants to accomplish and on the backgrounds of the students. If students are relatively proficient with *Lotus*, and if an instructor wants to emphasize financial modeling, then most of the cells should be erased, and students should be required to develop most (or even all) of the formulas for themselves. On the other hand, if the students do not have a very good background with *Lotus*, and if the instructor is more interested in having students see what spreadsheets can do than in having them do the actual modeling, then only the minimum number of cells should be erased. We solved this dilemma in the following way. A diskette with the completed instructor versions of the models is available to adopting instructors. However, the completed models contain three macros that permit instructors to create student versions of the models in three levels of difficulty—easy, medium, and difficult, with the easy models having relatively few cells erased. Thus, instructors can choose the type of model they want to make available to students on the basis of their students' *Lotus* skills and time constraints, for what is optimal for one group of students may not be so for another group.

At Florida, our students have widely varying backgrounds—some are quite good with *Lotus*, while others have managed to learn almost nothing about it prior to working the cases. Students with good *Lotus* skills can generally complete the easy student models in about a half hour (less for some models, slightly more for others), although they often get interested in the structure of the models and spend quite a bit of time going over them. The less computer-oriented students have to spend more time, at least early in the term. To force those students with only rudimentary *Lotus* skills to learn more, we typically start the course by making the easy student models available, then progress to medium, and finally end the course with one or two difficult models, where students must do most of the modeling.

To help those students that are using this casebook in conjunction with our finance textbook *Intermediate Financial Management*, we have included a spreadsheet tutorial (Appendix A) in the text. Also, a technology supplement that includes a spreadsheet tutorial is available to instructors who adopt *Financial Management: Theory and Practice*. This supplement can be copied and distributed to students. For students with limited *Lotus* skills who want to learn more about spreadsheets, we recommend *Finance with Lotus 1-2-3: Text and Models*, by Brigham, Aberwald, and Gapenski (Dryden Press, 1992). This book, which is a complete self-study course in spreadsheet basics and applications, was specifically designed to be used as a supplement in courses where *Lotus* cases are used and where students do not have access to a regular course on spreadsheets.

Acknowledgments

We have been working on these cases, and their predecessors, and also on the textbooks the cases illustrate, for a long time, and a great many individuals have contributed to the effort. Included are Mike Adler, Ed Altman, Bruce Anderson, Ron Anderson, Bob Angell, Vince Apilado, Bob Aubey, Gil Babcock, Peter Bacon, Bruce Bagamery, Kent Baker, Robert Balik, Stuart Bancroft, Tom Bankston, Les Barenbaum, Charles Barngrover, Chris Barry, Bill Beedles, Moshe Ben-Horim, Bill Beranek, Tom Berry, Bill Bertin, Scott Besley, Roger Bey, John Bildersee, Russ Boisjoly, Keith Boles, Geof Booth, Kenneth Boudreaux, Helen Bowers, Oswald Bowlin, Don Boyd, Pat Boyer, Joe Brandt, Elizabeth Brannigan, Greg Brauer, Mary Broske, Dave Brown, Kate Brown, Bill Brueggeman, Brian Butler, Kirt Butler, Bill Campsey, Bob Carleson, Severin Carlson, David Cary, Steve Celec, Don Chance, Antony Chang, Susan Chaplinsky, Jay Choi, S. K. Choudhury, Lal Chugh, Maclyn Clouse, Margaret Considine, Phil Cooley, Joe Copeland, David Cordell, John Cotner, Charles Cox, David Crary, Roy Crum, Brent Dalrymple, Bill Damon, Faramarz Damanpour, Joel Dauten, Steve Dawson, Sankar De, Miles Delano, Fred Dellva, James Desreumaux, Bernard Dill, Greg Dimkoff, Les Dlabay, Mark Dorfman, Gene Drycimski, Dean Dudley, David Durst, Ed Dyl, Dick Edelman, Charles Edwards, John Ellis, Dave Ewert, John Ezzell, Michael Ferri, Jim Filkins, John Finnerty, Susan Fischer, Steven Flint, Russ Fogler, Bruce Fredrikson, Dan French, Tim Gallagher, Michael Garlington, Jim Garvin, Adam Gehr, Jim Gentry, Philip Glasgo, Rudyard Goode, Walt Goulet, Bernie Grablowsky, Ed Grossnickle, John Groth, Alan Grunewald, Manak Gupta, Sam Hadaway, Don Hakala, Gerald Hamsmith, William Hardin, John Harris, Paul Hastings, Bob Haugen, Steve Hawke, Del Hawley, Robert Hehre, George Hettenhouse, Hans Heymann, Kendall Hill, Roger Hill, Tom Hindelang, Ralph Hocking, Ronald Hoffmeister, Robert Hollinger, Jim Horrigan, John Houston, John Howe, Keith Howe, Steve Isberg, Jim Jackson, Kose John, Craig Johnson,

Preface

Keith Johnson, Ramon Johnson, Ray Jones, Manuel Jose, Gus Kalogeras, Mike Keenan, Bill Kennedy, Carol Kiefer, Joe Kiernan, Rick Kish, Don Knight, Dorothy Koehl, Jaroslaw Komarynsky, Duncan Kretovich, Harold Krogh, Charles Kroncke, Joan Lamm, Larry Lang, P. Lange, Howard Lanser, Martin Laurence, Ed Lawrence, Wayne Lee, Jim LePage, John Lewis, Chuck Linke, Bill Lloyd, Susan Long, Judy Maese, Bob Magee, Ileen Malitz, Phil Malone, Terry Maness, Chris Manning, S. K. Mansinger, Terry Martell, D. J. Masson, John Mathys, John McAlhany, Andy McCollough, Tom McCue, Bill McDaniel, Robin McLaughlin, Jamshid Mehran, Larry Merville, Rick Meyer, Jim Millar, Ed Miller, John Mitchell, Carol Moerdyk, Bob Moore, Barry Morris, Gene Morris, Fred Morrissey, Chris Muscarella, David Nachman, Tim Nantell, Don Nast, Bill Nelson, Bob Nelson, Bob Niendorf, Timothy Nohr, Tom O'Brien, Dennis O'Connor, John O'Donnell, Jim Olsen, Robert Olsen, Jim Pappas, Stephen Parrish, Glenn Petry, Jim Pettijohn, Rich Pettit, Dick Pettway, Hugo Phillips, John Pinkerton, Gerald Pogue, R. Potter, Franklin Potts, R. Powell, Chris Prestopino, Jerry Prock, Howard Puckett, Herbert Quigley, George Racette, Bob Radcliffe, Bill Rentz, Ken Riener, Charles Rini, John Ritchie, Pietra Rivoli, Antonio Rodriguez, E. M. Roussakis, Dexter Rowell, Jim Sachlis, Abdul Sadik, Thomas Scampini, Kevin Scanlon, Mary Jane Scheuer, Carl Schweser, John Settle, Alan Severn, Sol Shalit, Frederic Shipley, Dilip Shome, Ron Shrieves, Neil Sicherman, J. B. Silvers, Mark Simmons, Clay Singleton, Joe Sinkey, Stacy Sirmans, Jaye Smith, Patricia Smith, Steve Smith, Don Sorenson, David Speairs, Ken Stanly, Ed Stendardi, Alan Stephens, Don Stevens, Jerry Stevens, Glen Strasburg, Philip Swensen, Ernie Swift, Sloan Swindle, Paul Swink, Gary Tallman, Dennis Tanner, Russ Taussig, Richard Teweles, Ted Teweles, Andrew Thompson, William Tozer, George Trivoli, George Tsetsekos, David Upton, Howard Van Auken, Pretorious Van den Dool, Pieter Vanderburg, Paul Vanderheiden, Jim Verbrugge, Patrick Vincent, Steve Vinson, Susan Visscher, John Wachowicz, Mike Walker, Sam Weaver, Kuo Chiang Wei, Bill Welch, Fred Weston, Norm Williams, Tony Wingler, Ed Wolfe, Larry Wolken, Don Woods, Michael Yonan, Dennis Zocco, and Kent Zumwalt.

We are also indebted to the following reviewers who carefully evaluated all or parts of the manuscript and offered valuable comments and suggestions for improvement: Hamdi Bilici, California State University, Long Beach; Jon Ewert, The College of Santa Fe; Janet Hamilton, Portland State University; Michael Schellenger, University of Wisconsin–Oshkosh. Special thanks are due to Pamela Coats, Harry Comeskey, Gregg Dimkoff, and Dilip Shome for their help and advice as we were making the final decisions on the original cases and on the

Preface

structure of the book. A number of Florida students provided us with many insightful comments plus invaluable help with the models and solutions, including Brian Butler, Randy Gressett, Andy Janssen, and Elizabeth Kantrowitz. Brent Gibbs and Dan Zinn deserve special thanks for their indispensable contributions to the most recent versions of the cases, including the models. In addition to students, several faculty members, especially Dana Aberwald, contributed to the book. The College of Business Administration at the University of Florida provided us with intellectual support in writing and testing the manuscript, and Carol Stanton did her usual great job typing, proofing, and coordinating the many revisions and last minute changes that had to be made. Finally, we want to express our appreciation to The Dryden Press staff, especially Diana Farrell, Rick Hammonds, Shana Lum, Jim Patterson, Mike Roche, Barbara Rosenberg, and Liz Widdicombe for their patience, under-standing, consideration, and unwavering support in bringing the book to completion.

The field of finance continues to undergo significant changes and advances. It is stimulating to participate in these developments, and we sincerely hope that these cases will help to communicate the important issues in finance to future generations of students.

Eugene F. Brigham
College of Business

Louis C. Gapenski
College of Business
College of Health Related Professions

University of Florida
Gainesville, Florida 32611

Contents

VI

Long-Term Financing Decisions 171

VII

Working Capital Decisions 233

I

Fundamental
Concepts

1

Discounted Cash Flow Analysis

Davis, Michaels, and Company

Tom Davis was born and raised in San Francisco and served as a Navy lieutenant in Vietnam. After his discharge he used the GI Bill to attend NYU, where he received his degree in finance and held a part-time job at Steel, Robbins, Hernandez, and Associates, a regional brokerage firm headquartered in New York City. After graduation he was offered a permanent position with Steel, which he gladly accepted. While at the firm, Tom became friends with Gene Michaels, a Stanford MBA who had been working as a financial analyst with the company for just over a year. Although Tom enjoyed his work, his ultimate goal was to open a financial consulting firm in his hometown. After five years, Tom managed to save enough commissions to realize his goal. He convinced Gene to become his partner and to move to San Francisco to open their own financial consulting firm, Davis, Michaels, and Company.

Davis, Michaels, and Company provides financial planning services to upper-middle-class professionals. Basically, the firm provides consulting services in the areas of income tax planning, investment planning, insurance planning, estate planning, and employee benefits planning for small, family-owned businesses. The firm is heavily involved in the Chinese community where Tom has close ties. Also, both he and Gene speak fluent Chinese. The firm does not have a tax lawyer or CPA on its staff, so Tom and Gene hire outside experts when a problem arises which they cannot handle, but this is rare.

Business has been good, perhaps too good. Tom and Gene have been working overtime to handle the load, and no end is in sight. In fact, Tom recently turned away several potential customers because he didn't think that the firm could offer them the high degree of personal service that it usually gives its customers. As a permanent solution, he is talking to career resource center personnel at several universities.

He hopes to hire a finance major who can start work immediately after graduation, but that is still several months away.

In the meantime, Tom believes that Janet Ho, the firm's top secretary, can handle various financial analysis duties after turning over some of her clerical duties to someone else. Janet has been taking night courses in business at a community college, and she is convinced that she can handle increased responsibilities. Tom has a great deal of faith in Janet—she has been with the firm from the very beginning, and her great personality and sound work ethic have contributed substantially to the firm's success. Still, Tom knows that there is little room for error in this business. Customers must be confident that their financial plans are soundly conceived and properly implemented. Any mistakes create instant mistrust, and the word spreads quickly.

To make sure that Janet has the skills to do the job, Tom plans to give her a short test. As far as Tom is concerned, the single most important concept in financial planning, whether it be personal or corporate, is discounted cash flow (DCF) analysis. He believes that if Janet has solid skills in this area, then she will be able to succeed in her expanded role with minimal supervision. The basis for the test is an actual analysis that Tom is currently working on for one of his clients. The client has $10,000 to invest with a goal of accumulating enough money in 5 years to pay for his daughter's first year of college at a prestigious Ivy League school. He has directed Tom to evaluate only fixed interest securities (bonds, bank certificates of deposit, and the like) since he does not want to put his daughter's future at risk.

One alternative is to invest the $10,000 in a bank certificate of deposit (CD) currently paying about 10 percent interest. CDs are available in maturities from 6 months to 10 years, and interest can be handled in one of two ways—the buyer can receive interest payments every 6 months or reinvest the interest in the CD. In the latter case, the buyer receives no interest during the life of the CD, but receives the accumulated interest plus principal amount at maturity. Since the goal is to accumulate funds over 5 years, all interest earned would be reinvested.

However, Tom must also evaluate some other alternatives. His client is considering spending $8,000 on home improvements this year, and hence he would have only $2,000 to invest. In this situation, Tom's client plans to invest an additional $2,000 at the end of each year for the following 4 years, for a total of 5 payments of $2,000 each. A final possibility is that the client might spend the entire $10,000 on home improvements and then borrow funds for his daughter's first year of college.

To check your skills at DCF analysis, place yourself in Janet's shoes and take the following test.

Questions

1. Consider a 1-year, $10,000 CD.

    a. What is its value at maturity (future value) if it pays 10.0 percent (annual) interest?

    b. What would be the future value if the CD pays 5.0 percent? If it pays 15.0 percent?

    c. The First National Bank of San Francisco offers CDs with a 10.0 percent nominal (stated) interest rate but compounded semiannually. What is the effective annual rate on such a CD? What would its future value be?

    d. Pacific Trust offers 10.0 percent CDs with daily compounding. What is such a CD's effective annual rate and its value at maturity?

    e. What nominal rate would the First National Bank have to offer to make its semiannual compounding CD competitive with Pacific's daily-compounding CD?

2. Now consider a 5-year CD. Rework Parts a through d of Question 1 using a 5-year ending date.

3. It is estimated that in 5 years the total cost for one year of college will be $20,000.

    a. How much must be invested today in a CD paying 10.0 percent annual interest in order to accumulate the needed $20,000?

    b. If only $10,000 is invested, what annual interest rate is needed to produce $20,000 after 5 years?

    c. If only $10,000 is invested, what stated rate must the First National Bank offer on its semiannual compounding CD to accumulate the required $20,000?

4. Now consider the second alternative—5 annual payments of $2,000 each. Assume that the payments are made at the end of each year.

   a. What type of annuity is this?

   b. What is the future value of this annuity if the payments are invested in an account paying 10.0 percent interest annually?

   c. What is the future value if the payments are invested with the First National Bank which offers semiannual compounding?

   d. What size payment would be needed to accumulate $20,000 under annual compounding at a 10.0 percent interest rate?

   e. What lump sum, if deposited today, would produce the same ending value as in Part b?

   f. Suppose the payments are only $1,000 each, but are made every 6 months, starting 6 months from now. What would be the future value if the 10 payments were invested at 10.0 percent annual interest? If they were invested at the First National Bank which offers semiannual compounding?

5. Assume now that the payments are made at the beginning of each period. Repeat the analysis in Question 4.

6. Now consider the following schedule of payments:

End of Year	Payment
0	$2,000
1	2,000
2	0
3	1,500
4	2,500
5	4,000

   a. What is the value of this payment stream at the end of Year 5 if the payments are invested at 10.0 percent annually?

   b. What payment today (Year 0) would be needed to accumulate the needed $20,000? (Assume that the payments for Years 1 through 5 remain the same.)

7. Consider Bay City Savings Bank, which pays 10.0 percent interest compounded continuously.

   a. What is the effective annual rate under these terms?

   b. What is the future value of a $10,000 lump sum after 5 years?

   c. What is the future value of a 5-year ordinary annuity with payments of $2,000 each?

8. The client is also considering borrowing the $20,000 for his daughter's first year of college and repaying the loan over a four-year period. Assuming that he can borrow the funds at a 10 percent interest rate, what amount of interest and principal will be repaid at the end of each year?

9. Assume that you are given a set of cash flows on a time line and asked to find their present value. How would you choose the discount rate to apply to these flows?

10. If you are using the *Lotus 1-2-3* model, first examine the model closely to see how it works and then complete the model. Don't hesitate to change input values to obtain a better grasp of the model. Also, don't forget to look at the graphs. After you are thoroughly familiar with the model, write a short summary of *Lotus's* DCF capabilities. Include not only what spreadsheets can do, but how they can be used in financial management decision making.

2

Risk and Return

Peachtree Securities, Inc. (A)

Peachtree Securities is a regional brokerage house based in Atlanta. Although the firm is only 20 years old, it has prospered by following a simple goal—providing quality personal brokerage services to small investors. Jake Taylor, the firm's founder and president, is well-satisfied with Peachtree's progress. However, he is apprehensive about the future, as more and more of the firm's customers are buying mutual funds rather than individual stocks and bonds. Thus, even though the number of customers per office has been increasing because of population growth, the number of transactions per customer has been decreasing, and hence sales growth has slackened.

Taylor believes this trend will continue, so he has been actively expanding his product line in an effort to increase sales volume. As a first step, Peachtree began offering trust and portfolio management services five years ago. Many of the trust clients are retirees who are interested primarily in current income rather than capital gains. Thus, an average portfolio consists mostly of bonds and high yield stocks. The stock component is heavily weighted with electric utilities, an industry that has traditionally paid high dividends. For example, the average electric company's dividend yield was about 6.3 percent in 1992, versus an average stock's yield of 3.1 percent.

Until 1993, Peachtree had no in-house security analysts—all stock and bond selections were based on research provided by subscription services. However, these services had become very costly, and the volume of portfolio management had reached the point where hiring an in-house analyst was now cost-effective. Because most of its portfolios were heavily weighted with electric utilities, Peachtree created its first analyst position to track this industry. Taylor hired Laura Donahue, a recent graduate of the University of Georgia, to fill the job.

Donahue reported to work in early January, 1993, jubilant at having the opportunity to use the skills she had worked so hard to learn. Taylor then informed her that her first task would be to conduct a seminar for a group of Peachtree customers on stock investments, including the effects of different securities on portfolio performance. Donahue was asked to pick an electric utility, assess its riskiness, develop an estimate of its required rate of return on equity, and then present her findings to a group of Peachtree's customers.

Donahue's first step—choosing the company—was simple. She had been born and raised in Tampa, Florida, so she picked TECO Energy, Inc., the holding company for Tampa Electric. Next, she searched for information on the company. Donahue remembered using the *Value Line Investment Survey* during her student days, so she turned to this source first. (See Figure 1 on the last page of this case.) Then, she spent a few days reviewing industry trends to gain an historical perspective.

Electric utilities are granted monopolies to provide electric service in a given geographical area. In exchange for the franchise, the company is subjected to regulation over both the prices it may charge and the quality of its service. In theory, regulation acts to prevent the company from abusing its monopoly position, and its prices are set to mimic those that would occur if the firm were operating under perfect competition. Under such competition, the firm would earn its cost of capital, no more and no less.

In the 1950s and much of the 1960s, electric utilities were in an ideal position. Their costs were declining because of technological advances and economies of scale in generation and distribution. This made everyone happy—managers, regulators, stockholders, and customers. However, the situation changed dramatically during the 1970s, when inflation, along with high gas and oil prices, pushed construction and operating costs to levels which were unimaginable just a few years earlier. The result was a massive change in the economics of the industry and in how investors viewed electric utilities.

Today, the industry is facing many challenges including cogeneration, diversification, deregulation, and nuclear generation. Cogeneration is the combined production of electricity and thermal power, usually steam. Most electric companies use coal or nuclear energy to generate electricity. In the 1980s, though, oil and gas prices dropped sharply, making it cheaper to generate with gas or oil. However, one cannot burn gas or oil in a coal or nuclear plant. The changed fuel cost situation, combined with a need for steam, made it profitable for many industrial customers to switch to cogeneration. This, in turn, has made it very difficult for utilities to forecast industrial demand. Also, since utilities must buy any surplus power generated by their former customers, companies with cogeneration plants are, in effect, competing with the electric companies.

Diversification, or expansion into nonregulated industries, is being evaluated by many utility companies. Due to large depreciation flows following completion of major plant construction programs in the early 1980's, many companies now have cash flows that exceed immediate needs. Industry officials believe that usage of these cash flows to diversify into nonregulated industries would smooth out the financial risks of the regulated business, while providing companies an opportunity to earn returns above those allowed by regulation. To facilitate diversification, many electric utilities, including TECO, have formed holding companies under which the parent company holds both regulated and nonregulated subsidiaries.

Diversification does have some potential downside for both utility customers (ratepayers) and stockholders. Ratepayers are supposed to pay the costs associated with producing and delivering power, plus enough to cover the utility's cost of capital. However, a diversified utility could, theoretically, allocate some corporate costs that should be assigned to the unregulated (diversified) subsidiaries to the regulated utility. This would cause reported profits to be abnormally high for the nonregulated business. In effect, ratepayers would be subsidizing the nonregulated businesses. The total corporation's overall rate of return would be excessive, because it would be earning the regulated cost of capital on utility operations and more than a competitive return on nonregulated operations. Of course, regulators are aware of all this, so their auditors are always on the alert to detect and prevent improper cost allocations.

There are two significant risks to stockholders from utility diversification programs. First, there is the chance that utility executives, who generally have limited exposure to intense competition, will fail in the competitive, nonregulated, markets they enter. In that case, money that could have been paid out as dividends will have been lost in business ventures that turned out to be unprofitable. Second, if the diversified activities are highly profitable, causing the overall corporation to earn a high rate of return, then regulators might reduce the returns allowed on the utility operations. There is always a question as to what a company's cost of capital really is—hence the rate of return the utility commission should allow it to earn—and it is easier for a commission to set the allowed rate of return at the low end of any reasonable range if the company is highly profitable because of successful nonregulated businesses. Thus, it has been argued that diversified utilities might be getting into a "can't-win" situation. As one analyst put it, a diversified utility's stockholders are in a "heads you win, tails I lose" situation.

There is also much discussion at present about the deregulation of the electricity markets per se, and there is much controversy over the forced use of "wheeling," whereby a customer (usually a large industrial customer) buys power from some other party but gets delivery over the transmission lines of the utility in whose service area it operates. This situation has occurred to a large extent in the gas industry, where large customers have contracted directly with producers and then forced (through legal actions) pipeline companies to deliver the gas.

Another problem facing many, but not all, electric companies relates to nuclear plants. A few decades ago, nuclear power was thought by many to be the wave of the future in electric generation. It was widely believed that nuclear was cleaner and cheaper than coal, oil, and gas generation. However, the 1979 accident at Three Mile Island almost instantly reversed the future of nuclear power. Many plants that were under construction at that time were canceled, while the costs of completing the remaining plants skyrocketed. Many partially completed plants had to be retrofitted with new safety devices. As a result, the cost of power from new nuclear plants rose dramatically. Further, several states have held referendums to close nuclear plants.

With this industry overview in mind, Laura Donahue developed the data in Table 1 on returns expected in the coming year. TECO is the stock of primary interest, Gold Hill is a domestic gold mining company, and the S&P 500 Fund is a mutual fund that invests in the stocks which make up the S&P 500 index. Donahue's final preparatory step was to outline some questions that she believed to be relevant to the task at hand. See if you can answer the questions she developed.

Table 1
Estimated Total Returns

		Estimated Total Returns			
State of the Economy	Probability	1-Year T-Bond	TECO	Gold Hill	S&P 500 Fund
Recession	0.10	8.0 %	− 8.0%	18.0 %	− 15.0 %
Below average	0.20	8.0	2.0	23.0	0.0
Average	0.40	8.0	14.0	7.0	15.0
Above average	0.20	8.0	25.0	− 3.0	30.0
Boom	0.10	8.0	33.0	2.0	45.0

Questions

1. Why is the T-bond return in Table 1 shown to be independent of the state of the economy? Is the return on a 1-year T-bond risk-free?

2. Calculate the expected rate of return on each of the four alternatives listed in Table 1. Based solely on expected returns, which of the potential investments appears best?

3. Now calculate the standard deviations and coefficients of variation of returns for the four alternatives. What type of risk do these statistics measure? Is the standard deviation or the coefficient of variation the better measure? How do the alternatives compare when risk is considered? (Hint: For the S&P 500, the standard deviation = 16.4%; for Gold Hill, the standard deviation = 9.1%.)

4. Suppose an investor forms a stock portfolio by investing $10,000 in Gold Hill and $10,000 in TECO.

    a. What would be the portfolio's expected rate of return, standard deviation, and coefficient of variation? How does this compare with values for the individual stocks? What characteristic of the two investments makes risk reduction possible?

    b. What do you think would happen to the portfolio's expected rate of return and standard deviation if the portfolio contained 75 percent Gold Hill? If it contained 75 percent TECO? If you are using the *Lotus 1-2-3* model for this case, calculate the expected returns and standard deviations for a portfolio mix of 0 percent TECO, 10 percent TECO, 20 percent TECO, and so on, up to 100 percent TECO.

5. Now consider a portfolio consisting of $10,000 in TECO and $10,000 in the S&P 500 Fund. Would this portfolio have the same risk-reducing effect as the Gold Hill-TECO portfolio considered in Question 4? Explain. If you are using the *Lotus* model, construct a portfolio using TECO and the S&P 500 Fund. What are the expected returns and standard deviations for a portfolio mix of 0 percent TECO, 10 percent TECO, 20 percent TECO, and so on, up to 100 percent TECO?

6. Suppose an investor starts with a portfolio consisting of one randomly selected stock.

    a. What would happen to the portfolio's risk if more and more randomly selected stocks were added?

    b. What are the implications for investors? Do portfolio effects impact the way investors should think about the riskiness of individual securities? Would you expect this to affect companies' costs of capital?

    c. Explain the differences between total risk, diversifiable (company-specific) risk, and market risk.

    d. Assume that you choose to hold a single stock portfolio. Should you expect to be compensated for all of the risk that you bear?

7. Now change Table 1 by crossing out the state of the economy and probability columns and replacing them with Year 1, Year 2, Year 3, Year 4, and Year 5. Then, plot three lines on a scatter diagram which shows the returns on the S&P 500 (the market) on the X axis and (1) T-bond returns, (2) TECO returns, and (3) Gold Hill returns on the Y axis. What are these lines called? Estimate the slope coefficient of each line. What is the slope coefficient called, and what is its significance? What is the significance of the distance between the plot points and the regression line, i.e., the errors? (Note: If you have a calculator with statistical functions, use linear regression to find the slope coefficients.)

8. Plot the Security Market Line. (Hint: Use Table 1 data to obtain the risk-free rate and the required rate of return on the market.) What is the required rate of return on TECO's stock using *Value Line's* beta estimate of 0.6 as reported in Figure 1? Based on the CAPM analysis, should investors buy TECO stock?

9. What would happen to TECO's required rate of return if inflation expectations increased by 3 percentage points above the estimate embedded in the 8.0 percent risk-free rate? Now go back to the original inflation estimate, where $k_{RF} = 8\%$, and indicate what would happen to TECO's required rate of return if investors' risk aversion increased so that the market risk premium rose from 7 percent to 8 percent. Now go back to the original conditions ($k_{RF} = 8\%$, $RP_M = 7\%$) and assume that TECO's beta rose from 0.6 to 1.0. What effect would this have on the required rate of return?

10. What is the efficient markets hypothesis (EMH)? What impact does this theory have on decisions concerning the investment in securities? Is it applicable to real assets such as plant and equipment? What impact does the EMH have on corporate financing decisions? Should Jake Taylor be concerned about the EMH when he considers adding to his staff of security analysts? Explain.

(The following questions require an introductory knowledge of business risk and financial risk. They may be assigned as part of the case or merely be discussed in class.)

11. *Value Line* indicates in Figure 1 that non-utility businesses will account for much of TECO's earnings growth. Suppose *Value Line* specified that an increasing portion of TECO's assets would be devoted to nonregulated businesses in the future (i.e. greater diversification). Would this fact affect the validity of *Value Line*'s 0.6 beta for decision purposes? If so, how? (Hint: *Value Line* bases its beta estimates on historical returns over the past 5 years.)

12. Notwithstanding the *Value Line* report, suppose TECO's long-term debt ratio (Long-term debt/Total assets) decreased during the period 1982 through 1992. Further, suppose this ratio was projected to continue decreasing in 1993 and beyond. What impact would this have on TECO's riskiness, hence on its beta and required rate of return on equity?

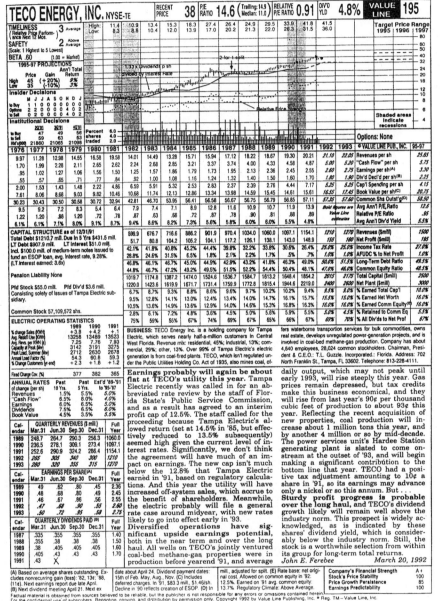

Figure 1. *Value Line Investment Survey* Report

3

Bond and Stock Valuation

Peachtree Securities, Inc. (B)

Laura Donahue, the recently hired utility analyst for Peachtree Securities, passed her first assignment with flying colors [see Case 2, Peachtree Securities, Inc. (A)]. After presenting her seminar on risk and return, many customers were clamoring for a second lecture. Therefore, Jake Taylor, Peachtree's president, gave Donahue her second task: determine the value of TECO Energy's securities (common stock, preferred stock, and bonds) and prepare a seminar to explain the valuation process to the firm's customers. (Note that it is not necessary to work Case 2 prior to working this case.)

To begin, Donahue reviewed the *Value Line Investment Survey* data (see Figure 1 in Case 2). Next, Donahue examined TECO's latest Annual Report, especially Note E to the Consolidated Financial Statements. This note lists TECO's long-term debt obligations, including its first-mortgage bonds, installment contracts, and term loans. Table 1 contains information on three of the first-mortgage bonds listed in the Annual Report.

Table 1
Partial Long-Term Debt Listing for TECO Energy

Face Amount	Coupon Rate	Maturity Year	Years to Maturity
$ 48,000,000	4 1/2%	1997	5
32,000,000	8 1/4	2007	15
100,000,000	12 5/8	2017	25

Note: The terms stated here are modified slightly from the actual terms to simplify the case.

A concern which immediately occurred to Donahue was the phenomenon of "event risk." Recently, many investors have shied away from the industrial bond market because of the wave of leveraged buyouts (LBOs) and debt-financed corporate takeovers that took place during the 1980s. These takeovers were financed by issuing large amounts of new debt—often high-risk "junk" bonds—which caused the credit rating of the firm's existing bonds to drop, the required rate of return to increase, and the price of the bonds to decline.

Donahue wondered if this trend would affect the required returns on TECO's outstanding bonds. Upon reflection, she concluded that TECO's bonds would be much less vulnerable to such event risk because TECO is a regulated public utility. Public utilities and banks are less vulnerable to takeovers and leveraged buyouts, primarily because their regulators would have to approve such restructurings, and it is unlikely that they would permit the level of debt needed for an LBO. Therefore, many investors have turned to government bonds, mortgage-backed issues, and utility bonds in lieu of publicly traded corporate bonds. As a result, Donahue concluded that the effect, if any, of the increased concern about event risk will be to *lower* TECO's cost of bond financing.

With these considerations in mind, your task is to help Donahue pass her second hurdle at Peachtree Securities by answering the following questions.

Questions

Preliminary note: Some of our answers were generated using a computer model which carried out calculations to 8 decimal places. Therefore, you can expect small rounding differences if your answers are obtained using a financial calculator. These differences are not material.

1. To begin, assume that it is now January 1, 1993, and that each bond in Table 1 matures on December 31 of the year listed. Further, assume that each bond has a $1,000 par value, each had a 30-year maturity when it was issued, and the bonds currently have a 10 percent required nominal rate of return.

    a. Why do the bonds' coupon rates vary so widely?

    b. What would be the value of each bond if they had annual coupon payments?

   c.   TECO's bonds, like virtually all bonds, actually pay interest semiannually. What is each bond's value under these conditions? Are the bonds currently selling at a discount or at a premium?

   d.   What is the effective annual rate of return implied by the values obtained in Part c?

   e.   Would you expect a semiannual payment bond to sell at a higher or lower price than an otherwise equivalent annual payment bond? Now look at the 5-year bond in Parts b and c. Are the prices shown consistent with your expectations? Explain.

2.   Now, regardless of your answers to Question 1, assume that the 5-year bond is selling for $800.00, the 15-year bond is selling for $865.49, and the 25-year bond is selling for $1,220.00.

   (Note: Use these prices, and assume semiannual coupons, for the remainder of the questions.)

   a.   Explain the meaning of the term "yield to maturity."

   b.   What is the nominal (as opposed to effective annual) yield to maturity (YTM) on each bond?

   c.   What is the effective annual YTM on each issue?

   d.   In comparing bond yields with the yields on other securities, should the nominal or effective YTM be used? Explain.

3.   Suppose TECO has a second bond with 25 years left to maturity (in addition to the one listed in Table 1), which has a coupon rate of 7 3/8 percent and a market price of $747.48.

   a.   What is (1) the nominal yield and (2) the effective annual YTM on this bond?

   b.   What is the current yield on each of the 25-year bonds?

   c.   What is each bond's expected price on January 1, 1994, and its capital gains yield for 1993, assuming no change in interest rates? (Hint: Remember that the nominal required rate of return on each bond is 10.18 percent.)

   d.   What would happen to the price of each bond over time? (Again, assume constant future interest rates.)

   e.   What is the expected total (percentage) return on each bond during 1993?

f.   If you were a tax-paying investor, which bond would you prefer? Why? What impact would this preference have on the prices, hence YTMs, of the two bonds?

4.   Consider the riskiness of the bonds.

a.   Explain the difference between interest rate (price) risk and reinvestment rate risk.

b.   Which of the bonds listed in Table 1 has the most price risk? Why?

c.   Assume that you bought 5-year, 15-year, and 25-year bonds, all with a 10 percent coupon rate and semiannual coupons, at their $1,000 par values. Which bond's value would be most affected if interest rates rose to 13 percent? Which would be least affected? If you are using the *Lotus* model, calculate the new value of each bond.

d.   Assume that your investment horizon (or expected holding period) is 25 years. Which of the bonds listed in Table 1 has the greatest reinvestment rate risk? Why? What is a type of bond you could buy to eliminate reinvestment rate risk?

e.   Assume that you plan to keep your money invested, and to reinvest all interest receipts, for 5 years. Assume further that you bought the 5-year bond for $800, and interest rates suddenly fell to 5 percent and remained at that level for 5 years. Set up a worksheet that could be used to calculate the actual realized rate of return on the bond, but do not (necessarily) complete the calculations. Note that each interest receipt must be compounded to the terminal date and summed, along with the maturity value. Then, the rate of return that equates this terminal value to the initial value of the bond is the bond's realized return. Assume that the answer is 9.16 percent. How does that value compare with your expected rate of return? What would have happened if interest rates had risen to 15 percent rather than fallen to 5 percent? How would the results have differed if you had bought the 25-year bond rather than the 5-year bond? Do these results suggest that you would be better off or worse off if you buy long-term bonds and then rates change? Explain.

f.   Today, many bond market participants are speculators, as opposed to long-term investors. If you thought interest rates were going to fall from current levels, what type of bond would you buy to maximize short-term capital gains?

5. Now assume that the 15-year bond is callable after 5 years at $1,050.

   a. What is its yield to call (YTC)?

   b. Do you think it is likely that the bond will be called?

6. TECO has $54,956,000 of preferred stock outstanding.

   a. Suppose its Series A, which has a $100 par value and pays a 4.32 percent cumulative dividend, currently sells for $48.00 per share. What is its nominal expected rate of return? Its effective annual rate of return? (Hint: Remember that dividends are paid quarterly. Also, assume that this issue is perpetual.)

   b. Suppose Series F, with a $100 par value and a 9.75 percent cumulative dividend, has a mandatory sinking fund provision. 60,000 of the 300,000 total shares outstanding must be redeemed annually at par beginning at the end of 1993. If the nominal required rate of return is 8.0 percent, what is the current (January 1, 1993) value per share?

7. Now consider TECO's common stock. *Value Line* estimates TECO's 5-year dividend growth rate to be 6.0 percent. (See Figure 1 in Case 2.) Assume that TECO's stock traded on January 1, 1992 for $22.26. Assume for now that the 6.0 percent growth rate is expected to continue indefinitely.

   a. What was TECO's expected rate of return at the beginning of 1992? (Hint: *Value Line* estimated D_1 to be $1.80 at the start of 1992. See Figure 1 in Case 2.)

   b. What was the expected dividend yield and expected capital gains yield on January 1, 1992?

   c. What is the relationship between dividend yield and capital gains yield over time under constant growth assumptions?

   d. What conditions must hold to use the constant growth (Gordon) model? Do many "real world" stocks satisfy the constant growth assumptions?

8. Suppose you believe that TECO's 6.0 percent dividend growth rate will only hold for 5 years. After that, the growth rate will return to TECO's historical 10-year average of 7.5 percent. Note that $D_6 = D_5 \times 1.075$. (Again, see Figure 1 in Case 2.)

    a. What was the value of TECO stock on January 1, 1992, if the required rate of return is 13.5 percent?

    b. What is the expected stock price at the end of 1992 assuming that the stock is in equilibrium?

    c. What is the expected dividend yield, capital gains yield, and total return for 1992?

    d. Suppose TECO's dividend was expected to remain constant at $1.80 for the next 5 years and then grow at a constant 6 percent rate. If the required rate of return is 13.5 percent, would TECO's stock value be higher or lower than your answer in Part a? If you are using the *Lotus* model for the case, calculate the dividend yield, capital gains yield, and total yield from 1992 through 1996.

    e. TECO's stock price was $22.26 at the beginning of 1992. Using the growth rates given in the introduction to this question, what is the stock's expected rate of return?

    f. Refer back to Figure 1 in Case 2. Look at the "% Earned Common Equity" estimated for 1995 through 1997 and at the projected earnings and dividends per share for the same period. Could those figures be used to develop an estimated long-run "sustainable" growth rate? Does this figure support the 7.5 percent growth rate given in the problem? [Hint: Think of the formula g = br = (Retention ratio)(ROE).]

9. Common stocks are usually valued assuming annual dividends even though dividends are actually paid quarterly. This is because the dividend stream is so uncertain that the use of a quarterly model is not warranted. The quarterly constant growth valuation model is:

$$\hat{P}_0 = \frac{D_{q1}(1+k)^{0.75} + D_{q2}(1+k)^{0.50} + D_{q3}(1+k)^{0.25} + D_{q4}(1+k)^0}{k-g} ,$$

    where P_0 is the stock's value and D_{qi} is the dividend in Quarter i. Note that this model assumes that dividend growth occurs once each year rather than at every quarter. Assume that TECO's next four quarterly dividends are $1.80/4 = $0.45 each; that k, the annual required rate of return, is 13.5 percent, and that g is a constant 6.0 percent. What is TECO's value according to the quarterly model?

II

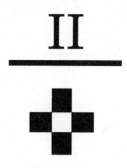

Cost of Capital

4

Cost of Capital

Silicon Valley Medical Technologies, Inc.

Silicon Valley Medical Technologies (SIVMED) was founded in San Jose, California, in 1982 by Kelly O'Brien, David Roberts, and Barbara Smalley. O'Brien and Roberts, both MDs, were on the research faculty at the UCLA Medical School at the time; O'Brien specialized in biochemistry and molecular biology, and Roberts specialized in immunology and medical microbiology. Smalley, who has a PhD, served as department chair of the Microbiology Department at UC-Berkeley.

The company started as a research and development firm which performed its own basic research, obtained patents on promising technologies, and then either sold or licensed the technologies to other firms which marketed the products. In recent years, however, the firm has also contracted to perform research and testing for larger genetic engineering and biotechnology firms, and for the U.S. government. Since its inception, the company has enjoyed enormous success—even its founders were surprised at the scientific breakthroughs made and the demand for its services. One event that contributed significantly to the firm's rapid growth was the AIDS epidemic. Both the U.S. government and private foundations have spent billions of dollars in AIDS research, and SIVMED had the right combination of skills to garner significant grant funds, as well as perform as a subcontractor to other firms receiving AIDS research grants.

The founders were relatively wealthy individuals when they started the company, and they had enough confidence in the business to commit most of their own funds to the new venture. Still, the capital requirements brought on by extremely rapid growth soon exhausted their personal funds, so they were forced to raise capital from outside sources. First, in 1984, the firm borrowed heavily, and then in 1986, when it used up its conventional debt capacity, it issued $15 million of preferred stock. Finally, in 1989, the firm had an initial public offering (IPO) which raised $50 million of common equity. Currently, the stock trades in the over-the-counter market, and it has been selling at about $25 per share.

SIVMED is widely recognized as the leader in an emerging growth industry, and it won an award in 1991 for being one of the 100 best-managed small companies in the United States. The company is organized into two divisions: (1) the Clinical Research Division and (2) the Genetic Engineering Division. Although the two divisions are housed in the same buildings, the equipment they use and their personnel are quite different. Indeed, there are few synergies between the two divisions. The most important synergies lie in the general overhead and marketing areas. Personnel, payroll, and similar functions are all done at the corporate level, while technical operations at the divisions are completely separate.

The Clinical Research Division conducts most of the firm's AIDS research. Since most of the grants and contracts associated with AIDS research are long-term in nature, and since billions of new dollars will likely be spent in this area, the business risk of this division is low. Conversely, the Genetic Engineering Division works mostly on in-house research and short-term contracts where the funding, duration, and payoffs are very uncertain. A line of research may look good initially, but it is not unusual to hit some snag which precludes further exploration. Because of the uncertainties inherent in genetic research, the Genetic Engineering Division is judged to have high business risk.

The founders are still active in the business, but they no longer work 70-hour weeks. Increasingly, they are enjoying the fruits of their past labors, and they have let professional managers take over day-to-day operations. They are all on the board of directors, though, and David Roberts is chairman.

Although the firm's growth has been phenomenal, it has been more random than planned. The founders would simply decide on new avenues of research, and then count on the skills of the research teams—and good luck—to produce commercial successes. Formal decision structures were almost nonexistent, but the company's head start and its bright, energetic founders easily overcame any deficiencies in its managerial decision processes. Recently, however, competition has become stiffer, and such large biotechnology firms as Genentech, Amgen, and even Bristol-Myers Squibb have begun to recognize the opportunities in SIVMED's research

28

lines. Because of this increasing competition, SIVMED's founders and board of directors have concluded that the firm must apply state-of-the-art techniques in its managerial processes as well as in its technological processes. As a first step, the board directed the financial vice president, Gary Hayes, to develop an estimate for the firm's cost-of-capital and to use this number in capital budgeting decisions. Hayes, in turn, directed SIVMED's treasurer, Julie Owens, to have a cost of capital estimate on his desk in one week. Owens has an accounting background, and her primary task since taking over as treasurer has been to deal with the banks. Thus, she is somewhat apprehensive about this new assignment, especially since one of the board members is a well-known San Jose State University finance professor.

Table 1

Silicon Valley Medical Technologies: Balance Sheet
for the Year Ended December 31, 1992
(In Millions of Dollars)

Cash and securities	$ 7.6	Accounts payable	$ 5.7
Accounts receivable	39.6	Accruals	7.5
Inventory	9.1	Notes payable	1.9
Current assets	$ 56.3	Current liabilities	$ 15.1
Net fixed assets	114.5	Long-term debt	61.2
		Preferred stock	15.0
		Common stock	79.5
Total assets	$ 170.8	Total claims	$ 170.8

To begin, Owens reviewed SIVMED's 1992 balance sheet, which is shown in Table 1. Next, she assembled the following data:

(1) SIVMED's long-term debt consists of 9.5 percent coupon, semiannual payment bonds with 15 years remaining to maturity. The bonds last traded at a price of $891 per $1,000 par value bond. The bonds are not callable, and they are rated BBB.

(2) The founders have an aversion to short-term debt, so the firm uses such debt only to fund cyclical working capital needs.

(3) SIVMED's federal-plus-state tax rate is 40 percent.

(4) The company's preferred stock pays a dividend of $2.50 per quarter; it has a par value of $100; it is noncallable and perpetual; and it is traded in the over-the-counter market at a current price of $104.00 per share. A flotation cost of $2.00 per share would be required on a new issue of preferred.

(5) The firm's last dividend (D_0) was $1.09, and dividends are expected to grow at about a 10 percent rate in the foreseeable future. Some analysts expect the company's recent growth rate to continue, others expect it to go to zero as new competition enters the market; the majority anticipate that a growth rate of about 10 percent will continue indefinitely. SIVMED's common stock now sells at a price of about $25 per share. The company has 5.0 million common shares outstanding.

(6) The current yield on long-term T-bonds is 8 percent, and a prominent investment banking firm has recently estimated that the market risk premium is 6 percentage points over Treasury bonds. The firm's historical beta, as measured by several analysts who follow the stock, is 1.2.

(7) The required rate of return on an average (A-rated) company's long-term debt is 10 percent.

(8) SIVMED is forecasting retained earnings of $1,800,000 and depreciation of $4,500,000 for the coming year.

(9) SIVMED's investment bankers believe that a new common stock issue would involve total flotation costs—including underwriting costs, market pressure from increased supply, and market pressure from negative signaling effects—of 30 percent.

(10) The market value target capital structure calls for 30 percent long-term debt, 10 percent preferred stock, and 60 percent common stock.

Now assume that you were recently hired as Julie Owens's assistant, and she has given you the task of helping her develop the firm's cost of capital. You will also have to meet with Gary Hayes and, possibly, with the president and the full board of directors (including the San Jose State finance professor) to answer any questions they might have. With this in mind, Owens wrote up the following questions to get you started with your analysis. Answer them, but keep in mind that you could be asked further questions about your answers, so be sure you understand the logic behind any formulas or calculations you use. In particular, be aware of potential conceptual or empirical problems that might exist.

Questions

1. What specific items of capital should be included in SIVMED's estimated weighted average cost of capital (WACC)? Should before-tax or after-tax values be used? Should historical (embedded) or new (marginal) values be used? Why?

2. a. What is your estimate of SIVMED's cost of debt?

   b. Should flotation costs be included in the component cost of debt calculation? Explain.

   c. Should the nominal cost of debt or the effective annual rate be used? Explain.

   d. How valid is an estimate of the cost of debt based on 15-year bonds if the firm normally issues 30-year long-term debt? If you believe the estimate is not valid, what could be done to make the 15-year cost a better proxy for the 30-year cost. (Hint: Think about the yield curve.)

   e. Suppose SIVMED's outstanding debt had not been recently traded; what other methods could be used to estimate the cost of debt?

   f. Would it matter if the currently outstanding bonds were callable? Explain.

3. a. What is your estimate of the cost of preferred stock?

   b. SIVMED's preferred stock is more risky to investors than its debt, yet you should find that its before-tax yield to investors is lower than the yield on SIVMED's debt. Why does this occur?

   c. Now suppose SIVMED's preferred stock had a mandatory redemption provision which specified that the firm must redeem the issue in 5 years at a price of $110 per share. What would SIVMED's cost of preferred be in this situation? (In fact, SIVMED's preferred does not have such a provision, so ignore this question when working the remainder of the case.)

4. a. Why is there a cost associated with retained earnings?

   b. What is SIVMED's estimated cost of retained earnings using the CAPM approach?

c. Why might one consider the T-bond rate to be a better estimate of the risk-free rate than the T-bill rate? Can you think of an argument that would favor the use of the T-bill rate?

d. How do historical betas, adjusted historical betas, and fundamental betas differ? Do you think SIVMED's historical beta would be a better or a worse measure of SIVMED's future market risk than the historical beta for an average NYSE company would be for its (the average NYSE company's) future market risk? Explain your answer.

e. How can SIVMED obtain a market risk premium for use in a CAPM cost-of-equity calculation? Discuss both the possibility of obtaining an estimate from some other organization and also the ways in which SIVMED could calculate a market risk premium in-house.

5. a. Use the discounted cash flow (DCF) method to obtain an estimate of SIVMED's cost of retained earnings.

b. Suppose SIVMED, over the last few years, has had a 14 percent average return on equity (ROE) and has paid out about 25 percent of its net income as dividends. Under what conditions could this information be used to help estimate the firm's expected future growth rate, g? Estimate k_s using this g estimate.

c. The firm's per share dividend payment over the past 5 years has been as follows:

Year	Dividend
1988	$0.72
1989	0.75
1990	0.85
1991	1.00
1992	1.09

What was the firm's historical dividend growth rate using the point-to-point method? Using linear regression?

6. Use the bond-yield-plus-risk-premium method to estimate SIVMED's cost of retained earnings.

7. What is your final estimate for k_s? Explain how you weighted the estimates of the three methods.

8. What is your estimate of SIVMED's cost of new common stock, k_e? What are some potential weaknesses in the procedures you used to obtain this estimate?

9. a. Construct SIVMED's marginal cost of capital (MCC) schedule. How large could the company's capital budget be before it is forced to sell new common stock? Ignore depreciation at this point.

    b. Would the MCC schedule remain constant beyond the retained earnings break point, no matter how much new capital it raised? Explain. Again, ignore depreciation.

    c. How does depreciation affect the MCC schedule? If depreciation were simply ignored, would this affect the acceptability of proposed capital projects? Explain.

10. Should the corporate cost of capital as developed above be used by both divisions and for all projects within each division? If not, what type of adjustments should be made?

11. a. What are SIVMED's book value weights of debt, preferred stock, and common stock? (Hint: Consider only long-term sources of capital.)

    b. What are SIVMED's market value weights of debt, preferred stock, and common stock?

    c. Should book value or market value weights be used when calculating the firm's weighted average cost of capital? Why?

5

Cost of Capital

Telecommunications Services, Inc.

Telecommunications Services, Inc. was founded in Dallas, Texas, in 1981 by Judi Estes, Gayle Daniels, and Jill Hays. Its purpose was to provide an "address and phone number" for small companies which did not have a full-time office staff, yet needed to respond rapidly to their customers' inquiries. For example, self-employed financial consultants could arrange to have their mail and telephone calls go to Telecommunications Services. Then, they could pick up mail at their convenience or have it forwarded to their homes. Also, they could have telephone calls routed to a mobile phone, or they could be "beeped" with a message to return a call. Telecommunications Services soon began to lease cellular phones and pagers, and it expanded into other eastern, southern, and midwestern cities.

Since its inception, the company has enjoyed enormous success. Even its founders were surprised at the demand for its services, and its founding coincided nicely with developments in both the telecommunications and personal computer (PC) industries, which made certain types of services feasible (for example, paging and mobile-phone services).

The founders were relatively wealthy individuals when they started the company, and they had enough confidence in the business to commit most of their own funds to the new venture. Still, the capital requirements brought on by extremely rapid growth soon exhausted their personal funds. Thus, they were forced to borrow heavily, and, eventually, to float an issue of common stock. Currently, the stock trades in the over-the-counter market, and it has been selling at about $50 per share.

Telecommunications Services is widely recognized as the leader in an emerging growth industry, and it won an award in 1992 for being one of the 100 best-managed companies in the United States. The company is organized into two divisions: (1) the Mail and Message Services Division and (2) the Cellular Phone and Pager Leasing Division. Although the two divisions are housed in the same buildings, the equipment they use and their personnel are quite different. Indeed, the only synergies lie in the marketing area, but since marketing is of overwhelming importance in the personal service industry, no thought has been given to breaking up the company. However, Telecommunications Services' management regards the Cellular Phone and Pager Leasing Division as being subject to the greatest threat from potential competition.

The founders are still active in the business, but they no longer work 70-hour weeks. Increasingly, they are enjoying the fruits of their past labors, and they have let professional managers take over day-to-day operations. They are all on the board of directors, though, and Judi Estes is chairman.

Although its growth has been phenomenal, it has been more random than planned. The founders would simply decide on a location for a new facility, run an ad in a local newspaper for employees, send in an experienced manager from one of the established offices, and begin to make money almost immediately. Formal decision structures were almost nonexistent, but the company's head start and its bright, energetic founders easily overcame any deficiencies in its managerial decision processes.

Recently, however, competition has become stiffer, and such giant firms as GTE, BellSouth, and Nynex have begun to recognize the opportunities in Telecommunications Services' markets. Because of this increasing competition, Telecommunications Services' founders and board of directors have concluded that the firm must apply state-of-the-art techniques in its managerial processes as well as in its technological processes.

As a first step, the board directed the financial vice president, Bruce Holden, to develop an estimate for the firm's cost-of-capital and to use this number in capital budgeting decisions. Holden, in turn, directed Telecommunications Services' treasurer, Will Shire, to have a cost of capital estimate on his desk in one week. Shire has an accounting background, and his primary task since taking over as treasurer has been to deal with the banks. Thus, he is somewhat apprehensive about this new assignment, especially since one of the board members is a famous University of Texas finance professor.

Table 1

Telecommunications Services: Balance Sheet
for the Year Ended December 31, 1992
(In Millions of Dollars)

Cash and securities	$ 22.9	Accounts payable	$ 17.1
Accounts receivable	118.8	Accruals	22.5
Inventory	27.5	Notes payable	5.9
Current assets	$ 169.2	Current liabilities	$ 45.5
Net fixed assets	343.4	Long-term debt	183.6
		Preferred stock	43.6
		Common stock	239.9
Total assets	$ 512.6	Total claims	$ 512.6

To begin, Shire reviewed Telecommunications Services' 1992 balance sheet, which is shown in Table 1. Next, he assembled the following data:

(1) Telecommunications Services' long-term debt consists of 13 percent coupon, semiannual payment bonds with 15 years remaining to maturity. The bonds last traded at a price of $1,230.58 per $1,000 par value bond. The bonds are not callable, and they are rated BBB.

(2) The founders have an aversion to short-term debt, so Telecommunications Services uses such debt only to fund cyclical working capital needs.

(3) Telecommunications Services' federal-plus-state tax rate is 40 percent.

(4) The company's preferred stock pays a dividend of $2.50 per quarter; it has a par value of $100; it is noncallable and perpetual; and it is traded in the over-the-counter market at a current price of $113.10 per share. A flotation cost of $2.00 per share would be required on a new issue of preferred.

(5) The firm's last dividend (D_0) was $1.73, and dividends are expected to grow at about a 10 percent rate in the foreseeable future. Some analysts expect the company's recent growth rate to continue, others expect it to go to zero as new competition enters the market; the majority anticipate that a growth rate of about 10 percent will continue indefinitely. Telecommunications Services' common stock now sells at a price of about $50 per share. The company has 7.5 million common shares outstanding.

(6) The current yield on long-term T-bonds is 7 percent, and a prominent investment banking firm has recently estimated that the market risk premium is 6 percentage points over Treasury bonds. The firm's historical beta, as measured by several analysts who follow the stock, is 1.2.

(7) The required rate of return on an average (A-rated) company's long-term debt is 9 percent.

(8) Telecommunications Services is forecasting retained earnings of $5,400,000 and depreciation of $13,500,000 for the coming year.

(9) Telecommunications Services' investment bankers believe that a new common stock issue would involve total flotation costs—including underwriting costs, market pressure from increased supply, and market pressure from negative signaling effects—of 30 percent.

(10) The market value target capital structure calls for 30 percent long-term debt, 10 percent preferred stock, and 60 percent common stock.

Now assume that you were recently hired as Will Shire's assistant, and he has given you the task of helping him develop a cost of capital. You will also have to meet with Bruce Holden and, possibly, with the president and the full board of directors (including the Texas finance professor) to answer any questions they might have. With this in mind, Shire wrote up the following questions to get you started with your analysis. Answer them, but keep in mind that you could be asked further questions about your answers, so be sure you understand the logic behind any formulas or calculations you use. In particular, be aware of potential conceptual or empirical problems that might exist

Questions

1. What specific items of capital should be included in Telecommunications Services' estimated weighted average cost of capital (WACC)? Should before-tax or after-tax values be used? Should historical (embedded) or new (marginal) values be used? Why?

2. a. What is your estimate of Telecommunications Services' cost of debt?

b. Should flotation costs be included in the component cost of debt calculation? Explain.

c. Should the nominal cost of debt or the effective annual rate be used? Explain.

d. How valid is an estimate of the cost of debt based on 15-year bonds if the firm normally issues 30-year long-term debt?

e. Suppose Telecommunications Services' outstanding debt had not been recently traded; what other methods could be used to estimate the cost of debt?

f. Would it matter if the currently outstanding bonds were callable? Explain.

3. a. What is your estimate of the cost of preferred stock?

b. Telecommunications Services' preferred stock is more risky to investors than its debt, yet you should find that its before-tax yield to investors is lower than the yield on Telecommunications Services' debt. Why does this occur?

c. Now suppose Telecommunications Services' preferred stock had a mandatory redemption provision which specified that the firm must redeem the issue in 5 years at a price of $110 per share. What would Telecommunications Services' cost of preferred be in this situation? (In fact, Telecommunications Services' preferred does not have such a provision, so ignore this question when working the remainder of the case.)

4. a. Why is there a cost associated with retained earnings?

b. What is Telecommunications Services' estimated cost of retained earnings using the CAPM approach?

c. Why might one consider the T-bond rate to be a better estimate of the risk-free rate than the T-bill rate? Can you think of an argument that would favor the use of the T-bill rate?

d. How do historical betas, adjusted historical betas, and fundamental betas differ? Do you think Telecommunications Services' historical beta would be a better or a worse measure of its future market risk than the historical beta for an average NYSE company would be for its (the average NYSE company's) future market risk? Explain your answer.

e. How can Telecommunications Services obtain a market risk premium for use in a CAPM cost-of-equity calculation? Discuss both the possibility of obtaining an estimate from some other organization, and also the ways in which Telecommunications Services could calculate a market risk premium in-house.

5. a. Use the discounted cash flow (DCF) method to obtain an estimate of Telecommunications Services' cost of retained earnings.

    b. Suppose Telecommunications Services, over the last few years, has had a 15 percent average return on equity (ROE) and has paid out about 20 percent of its net income as dividends. Under what conditions could this information be used to help estimate the firm's expected future growth rate, g? Estimate k_s using this g estimate.

6. Use the bond-yield-plus-risk-premium method to estimate Telecommunications Services' cost of retained earnings.

7. What is your final estimate for k_s? Explain how you weighted the estimates of the three methods.

8. What is your estimate of Telecommunications Services' cost of new common stock, k_e? What are some potential weaknesses in the procedures you used to obtain this estimate?

9. a. Construct Telecommunications Services' marginal cost of capital (MCC) schedule. How large could the company's capital budget be before it is forced to sell new common stock? Ignore depreciation at this point.

    b. Would the MCC schedule remain constant beyond the retained earnings break point, no matter how much new capital it raised? Explain. Again, ignore depreciation.

    c. How does depreciation affect the MCC schedule? If depreciation were simply ignored, would this affect the acceptability of proposed capital projects? Explain.

10. Should the corporate cost of capital as developed above be used by both divisions and for all projects within each division? If not, what type of adjustments should be made?

11. a. What are Telecommunications Services' book value weights of debt, preferred stock, and common stock? (Hint: Consider only long-term sources of capital.)

b. What are Telecommunications Services' market value weights of debt, preferred stock, and common stock?

c. Should book value or market value weights be used when calculating the firm's weighted average cost of capital? Why?

6

Divisional Hurdle Rates

Randolph Corporation

Randolph Corporation is a multidivisional producer of (1) abrasive products, especially high-quality electric sanders and sandpaper for home use, (2) industrial grinders and sharpeners, and (3) coated ceramics used in aerospace and other industries that require surface bonding agents with high strength and resistance to high temperatures. The company also has a division which is active in real estate development. This division was started several years ago, when a large tract of land just west of Phoenix, Arizona, which Randolph had acquired for its mineral potential many years ago, became valuable for residential real estate development. Because of the nature of the various product lines, the company was divided into four separate divisions in 1990: the Home Products Division, the Equipment Manufacturing Division, the Ceramic Coatings Division, and the Residential Real Estate Division. This arrangement has worked reasonably well, but frictions have developed among the divisions, and Randolph's stock has not performed as well as that of others in the industry.

A special committee was appointed by the board of directors to evaluate this situation. The committee has asked all senior executives, including Tony Gianneti, the firm's financial vice president, to identify problems and then to recommend ways to eliminate them. Gianneti found numerous small ways in which financial operations could be changed for the better, but only one area presented a major problem—the financial planning process and, specifically, the way risk is taken into consideration in this process. Currently, Randolph does not formally incorporate differential risk into project evaluations. The capital budgeting process works like this:

(1) A corporate hurdle rate is developed by the corporate treasurer.

(2) Projected cash inflows and outflows are estimated for each potential project by each division, and these project data are entered into the computerized capital budgeting system, which then calculates each project's NPV, IRR, MIRR, and payback.

(3) If a project's NPV is positive and large, if its IRR and MIRR are at least 3 percentage points above the corporate hurdle rate, and if its payback is four years or less, then the project will usually be accepted. On the other hand, if the NPV is negative, if the IRR and MIRR are well below the corporate hurdle rate, and if the payback period is long (eight years or more), the project will almost always be rejected.

(4) Projects with NPVs close to zero, IRRs and MIRRs close to the corporate hurdle rate, and paybacks in the five-to-seven-year range are considered marginal. These projects are accepted or rejected depending on management's confidence in the cash flow forecasts, on the project's long-run, strategic effects on the firm, and on the availability of capital.

Although everyone agrees that an average project in the Ceramic Coatings Division is substantially riskier than an average project in the Home Products Division, no explicit allowance is made for this differential risk. As a result, substantially more capital has been invested in the Ceramic Coatings Division (and in riskier projects from all divisions), than otherwise would have occurred, because high-risk projects typically offer high returns. Gianneti recognizes that such problems are inherent in an informal risk-adjustment process. Also, his assistant, Barbara Kravitz, a University of Arizona graduate with an MBA, recently concluded her annual review of the company's budgeting process with two strong recommendations: (1) that project risk be given more-formal consideration in the capital budgeting process, and (2) that the idea of different hurdle rates for different divisions be investigated.

Gianneti appreciates the need for some sort of formal risk evaluation system, but he is afraid that top management will resist such an approach unless he can document why so radical a departure from past practices is necessary and also show how not using such procedures has hurt the company in the past. The job of proving the need for, and then designing, a risk evaluation system will not be easy—it will require the cooperation of many managers from all parts of the organization.

With the annual budget completed and no urgent problems facing him, Gianneti set up a team to study the question of risk-adjusted hurdle rates. Marion Hale, the corporate treasurer, Jim Benson, the corporate capital budgeting director, and the four divisional controllers comprised the study group. Barbara Kravitz was also assigned to the study group and was asked to research the following questions, plus any others she regarded as important:

(1)   Should hurdle rates be established for each division, for each product line within a division, or on an individual project basis?

(2)   How should project risk be measured?

(3)   How should capital structure, or debt capacity, be handled? This issue is important because the Real Estate division manager, Emmit Jones, has been complaining that he needs to use more debt if he is to compete effectively with other firms in the real estate development business.

Kravitz decided that a reasonable place to start her inquiry was to focus on the concept of market risk which she had studied as an MBA student. After several discussions, she found that Randolph's senior management agreed that the firm's risk, as seen by well-diversified investors, is the key determinant of its cost of equity capital. The senior managers also agreed that investors estimate risk, in large part although not exclusively, by a stock's relative volatility as measured by its beta coefficient. Kravitz had earlier conducted a study of the determinants of Randolph's beta and had concluded that the corporate beta is a weighted average of the betas that the four divisions would have if they were operated as separate firms. Kravitz then set up the following table:

Division	Percentage of Corporate Assets	Estimated Divisional Beta	Product
Real Estate	0.10	0.60	0.060
Ceramic Coatings	0.10	1.95	0.195
Equipment Manufacturing	0.30	1.05	0.315
Home Products	0.50	0.65	0.325
	1.00		
	Weighted average corporate beta =		0.895 ≈ 0.90.

In estimating the divisional betas, Kravitz (1) examined the betas for publicly held real estate, abrasives, general manufacturing, and special coatings companies, and (2) looked at the volatility of earnings in each division vis-a-vis earnings on the Standard & Poor's 500 index. The betas, as estimated by both of these methods for each division, were then averaged, and this average was used as the divisional beta reported in the tabulation. The weighted average of the divisional betas, 0.9, is quite close to Randolph's beta coefficient as reported by leading brokerage houses.

Barbara Kravitz then used these divisional betas to set basic risk-adjusted costs of capital for each division. First, she estimated the required rate of return on equity, k_s, by using the Security Market Line (SML) equation:

$$k_s = k_{RF} = (k_M - k_{RF})b.$$

Here k_M is the return on an "average" stock, k_{RF} is the riskless rate, b is the stock's (or division's) beta coefficient, and the term $(k_M - k_{RF})b$ is the stock's (or division's) risk premium above the risk-free rate. Using the current Treasury bond rate as the riskless rate, $k_{RF} = 8.0\%$, and the Goodman Saks estimate of the long-run return on the market, $k_M = 13.5\%$, Kravitz concluded that the corporate cost of equity for Randolph is 13.0 percent:

$$
\begin{aligned}
k_s &= 8.0\% + (13.5\% - 8.0\%)0.9 \\
&= 8.0\% + (5.5\%)0.9 \\
&= 12.95\% \approx 13.0\%.
\end{aligned}
$$

Under current procedures, this 13 percent would be averaged in with debt to find the corporate weighted average cost of capital (WACC), which would then be used to evaluate all projects in all divisions. However, Kravitz feels that the data clearly show that each division's cost of equity differs from the 13.0 percent corporate cost, depending on the division's own beta.

The next question Kravitz must consider is capital structure: Should different divisions be assigned different capital structures and debt costs, or should they be assigned the corporate average? If different capital structures are to be used, how should they be derived? What interest rate should be used for debt? How should divisional equity costs be adjusted to reflect varying capital structures?

Kravitz decided to use the corporate target capital structure of 45 percent debt for each division for the following reasons:

(1) Her old finance professor argued that the WACC is not very sensitive to capital structure over a fairly wide range of debt ratios; therefore, the issue is not as critical as it might first appear.

(2) If a division were assigned a high debt ratio, its costs of debt and equity would rise, and this would tend to offset the greater use of lower-cost debt capital.

(3) Kravitz reasoned that she was already going to have a hard time persuading management to accept multiple hurdle rates, and the simpler her approach, the greater her chance of success.

Now that she has cost-of-equity estimates for each division, as well as the appropriate capital structure weights, Kravitz can calculate benchmark hurdle rates for each division. Randolph's before-tax cost of debt is 11.0 percent; its federal-plus-state marginal tax rate is 40 percent.

When Kravitz presented her initial ideas at the first committee meeting, the representative from the Real Estate Division voiced a strong objection. Debra Brown, the division's vice president, was displeased with the fact that a uniform capital structure of 45 percent debt was proposed. She argued that firms in the real estate industry averaged close to 75 percent debt—even the most conservative ones used about 60 percent debt—and, based on the conservative firms' bond ratings, their before-tax cost of debt averaged only 10.5 percent, or 50 basis points below Randolph's overall cost of debt. Their cost of equity, using beta coefficients provided by several financial services companies, is about 13.0 percent, which, assuming a tax rate of 40 percent, results in a hurdle rate of about 9.0 percent:

$$\text{WACC} = w_d(k_d)(1 - T) + w_s(k_s)$$
$$= 0.6(10.5\%)(0.6) + 0.4(13.0\%) = 8.98\% \approx 9.0\%.$$

Brown argued that if she is forced to use a higher hurdle rate while competing firms use 9.0 percent, Randolph will lose ground in the real estate business. Jim Benson backed her up, noting that he had recently attended a conference at which a case study involving Continental Foods' problem in setting divisional hurdle rates was used. The restaurant industry tends to have debt ratios of about 70 percent, as compared to 38 percent for the major divisions of Continental Foods. Continental decided to use a 70 percent debt ratio for its restaurant division, compared to 40 percent for its frozen foods division, so that comparability with stand-alone competitors could be achieved. Other attendees had pointed out that Zenith Steel Corporation's Equipment Lease Financing Division also has a high debt ratio (about 80 percent debt, as opposed to 42 percent for its other divisions). In both situations, the companies indicated that they could remain competitive only if their divisions could follow industry practice for capital structure when calculating hurdle rates.

When Benson finished, Marion Hale noted that both the restaurant and equipment leasing industries have recently been experiencing financial difficulties. Regarding Continental, Hale cited the following quote from *The Wall Street Journal*:

> *Continental Foods disclosed some more bad news about its earnings, and it received some bad news itself from a major credit service, which reduced the rating on the food processor's debentures . . . net income fell 22% while sales rose 18% . . . debentures were downgraded to Single-A-plus from double A because of the "continuing deterioration in earnings and fixed charge coverage."*

Hale then suggested that these problems might have been brought on in part by an overexpansion resulting from the use of hurdle rates that were unrealistically low. Others agreed with her point, but no conclusions were reached at the meeting; the study group decided to defer action until Kravitz's report was finalized.

After the meeting, Kravitz had extended discussions with operating personnel regarding various ways of accounting for individual project risk. She concluded that any system would necessarily be somewhat arbitrary and imprecise. Most individual projects are parts of larger processes, and the results of a given capital project are highly sensitive to market and production conditions for the product.   Still, experienced operating personnel admitted that they are more confident about the projected cash flows from some projects than from others, and they recognized that some projects are simply riskier than others. Also, Benson reported that some operating personnel have better "track records" in forecasting cash flows than others have, and Benson takes this fact into account in his own assessment of project risk.

For large projects, generally those involving entirely new technologies or product lines, Barbara Kravitz believes that Monte Carlo simulation or scenario analysis should be used to generate distributions of rates of return. Probabilities would be assigned to sales prices, sales quantity, and so on, and both an expected rate of return and the standard deviation of returns would be developed. However, the vast majority of proposed capital projects would not be   subjected to such analyses. Kravitz feels that the costs would outweigh the benefits of such approaches for smaller projects, especially in view of the highly subjective nature of the estimation process that would have to be used for the probability data.

Still, Kravitz recommended that divisional managers be required to classify projects into one of three groups: high risk, average risk, and low risk. Risky projects would be evaluated at a hurdle rate 1.2 times the divisional rate; average projects would be evaluated at the divisional rate; and low-risk projects would be evaluated at a hurdle rate 0.9 times the divisional rate. When this was discussed at the next study group meeting, the members agreed that the recommended procedure was arbitrary, but most felt that it would be superior to what was currently being done. Moreover, they could suggest no better procedure.

In drafting her final conclusions, Kravitz remained convinced that capital budgeting must involve judgment as well as quantitative analyses. At present, the capital budgeting process is as follows: (1) one hurdle rate is used throughout the entire corporation; (2) NPVs, IRRs, MIRRs, and paybacks are calculated; and (3) these quantitative data are used, along with such qualitative factors as "what the project does for our strategic position in the market," in making the final "accept, reject, or defer" decision. Kravitz's report emphasized that this general procedure should be retained, but that the quantitative inputs used in the final decision would be better if differential risk-adjusted discount rates were used.

The day before her final report was due, Kravitz received a call for jury duty. She had avoided serving the last two times she was called, so there was no way out this time—it was jury duty or jail for contempt of court. Assume that you have been assigned to take over the task of completing the report and defending it before the study group. Kravitz did leave you with the following list of questions to help you complete the task. She also informed you that Tony Gianneti, the financial VP, was thinking of giving you a significant promotion, but your chances for the promotion will be ruined if you don't do a good job writing up the report and then answering questions about it.

Questions

1. Estimate the divisional hurdle rates for each division. Assume that all divisions use a 45 percent debt ratio for this purpose.

2. Now assume that, within divisions, projects are identified as being high risk, average risk, or low risk. What hurdle rates would be assigned to projects in those risk categories within each division?

3. How comfortable are you with the 1.2 and 0.9 project risk-adjustment factors? Is there a theoretical foundation for the size of these adjustments?

4. Suppose the Ceramic Coatings Division has an exceptionally large number of projects whose returns exceed the risk-adjusted hurdle rates, so its growth rate substantially exceeds the corporate average. What effect would this have, over time, on Randolph's corporate beta and on the overall cost of capital? (Assume that the aggregate risk of the division remains unchanged.)

5. Suppose that, despite the higher cost of capital for risky projects (1.2 times divisional cost), the Equipment Manufacturing Division made relatively heavy investments in projects deemed to be more risky than average. What effect would this have on the firm's corporate beta and overall cost of capital? How long would it take for the effects of these relatively risky investments to show up in the corporate beta as reported by brokers and investment advisory services?

6. Do you agree with Kravitz on the capital structure issue? How would your thinking be affected if: (a) each division raised its own debt, that is, if the divisions were set up as wholly owned subsidiaries, which then issued their own debt (in fact, Randolph raises debt capital at the corporate level, and funds are then made available by headquarters to the various divisions); (b) divisions issued their own debt, but the corporation guaranteed the divisional debt; or (c) all debt was issued by the corporation (which is actually the case).

7. One problem with a market risk analysis such as the one Kravitz is conducting relates to differences in reported market beta coefficients. Some services calculate and report straight historical betas, while others make adjustments for the tendency of betas to approach 1.0 over time. A few services even attempt to include fundamental economic factors in their beta calculations. Explain why reported beta values (even pure historical betas) are so inconsistent. Do historical betas provide good measures of the future riskiness of firms (or divisions)?

8. Kravitz's analysis requires that betas be estimated for Randolph's four divisions, and she used both the pure play and the accounting beta methods for these estimates. Suppose she did not feel comfortable with beta analysis. Could divisional (and project) hurdle rates be established using total risk analysis? If so, describe how this

might be done. (Hint: The risk of divisions (and projects) can be viewed on a stand-alone basis or on a within-firm basis, which treats the firm as a portfolio of assets.)

9. Randolph uses an incentive-based compensation plan for its upper management personnel. Division managers receive approximately half of their annual compensation, on average, as bonuses or incentive stock. These percentages vary greatly, of course, from year to year, depending on the state of the economy and on how both the corporation and the divisions did during the recent past. The incentive compensation at the division level is based on three factors: (1) the division's ROE, (2) its sales growth, and (3) its earnings growth, all averaged over the last 3 years. The incentive compensation of the senior corporate executives is based on the same three factors, but measured for the entire corporation.

   a. Do you see any obvious conceptual problems with the company's compensation program?

   b. How would you expect the compensation plan to influence managers' reaction to Kravitz's recommendations? Would these reactions be good or bad from the standpoint of maximizing the price of Randolph's stock?

   c. Should Randolph change either its compensation plan or its capital budgeting procedures to make them more consistent with one another and with the goal of stock price maximization?

Be sure to discuss fully your answers to these questions.

III

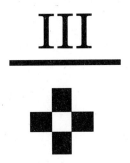

Capital Structure

7

Capital Structure
Theory

Seattle Steel Products

Seattle Steel Products was founded shortly after World War II by Leonard Freeman. Prior to the war, Freeman had owned a small steel foundry in Pittsburgh, Pennsylvania. The business was hit particularly hard by the Great Depression of the 1930s, driving it into bankruptcy. In 1940, Freeman moved his family west and went to work as a mill foreman for American Steel Corporation in Seattle, Washington. After the war ended, Freeman decided that he again wanted to run his own business. Thus, Seattle Steel Products was founded in 1946.

With the memory of his last disastrous business experience still etched clearly in his mind, Freeman vowed that his new firm would be operated so as to minimize vulnerability to general business downturns. Freeman's management style, and his dedication to making the business prosper, proved to be successful, as the firm has enjoyed relatively rapid growth for over four decades. Moreover, it has maintained a consistently strong financial position.

In late 1992, Freeman, still very energetic at the age of 85, retired from active participation in the day-to-day operations, but retained the position of Chairman of the Board. Steve Freeman, Leonard's grandson, was simultaneously appointed as the new Chief Executive Officer. Steve Freeman was well prepared for his new position. He graduated with high honors from Cornell University, obtaining a degree in materials engineering. Afterwards, he spent 10 years in various sales and technical positions with Seattle Steel. His one weakness is in the financial area, where he has had no experience or training.

Steve Freeman spent the first several weeks in his new job trying to obtain a better feel for the accounting and financial side of the business. One area of concern is the firm's heavy reliance on equity financing. Seattle Steel uses short-term debt to finance its temporary working capital requirements, but it does not use any permanent debt capital. Other firms in the steel industry generally have between 25 and 35 percent of their long-term capitalization in debt. Steve Freeman wonders if this difference should continue, and what affect a movement toward a greater use of debt would have on the company's earnings and stock price.

As part of the process of familiarizing himself with the operations of the firm, Steve Freeman had extensive meetings with the managers of each of the firm's major functional departments. From Doug Howser, the financial vice president, Freeman learned that the firm was projecting earnings before interest and taxes of $3.0 million for 1993. Since Seattle Steel will have essentially zero interest expense in 1993, this figure would also be the firm's earnings before taxes for 1993. Howser also reported that the firm's federal-plus-state income tax rate for 1993, and the foreseeable future, should be 40 percent.

Steve Freeman also learned from Howser, who obtained his information from the firm's investment bankers, that the firm's cost of equity—hence its weighted-average cost of capital—was approximately 15 percent. The investment bankers had indicated, though, that the firm could issue at least $10 million of long-term debt at a cost of 10 percent. Unless the company used quite a lot of debt, its bonds would be highly rated and would carry a low coupon because the firm currently has no outstanding long-term debt.

In part because of Leonard Freeman's depression experience—he had observed that companies with high dividend payouts had rarely gone bankrupt—Seattle Steel has always followed a policy of paying out 100 percent of its earnings as dividends. In lieu of retaining earnings to reinvest in the business, the firm has used cash flows from depreciation and deferred taxes to meet its funding needs, but it also issued additional equity capital (80 percent of which is currently held by members of the Freeman family) when its financing needs were exceptionally high.

Steve Freeman has done some reading in the area of financial management, so he is vaguely familiar with some key terms and with the works of a few of the better-known financial theorists. To gain additional insights into the capital structure issue, he asked Doug Howser to give him a briefing on the subject. Howser, in turn, asked his assistant to help him prepare a briefing report which the two of them would use in a meeting with Steve Freeman the following week. To begin, Howser and his assistant prepared the following list of questions, and the assistant must now draft answers to them prior to a meeting with Howser. Assume that you are Howser's assistant, and prepare answers to the questions. Think also about other relevant questions that Freeman might ask—he may not know much finance, but he is a very bright individual and has a reputation for "asking the right questions" and for making life difficult for subordinates who are not prepared to answer them.

Questions

1. a.   What is a firm's capital structure? What is its capitalization?

   b.   What is capital structure theory?

2. a.   Who are Modigliani and Miller (MM)?

   b.   List the assumptions of MM's no-tax (1958) model.

   c.   What were the two main propositions MM developed in their no-tax model? State the propositions algebraically and discuss their implications.

   d.   Describe briefly how MM proved their propositions.

3. Using Seattle Steel's projected 1993 EBIT of $3.0 million, and assuming that the MM conditions hold, we can compare Seattle Steel's value as an unlevered firm (V_U) with a 15 percent cost of equity (k_{sU}), with the value the firm would have, under the MM no-tax model, if it had $10 million of 10 percent debt (V_L).

   a.   What are the values for V_U, V_L, and k_{sL}?

   b.   Use the WACC formula to find Seattle Steel's WACC if it used debt financing.

   c.   Use the formula WACC = EBIT/V to verify that Firm L's WACC is 15 percent.

   d.   Graph the MM no-tax relationships between capital costs and leverage, plotting D/V on the horizontal axis. Also, graph the relationship between the firm's value and D/V.

4. Now consider MM's later (1963) model, in which they relaxed the no-tax assumption and added corporate taxes.

   a.   What are their new Propositions I and II?

b.   Repeat the analysis in Question 3 under the assumption that both the levered and unlevered firm would have a 40 percent tax rate.

5.   Miller, in his 1976 Presidential Address to the American Finance Association, added personal taxes to the model.

a.   What is Miller's basic equation (his Proposition I)?

b.   What happens to Miller's model if there are no corporate or personal taxes? What happens if only corporate taxes exist?

c.   Now assume that T_c = Corporate tax rate = 40%, T_d = Personal rate on debt income = 28%, and T_s = Personal tax rate on stock income = 20%. What is the gain from leverage according to the Miller model? How does this compare with the MM gain from leverage, where only corporate taxes are considered?

d.   What generalizations can we draw from the Miller model regarding the value to a corporation of using debt when personal taxes are considered?

6.   What are the implications of the three theories (MM no-tax, MM with corporate taxes, and Miller with corporate and personal taxes) for financial managers regarding the optimal capital structure? Do firms appear to follow one of these theoretical guidelines consistently?

7.   How does the addition of financial distress and agency costs change the MM (with corporate taxes) model and the Miller model? (Express your answer in both equation and graphical forms, and also discuss the results.)

8.   Briefly describe the asymmetric information theory of capital structure. What are its implications for financial managers?

9.   Now prepare a summary of the implications of capital structure theory which can be presented to Steve Freeman. Consider specifically these issues: (a) Are the tax tradeoff and asymmetric information theories mutually exclusive? (b) Can capital structure theory be used to actually establish a firm's optimal capital structures with precision? If not, then what insights can capital structure theory provide managers regarding the factors which influence their firms' optimal capital structures?

8

Optimal Operating and Financial Leverage

Johnson Window Company

As a builder in San Diego, Mark Johnson observed a rapid expansion in the use of custom windows and window treatments such as vertical blinds and drapes in both residential and commercial construction. People wanted to bring as much natural light as possible into their buildings, but large window footages typically increased the cost of heating and cooling by an unreasonable amount. The obvious solution was an improved-design, better-quality window. To capitalize on what he thought was a huge potential market, Johnson designed and patented a new type of tinted glass window which changed tint as the brightness of the sun changed. As the sun became brighter, the glass in the window would become darker and vice versa. In addition, the customer could select the initial tint level and tint color. Johnson felt the new glass would be particularly well-suited for office and apartment buildings which contain a lot of window footage. Although windows made with the new glass were nearly 75 percent greater in price than traditional glass windows, a feasibility study conducted by an outside engineering firm estimates that, over a period of five years, the savings associated with lower heating and cooling costs would more than make up for the price difference. Furthermore, the advantage of maintaining a constant level of brightness inside the building would be a plus to many purchasers.

Even before the patent was issued, Johnson began to organize a firm to manufacture the tinted windows. To start, he teamed up with a production engineer and a finance specialist. John Phillips, the engineer, brought manufacturing know-how to the firm, while Lori Gibbs, who had majored in finance, was responsible for finance and accounting. Each of them agreed to invest both time and money in the new business. They, along with Johnson, would have a significant ownership interest. Although the three founders would need additional capital, they anticipated little trouble in raising outside debt or equity capital because of good reports on the product and strong population growth in the sunbelt region. In fact, several local banks and regional insurance companies had already expressed an interest in providing debt capital, and a regional brokerage firm which specializes in start-up financing had expressed an interest in supplying equity venture capital.

A local attorney advised Johnson, Phillips, and Gibbs that the business should be incorporated immediately, before any outside capital is raised. The attorney also suggested that 10 million shares be authorized in the corporate charter and that a par value of $0.10 per share be assigned. The founders agreed with these recommendations and decided to issue shares to themselves at a price of $0.10 each, to assign a value of $1 to the patent, and to issue shares to outside investors at a price of $10 per share. However, before the charter could be filed, it was necessary to determine the number of shares that could be issued to the founders at $0.10 each and still have sufficient value left in the firm to raise enough equity capital at $10 per share to meet the firm's initial capital requirements. Thus, Gibbs concluded that she should create a business plan that not only described the product, the markets to be served, and the firm's production plans, but which also outlined the anticipated financing requirements in some detail.

The initial marketing plan called for selling the tinted windows directly to large contractors and using several wholesalers to distribute the items to architects and small contractors. At a projected average selling price of $750 per unit, they had little doubt that sales would be strong. However, the tinted windows will be used primarily in new construction, and this industry has always been subject to highly cyclical sales. Further, although the sunbelt region is continuing to experience relatively strong commercial and residential markets, other sunbelt areas such as Houston have been suffering from high commercial vacancy rates and depressed residential markets. Thus, Gibbs felt uncomfortable about using a point estimate for unit sales, so she developed estimates for three possible scenarios: most likely, optimistic, and pessimistic, with probabilities of occurrence of 0.50, 0.25, and 0.25, respectively. Of course, Gibbs realizes that unit sales could assume almost any value, but her discrete distribution is roughly comparable to a continuous normal distribution which has a range of plus or minus 2 standard deviations about the mean:

Scenario	Probability	Unit Sales	Dollar Sales
Pessimistic	0.25	52,200	$39,150,000
Most likely	0.50	67,500	50,625,000
Optimistic	0.25	82,800	62,100,000

After an in-depth study, Phillips, the engineer-production manager, identified two alternative production processes that could be employed, and he asked Gibbs to evaluate the financial implications of the alternatives and to recommend a course of action. Plan A involves only a small amount of automated equipment, as most of the window components would be purchased from local subcontractors. Under this plan, annual fixed costs are estimated to be $7,769,900, while variable costs would be $585 per unit produced. The second alternative, Plan B, would require the firm to make a significant investment in fabrication machinery, resulting in a fixed cost estimate of $17,845,000 per year and variable costs of $415 per unit. Neither fixed cost estimate includes interest expense, since the capitalization mix is still uncertain. The company plans to set the initial sales price at $750 per unit regardless of which production process is chosen. Total capital requirements for both current and fixed assets, as well as start-up operating funds, are estimated to be $14.0 million under Plan A and $20.0 million under Plan B.

To help with the capitalization decision, Gibbs had extensive meetings with investment bankers, venture capitalists, commercial bankers, insurance executives, and mutual-fund managers. On the basis of these meetings, she constructed the following estimates for the relationship between financial leverage and capital costs:

Amount Borrowed	Cost of Debt	Cost of Equity
$ 0 million	0.0%	14.0%
4 million	11.0	15.0
8 million	12.0	17.0
12 million	14.0	20.0
16 million	17.0	24.0

The total potential output would be much higher under Plan B than under Plan A. Thus, if the market really takes off, the company could move rapidly to meet this demand if it goes with Plan B. This might head off potential entry and competition. Of course, if demand is way below expectations, going with Plan B could prove to be a disaster. With all this in mind, Gibbs now must develop recommendations for the production method and financing mix. To help with the decision, Gibbs has prepared the following set of questions, which she passed to you, her assistant, to answer.

Questions

1. Which production plan should Gibbs recommend? (Hint: Calculate the breakeven point and the expected EBIT and ROI [return on investment] under both plans and then assess the riskiness of each. Note that the final decision is a joint decision that involves both production and financing decisions, but for this question think only about the issues involved with the production decision. Use Table 1 as a guide.)

2. Regardless of your conclusion in Question 1, assume that the decision is made to adopt Plan B, that the total capital required by Johnson Window to effect this plan is $20.0 million, and that the estimates of the relationships between financial leverage and component costs of capital given in the case are based on Plan B. Johnson's investment bankers indicated that if no debt is used, 2.0 million shares can be sold at $10 per share to raise the required $20.0 million of capital. However, Gibbs's goal is to choose that capital structure which will maximize the value of the stock held by the firm's founders. Since the stock price is to be set at $10, Gibbs has to find the number of shares that the founders can issue to themselves and still induce outside investors to pay the $10 per share price. To simplify the analysis, Gibbs has made two assumptions: (1) Since the $0.10 per share paid by the founders is 1/100th of the issue price, the founders' contribution can be ignored; hence, for simplicity, Gibbs assumed that the founders paid nothing for their stock. (2) Gibbs also assumed perpetual cash flows, so the value of the firm, V, can be estimated on the basis of expected EBIT as follows:

    $$V = D + S$$

    $$= D + \frac{(EBIT - k_d D)(1 - T)}{k_s}.$$

Here, D = market value of debt, S = market value of equity, k_d = cost of debt, and k_s = cost of equity.

Note that Gibbs will estimate the value of the equity, divide by the specified price per share to determine the number of shares that will be outstanding, assign the required number of shares to outside investors, and then leave the founders with the remaining shares. An alternative procedure would be to find the value of the equity, specify some number of shares to issue, divide equity by shares to get the equilibrium price per share, and then divide the required outside equity by this equilibrium price to get the shares issued to outsiders and remaining for the founders. The calculated wealth to the investors will be identical under either procedure, as the product Price × Shares = Value will be the same under either procedure. The procedure called for in the case is the one investment bankers typically use to estimate a "first approximation" number of shares and share price, then they make subsequent adjustments to the market price to reflect market conditions. Incidently, the investment bankers invariably put on a "road show" where they, along with company executives, travel around the country and meet with institutional investors and security analysts to pre-sell the stock and get an idea of the interest in the company. The final price is adjusted to reflect investor reactions. With this background, answer the following questions:

a. If the firm's tax rate, T, is estimated at 40 percent, what amount of financial leverage would maximize the value of the firm?

b. How many shares will the founders receive? What is the value of their shares?

c. Calculate Johnson Window's weighted average cost of capital (WACC) at each debt level. What is the relationship between Johnson's value and its WACC?

d. Suppose an investor purchased shares at $10, learned that the founders had bought their shares for only $0.10, and then felt cheated and threatened to sue the company and its founders. Would this person have a good case? Should the SEC protect investors from this kind of thing?

3. Gibbs is well aware of the fact that the average manufacturing company has a times-interest-earned (TIE) ratio of about 6×. Using

TIE as a risk measure, together with your answer to Question 2, how risky does the company appear to be?

4. Suppose Johnson is planning to raise debt by issuing a 20-year term loan. What would be the annual payment, including both interest and principal amortization? Use this information to calculate Johnson's expected first-year debt service coverage ratio, defined here as EBIT/(Interest expense + Before-tax principal repayment). If the average manufacturing firm has a coverage ratio of about 4×, what does this indicate about Johnson's riskiness?

5. Suppose this were your company. Would your choice of debt level be influenced by your other asset holdings? That is, would it matter whether your entire net worth was invested in the company as opposed to the situation where you owned millions of dollars of stocks in other companies in addition to your holdings in Johnson Window?

6. The entire analysis depends on (a) Gibbs's estimates of the costs of debt and equity at different capital structures, and (b) the validity of the equation given in Question 2.

    a. How confident are you in Gibbs's estimates of k_d and k_s? Could changes in these estimates affect the capital structure decision?

    b. What assumptions underlie the equity valuation equation? Is it likely that Johnson meets these assumptions?

7. A theory has been expressed in the finance literature that "information asymmetries" cause investors to interpret the sale of stock by a company as a "signal" that things may get worse in the future, whereas the use of debt is taken as a positive signal. In general, what implications does this have for capital structure policy? Does it matter if the firm in question is a mature company or a start-up firm? Would it matter if the founders planned to sell some of their shares at the time of the initial public offering, to make a further investment of their own capital by buying some more stock, or to neither buy nor sell shares?

8. Should the issue of control of the company be taken into account in the capital structure decision? If so, how would it affect things?

9. Gibbs has heard rumors that California may repeal its corporate taxes, resulting in a lower, 34 percent, tax rate. What impact might this have on Johnson's optimal debt level? If you are using the *Lotus*

model, calculate Johnson's value at the different debt levels assuming a 34 percent tax rate.

10. Gibbs has read several articles in *The Wall Street Journal* which indicate that labor costs will rise over the next few years, and she begins to wonder whether the variable cost estimates are realistic. Thus, Gibbs revises her original variable cost estimate for Plan A to $625 per unit. What impact do you believe this would have on the production decision? If you are using the *Lotus* model for this case, determine the ROI under each scenario for Plan A. Does this change your views toward the two production plans?

Table 1

Selected Case Data

Plan A - EBIT and ROI Calculations:

	Pessimistic	Most Likely	Optimistic
Sales revenue	$39,150,000	$50,625,000	X
Fixed costs	7,769,900	7,769,900	X
Variable costs	X	39,487,500	$48,438,000
EBIT	X	$ 3,367,600	$ 5,892,100
ROI	6.02%	X	42.09%
E(EBIT)		$ 3,367,600	
SD(EBIT)		X	
CV(EBIT)		0.53	
E(ROI)		X	
SD(ROI)		12.75%	
CV(ROI)		0.53	

Plan B - EBIT and ROI Calculations:

	Pessimistic	Most Likely	Optimistic
Sales revenue	$39,150,000	X	$62,100,000
Fixed costs	17,845,000	X	17,845,000
Variable costs	21,663,000	X	$34,362,000
EBIT	($ 358,000)	X	$ 9,893,000
ROI	−1.79%	X	49.47%
E(EBIT)		$ 4,767,500	
SD(EBIT)		$ 3,624,276	
CV(EBIT)		0.76	
E(ROI)		23.84%	
SD(ROI)		18.12%	
CV(ROI)		0.76	

Value Calculations:

Cost of Debt	Cost of Equity	Debt	Firm Value	Number of Founders' Shares
0.00%	14.00%	$ 0	$20,432,143	43,214
11.00	15.00	4,000,000	21,310,000	131,000
12.00	17.00	8,000,000	X	X
14.00	20.00	12,000,000	X	X
17.00	24.00	16,000,000	21,118,750	111,875

Table 1
Selected Case Data (continued)

Cost of Capital Calculations:

After-Tax Cost of Debt	Cost of Equity	Debt	Equity	Weight of Debt	Weight of Equity	Cost of Capital
0.00%	14.00%	$ 0	$20,432,143	0.00%	100.00%	14.00%
6.60	15.00	4,000,000	17,310,000	18.77	81.23	13.42
X	X	X	X	X	X	X
8.40	20.00	12,000,000	9,262,500	56.44	43.56	13.45
10.20	24.00	16,000,000	5,118,750	75.76	24.24	13.54

9

*Capital Structure
Policy*

Kleen Kar, Inc.

Kleen Kar, Inc., franchises automobile care centers throughout the southern United States. A complete Kleen Kar center includes a building with an automatic car washing bay and four service bays. The company also offers 10-minute oil changes and wax jobs for $15.95 each. Basically, the franchisee buys the exclusive right to use the Kleen Kar name within a given territory. In addition, franchisees receive marketing and management support and have access to low-cost supplies such as soap, wax, and oil.

Todd Lyle, a Louisiana State University graduate who founded the company in 1981, recognized the need for a fast and convenient automobile car care center. Customers of Kleen Kar could receive an oil change, wash, and wax in less than 30 minutes. Kleen Kar expanded rapidly from its base in New Orleans, first by opening company-owned stores in large cities in the South such as Miami, Orlando, Atlanta, and New Orleans, and then by franchising into other southern cities and towns. Todd was a firm believer in the virtues of equity financing. Although the company had used debt financing in the early years to finance the company-owned store expansion, Todd always used Kleen Kar's cash flows to retire the debt as soon as possible. Recent growth has occurred from franchising, where the franchisee puts up the required capital. Thus, the company has not required outside capital in several years.

Todd believes that the market for his company's services has finally matured. First, numerous competing chains, such as the Mad Hatter, $12.95 Handwax, and Oil Can Henry's, have appeared on the scene, and it now seems as if every town in the country with a population over 10,000 has at least one fast-food and one car care center franchise. Second, self-service gas stations, such as Mobil and British Petroleum, offer free automatic car washes with the purchase of gasoline. Third, many large oil companies, such as Pennzoil and Shell Oil, are entering the oil-change market and offering even lower prices in order to gain market share. Thus, Todd expects Kleen Kar's 1993 earnings before interest and taxes (EBIT) of $17 million to remain relatively constant into the foreseeable future.

Kleen Kar has 10 million shares of common stock outstanding, which is traded in the over-the-counter market. The current stock price is $6, so the total value of Kleen Kar's equity is $60 million. The book value of the firm's stock is also $60 million, so the stock now sells at its book value. Todd owns 20 percent of the outstanding shares, and others in the management group collectively own an additional 10 percent. The company's financial manager, Bill Joseph, has been preaching for years that Kleen Kar should use debt in its capital structure. "After all," says Bill, "everybody else is using at least some debt, and many firms use a great deal of debt financing. I don't want to put the firm into the junk bond category—that market has been hammered over the past few years—but I do think that judicious use of debt can benefit everyone. Also, by being unleveraged, we are just inviting some raider to line up a lot of debt financing and then make a run at our company." Todd's reaction to Bill's prodding was cautious. However, since one of Todd's friends just lost her unleveraged company to a raider, he was willing to give Bill a chance to prove his point.

Bill had worked with Todd for the past six years, and he knew that the only way he could ever convince Todd that the firm should use debt financing would be to conduct a comprehensive quantitative analysis. To begin, Bill arranged for a joint meeting with his former finance professor and an investment banker who specializes in corporate financing for service companies. After several hours, the trio agreed on these estimates for the relationships between the amount of debt financing and Kleen Kar's capital costs:

Amount Borrowed (in Millions of Dollars)	Cost of Debt	Cost of Equity
$ 0.0	0.0%	17.0%
12.5	12.0	17.5
25.0	13.0	18.5
37.5	15.0	20.0
50.0	18.0	22.0
62.5	22.0	27.0

If Kleen Kar recapitalizes, the borrowed funds would be used to repurchase the firm's stock in the over-the-counter market. The firm's federal-plus-state tax bracket is 40 percent.

With these data at hand, Bill must now complete an analysis designed to convince Todd to use some debt financing. The analysis is going to be presented in question-and-answer format, because Todd seems partial to this approach for conveying ideas. Thus, Bill's first task was to develop the set of questions to be answered. Assume that Bill has passed the questions on to you, his assistant, for answers. Remember that Bill has a strong finance background, and Todd is an excellent businessman with good instincts. Be sure to answer the questions thoroughly and be prepared for follow-up questions.

Questions

1. a. What is the difference between business risk and financial risk?

   b. How can these risks be measured in a total risk sense?

   c. How can these risks be measured in a market risk framework?

   d. How does business risk affect capital structure decisions?

2. Although Kleen Kar's EBIT is expected to be $17 million, there is a great deal of uncertainty in the estimate, as indicated by the following probability distribution:

Probability	EBIT
0.25	$ 5,000,000
0.50	17,000,000
0.25	29,000,000

   Assume that Kleen Kar has only two capitalization alternatives: Either an all-equity capital structure with $60 million of stock or $30 million of 14 percent debt plus $30 million of equity.

   a. Conduct a ROE and TIE analysis. That is, construct partial income statements for each financing alternative at each EBIT level. (Hint: Use the upper half of Table 1 as a guide.)

   b. Now calculate the return on equity (ROE) and times-interest-earned (TIE) ratio for each alternative at each EBIT level.

c. Finally, discuss the risk/return tradeoffs under the two financing alternatives. In your discussion, consider the expected ROE and the standard deviation of ROE under each alternative.

3. Since Kleen Kar is not expected to grow, Bill believes that the following equations can be used in the valuation analysis:

(1) $S = [EBIT - k_d(D)](1 - T)/k_s$.

(2) $V = S + D$.

(3) $P = (V - D_0)/n_0$.

(4) $n_1 = n_0 - D/P$.

Here,

S	= market value of equity
EBIT	= earnings before interest and taxes
k_d	= cost of debt
D	= market (and book) value of new debt
D_0	= market value of old debt
T	= tax rate
k_s	= cost of equity
V	= total market value
P	= stock price after recapitalization
n_0	= number of shares before recapitalization
n_1	= number of shares after recapitalization

a. Explain the logic of Equation (1) for a zero-growth firm.

b. Describe briefly, without using numbers, the sequence of events that would occur if Kleen Kar decided to recapitalize.

4. Now, use the data given in the case as the basis for a valuation analysis.

a. Estimate Kleen Kar's stock price at the six levels of debt given in the case. (Hint: Use the lower half of Table 1 as a guide. Assume that all debt issued by the firm is perpetual.)

b. How many shares would remain after recapitalization under each debt scenario?

c. Considering only the six levels of debt proposed in the case, what is Kleen Kar's optimal capital structure?

5. Now assume that Kleen Kar recapitalized with $12.5 million of debt, hence S = $53,142,857; D = $12,500,000; V = $65,642,857; P = $6.56; and n = 8,095,756.

a. What would Kleen Kar's share price and ending number of shares be if it increased its debt to $25 million by issuing $25 million of new debt and using half to refund the existing issue and half to repurchase stock? (Assume that the indenture for the first $12.5 million debt issue prohibits the firm from issuing additional debt without refunding.)

b. Now assume that Kleen Kar issues $12.5 million of new debt without refunding the first issue. What would be the stock price and ending number of shares in this situation? (Assume that the old and the new debt issues have the same priority of claims. Also, remember that if the firm has $25 million of debt in total, its cost of debt is 13 percent, so the new $12.5 million debt issue will have an interest rate of 13 percent, and the old debt issue will have a required rate of return of 13 percent.)

c. Explain why the prices are higher in Parts a and b than those obtained in Question 4.

6. In addition to valuation estimates, most managers are also concerned with the impact of financial leverage on the firm's earnings per share (EPS) and weighted average cost of capital (WACC).

a. Calculate the EPS at each debt level, assuming that Kleen Kar begins with zero debt and raises new debt in a single issue.

b. Is EPS maximized at the same debt level that maximizes stock price?

c. Calculate the WACC at each debt level.

d. What are the relationships between the amount of debt, stock price, and WACC?

7. Consider what would happen if Kleen Kar's business risk were considerably different than that used to estimate the financial leverage/capital cost relationships given in the case.

a.   Describe how the analysis would change if Kleen Kar's business
     risk were significantly higher than originally estimated. If you
     are using the *Lotus* model for this case, assume that the
     following set of leverage/cost estimates applies:

Amount Borrowed (in Millions of Dollars)	Cost of Debt	Cost of Equity
$ 0.0	0.0 %	18.0 %
12.5	13.0	19.0
25.0	15.0	21.0
37.5	18.0	24.0
50.0	22.0	28.0
62.5	27.0	33.0

What would be Kleen Kar's optimal capital structure in this
situation?

b.   How would things change if the firm's business risk were
     considerably lower than originally estimated? If you are using
     the *Lotus* model for this case, assume that the following set of
     leverage/cost estimates applies:

Amount Borrowed (In Millions of Dollars)	Cost of Debt	Cost of Equity
$ 0.0	0.0 %	15.0 %
12.5	10.0	15.3
25.0	10.5	16.0
37.5	11.5	17.0
50.0	13.5	18.5
62.5	15.5	20.0

What would be the firm's optimal capital structure in this situation?

8.   Now consider two capital structure theories: Modigliani-Miller with
     corporate taxes (MM63) and the Miller model.

a.   What would Kleen Kar's value at $37.5 million of debt be,
     according to the MM63 model?

b.   What would the firm's value be, according to the Miller model?
     (Assume that the personal tax rate on income from stock $[T_s]$ is
     25 percent, and the personal tax rate on income from debt $[T_d]$ is
     30 percent. Also, use $60 million as the value of the unlevered
     firm $[V_U]$ in both the MM and Miller models, even though it
     should be less in the Miller model.)

c. Why do the values differ when calculated by the equations in Question 3, the MM63 model, and the Miller model?   (Hint: Consider the assumptions that underlie each model.)

9. How do control issues affect the capital structure decision?

10. Consider the usefulness of this analysis for most firms.

a. What are the major weaknesses of the type of analysis called for in the case?

b. What other approaches could managers use to help determine an appropriate target capital structure?

c. Is the target capital structure best thought of as a point estimate or as a range?

d. What other factors should managers consider when setting their firms' target capital structures?

Table 1
Selected Case Data

ROE and TIE Analyses:

	All Equity			50% Debt		
Probability	0.25	0.50	0.25	0.25	0.50	0.25
EBIT	$5,000,000	$17,000,000	$29,000,000	$5,000,000	$17,000,000	$29,000,000
Interest	0	0	0	4,200,000	4,200,000	4,200,000
EBT	$5,000,000	X	X	$ 800,000	$12,800,000	$24,800,000
Taxes	2,000,000	X	X	320,000	5,120,000	9,920,000
Net Income	X	$10,200,000	$17,400,000	$ 480,000	$ 7,680,000	$14,880,000
ROE	5.0%	X	29.0%	1.6%	25.6%	X
TIE	n.a.	n.a.	n.a.	1.19	4.05	X
E(ROE)		17.0%			X	
σROE		8.5%			17.0%	
CV		0.50			0.66	

Valuation Analysis:

D (000s)	S	V	D/V	P	WACC	Number of Shares	EPS
$ 0	$60,000,000	$60,000,000	0%	$6.00	17.0%	10,000,000	$1.02
12,500	53,142,857	65,642,857	19	6.56	15.5	8,095,756	1.15
X	X	X	X	X	X	X	X
X	X	X	X	X	X	X	X
50,000	21,818,182	71,818,182	70	7.18	14.2	3,037,975	1.58
62,500	7,222,222	69,722,222	90	6.97	14.6	1,035,857	1.88

10

Capital Structure Policy

Aspeon Sparkling Water, Inc.

Aspeon Sparkling Water, Inc., bottles pure Rocky Mountain spring water and sells it through independent distributors located throughout the continental United States. The company owns and operates regional warehouses in St. Louis, Buffalo, Jacksonville, and Los Angeles. Basically, Aspeon sells its water to wholesale distributors who have exclusive rights to a given territory. Then, the distributors sell it to supermarkets within their region. Additionally, Aspeon is responsible for marketing the product nationally.

The company was founded in 1981 by Beth Poe, then a recent graduate of the University of Michigan. Beth grew up in Aspen, Colorado. She knew that consumers were becoming more health conscious, and she recognized a demand for clean, fresh-tasting water. After returning to Colorado upon graduation and convincing her wealthy parents to become silent partners, she obtained the necessary equity capital to build a plant. Aspeon grew rapidly from its initial customer base in Colorado, and by 1988 Aspeon water was on virtually every supermarket shelf in America. Beth was a dedicated believer in the virtues of equity financing. Although the company had used debt financing in the early years to finance the regional warehouses, Beth always used Aspeon's cash flows to retire the debt as soon as possible.

Beth believes that the market for her company's product has finally matured. First, numerous bottled-water companies, such as Zephyrhills and Evian, have appeared on the scene. Second, it is extremely difficult to differentiate Aspeon from other brands of water. Third, the product is currently sold throughout the country, and there are no additional markets to enter. Thus, Beth expects Aspeon's 1993 earnings before interest and taxes (EBIT) of $32 million to remain relatively constant into the foreseeable future.

Aspeon has 10 million shares of common stock outstanding, which is traded in the over-the-counter market. The current stock price is $12.00, so the total value of Aspeon's equity is $120 million. The book value of the firm's stock is also $120 million, so the stock now sells at its book value. Beth owns 20 percent of the outstanding shares, and others in the management group own an additional 10 percent. The company's financial manager, Emily Martin, has been preaching for years that Aspeon should use debt in its capital structure. "After all," says Emily, "everybody else is using at least some debt, and many firms use a great deal of debt financing. I don't want to put the firm into the junk bond category—that market has been hammered over the past few years—but I do think that the judicious use of debt can benefit everyone. Also, by being unleveraged, we are just inviting some raider to line up a lot of debt financing and then make a run at our company." Beth's reaction to Emily's prodding was cautious. However, since one of Beth's friends just lost his unleveraged company to a raider, she was willing to give Emily a chance to prove her point.

Emily had worked with Beth for the past six years, and she knew that the only way she could ever convince Beth that the firm should use debt financing would be to conduct a comprehensive quantitative analysis. To begin, Emily arranged for a joint meeting with her former finance professor and an investment banker who specializes in corporate financing for service companies. After several hours, the trio agreed on these estimates for the relationships between the amount of debt financing and Aspeon's capital costs:

Amount Borrowed (In Millions of Dollars)	Cost of Debt	Cost of Equity
$ 0.0	0.0 %	16.0 %
25.0	10.0	16.5
50.0	11.0	17.5
75.0	13.0	19.0
100.0	16.0	21.0
125.0	20.0	26.0

If Aspeon recapitalizes, the borrowed funds would be used to repurchase the firm's stock in the over-the-counter market. The firm's federal-plus-state tax bracket is 40 percent.

With these data at hand, Emily must now complete an analysis designed to convince Beth to use some debt financing. The analysis is going to be presented in question-and-answer format, because Beth seems partial to this approach for conveying ideas. Thus, Emily's first task was to develop the set of questions to be answered. Assume that Emily has passed the questions on to you, her assistant, for answers. Emily has a strong finance background, and Beth is an excellent businesswoman with good instincts. Be sure to answer the questions thoroughly and be prepared for follow-up questions.

Questions

1. a. What is the difference between business risk and financial risk?

    b. How can these risks be measured in a total risk sense?

    c. How can these risks be measured in a market risk framework?

    d. How does business risk affect capital structure decisions?

2. Although Aspeon's EBIT is expected to be $32 million, there is a great deal of uncertainty in the estimate, as indicated by the following probability distribution:

Probability	EBIT
0.25	$ 10,000,000
0.50	32,000,000
0.25	54,000,000

Assume that Aspeon had only two capitalization alternatives: Either an all-equity capital structure with $120 million of stock or $60 million of 13 percent debt plus $60 million of equity.

    a. Conduct a ROE and TIE analysis. That is, construct partial income statements for each financing alternative at each EBIT level. (Hint: Use the upper half of Table 1 as a guide.)

    b. Now calculate the return on equity (ROE) and times-interest-earned (TIE) ratio for each alternative at each EBIT level.

    c. Finally, discuss the risk/return tradeoffs under the two financing alternatives. In your discussion, consider the expected ROE and the standard deviation of ROE under each alternative.

Part III *Capital Structure*

3. Since Aspeon is not expected to grow, Emily believes that the following equations can be used in the valuation analysis:

    (1) $S = [EBIT - k_d(D)](1 - T)/k_s$.

    (2) $V = S + D$.

    (3) $P = (V - D_0)/n_0$.

    (4) $n_1 = n_0 - D/P$.

    Here,

S	=	market value of equity
EBIT	=	earnings before interest and taxes
k_d	=	cost of debt
D	=	market (and book) value of new debt
D_0	=	market value of old debt
T	=	tax rate
k_s	=	cost of equity
V	=	total market value
P	=	stock price after recapitalization
n_0	=	number of shares before recapitalization
n_1	=	number of shares after recapitalization

    a. Explain the logic of Equation (1) for a zero-growth firm.

    b. Describe briefly, without using numbers, the sequence of events that would occur if Aspeon decided to recapitalize.

4. Now, use the data given in the case as the basis for a valuation analysis.

    a. Estimate Aspeon's stock price at the six levels of debt given in the case. (Hint: Use the lower half of Table 1 as a guide. Assume that all debt issued by the firm is perpetual.)

    b. How many shares would remain after recapitalization under each debt scenario?

    c. Considering only the six levels of debt proposed in the case, what is Aspeon's optimal capital structure?

5. Now assume that Aspeon recapitalized with $25.0 million of debt, hence S = $107,272,727; D = $25,000,000; V = $132,272,727; P = $13.23; and n = 8,109,966.

    a. What would Aspeon's share price and ending number of shares be if it increased its debt to $50 million by issuing $50.0 million of new debt and using half to refund the existing issue and half to repurchase stock? (Assume that the indenture for the first $25.0 million debt issue prohibits the firm from issuing additional debt without refunding.)

    b. Now assume that Aspeon issues $25.0 million of new debt without refunding the first issue. What would be the stock price and ending number of shares in this situation? (Assume that the old and the new debt issues have the same priority of claims. Also, remember that if the firm has $50 million of debt in total, its cost of debt is 11 percent, so the new $25.0 million debt issue will have an interest rate of 11 percent, and the old debt issue will have a required rate of return of 11 percent.)

    c. Explain why the prices are higher in Parts a and b than those obtained in Question 4.

6. In addition to valuation estimates, most managers are also concerned with the impact of financial leverage on the firm's earnings per share (EPS) and weighted average cost of capital (WACC).

    a. Calculate the EPS at each debt level, assuming that Aspeon begins with zero debt and raises new debt in a single issue.

    b. Is EPS maximized at the same debt level that maximizes stock price?

    c. Calculate the WACC at each debt level.

    d. What are the relationships between the amount of debt, stock price, and WACC?

7. Consider what would happen if Aspeon's business risk were considerably different than that used to estimate the financial leverage/capital cost relationships given in the case.

    a. Describe how the analysis would change if Aspeon's business risk were significantly higher than originally estimated. If you are using the *Lotus* model for this case, assume that the following set of leverage/cost estimates applies:

Part III *Capital Structure*

Amount Borrowed (in Millions of Dollars)	Cost of Debt	Cost of Equity
$ 0.0	0.0 %	17.0 %
25.0	11.0	18.0
50.0	13.0	20.0
75.0	16.0	23.0
100.0	20.0	27.0
125.0	25.0	32.0

What would be Aspeon's optimal capital structure in this situation?

b. How would things change if the firm's business risk were considerably lower than originally estimated? If you are using the *Lotus* model for this case, assume that the following set of leverage/cost estimates applies:

Amount Borrowed (in Millions of Dollars)	Cost of Debt	Cost of Equity
$ 0.0	0.0 %	14.0 %
25.0	8.0	14.3
50.0	8.5	15.0
75.0	9.5	16.0
100.0	11.5	17.5
125.0	13.5	19.0

What would be the firm's optimal capital structure in this situation?

8. Now consider two capital structure theories: Modigliani-Miller with corporate taxes (MM63) and the Miller model.

   a. What would Aspeon's value at $75.0 million of debt be, according to the MM63 model?

   b. What would the firm's value be, according to the Miller model? (Assume that the personal tax rate on income from stock $[T_s]$ is 25 percent, and the personal tax rate on income from debt $[T_d]$ is 30 percent. Also, use $120 million as the value of the unlevered firm $[V_U]$ in both the MM63 and Miller models, even though it should be less in the Miller model.)

   c. Why do the values differ when calculated by the equations in Question 3, the MM63 model, and the Miller model? (Hint: Consider the assumptions that underlie each model.)

9. How do control issues affect the capital structure decision?

10. Consider the usefulness of this analysis for most firms.

    a. What are the major weaknesses of the type of analysis called for in the case?

    b. What other approaches could managers use to help determine an appropriate target capital structure?

    c. Is the target capital structure best thought of as a point estimate or as a range?

    d. What other factors should managers consider when setting their firms' target capital structures?

Table 1

Selected Case Data

ROE and TIE Analyses:

	All Equity			50% Debt		
Probability	0.25	0.50	0.25	0.25	0.50	0.25
EBIT	$10,000,000	$32,000,000	$54,000,000	$10,000,000	$32,000,000	$54,000,000
Interest	0	0	0	7,800,000	7,800,000	7,800,000
EBT	$10,000,000	X	X	$ 2,200,000	$24,200,000	$46,200,000
Taxes	4,000,000	X	X	880,000	9,680,000	18,480,000
Net Income	X	$19,200,000	$32,400,000	$ 1,320,000	$14,520,000	$27,720,000
ROE	5.0%	X	27.0%	2.2%	24.2%	X
TIE	n.a.	n.a.	n.a.	1.28	4.10	X
E(ROE)		16.0%			X	
σROE		7.8%			15.6%	
CV		0.49			0.64	

Valuation Analysis:

D (000s)	S	V	D/V	P	WACC	Number of Shares	EPS
$ 0	$120,000,000	$120,000,000	0%	$12.00	16.0%	10,000,000	$1.92
25,000	107,272,727	132,272,727	19	13.23	14.5	8,109,966	2.18
X	X	X	X	X	X	X	X
X	X	X	X	X	X	X	X
100,000	45,714,286	145,714,286	69	14.57	13.2	3,137,255	3.06
125,000	16,153,846	141,153,846	89	14.12	13.6	1,144,414	3.67

IV

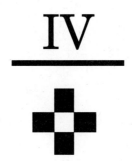

Capital Budgeting

11

Capital Budgeting
Decision Methods

Chicago Valve Company

Although he was hired as a financial analyst after completing his MBA, Richard Houston's first assignment at Chicago Valve was with the firm's marketing department. Historically, the major focus of Chicago Valve's sales effort was on demonstrating the reliability and technological superiority of the firm's product line. However, many of Chicago Valve's traditional customers have embarked on cost-cutting programs in recent years. As a result, Chicago Valve's marketing director asked Houston's boss, the financial VP, to lend Houston to marketing to help them develop some analytical procedures that the salesforce can use to demonstrate the financial benefits of buying Chicago Valve's products.

Chicago Valve manufactures valve systems that are used in a wide variety of applications including sewage treatment systems, petroleum refining, and pipeline transmission. The complete systems include sophisticated pumps, sensors, valves, and control units that continuously monitor the flow rate and the pressure along a line and automatically adjust the pump to meet pre-set pressure specifications. Most of Chicago Valve's systems are made up of standard components, and most complete systems are priced from $100,000 to $250,000. Because of the somewhat technical nature of the products, the majority of Chicago Valve's salespeople have a background in engineering.

As he began to think about his assignment, Houston quickly came to the conclusion that the best way to "sell" a system to a cost-conscious customer would be to conduct a capital budgeting analysis which would demonstrate the cost effectiveness of the system. Further, Houston concluded that the best way to begin was with an analysis for one of Chicago Valve's actual customers.

From discussions with the firm's salespeople, Houston concluded that a proposed sale to Lone Star Petroleum, Inc., was perfect to use as an illustration. Lone Star is considering the purchase of one of Chicago Valve's standard petroleum valve systems which costs $200,000, including taxes and delivery. It would cost Lone Star another $12,500 to install the equipment, and this expense would be added to the invoice price of the equipment to determine the depreciable basis of the system. A MACRS class-life of 5 years would be used, but the system has an economic life of 8 years, and it will be used for that period. After 8 years, the system will probably be obsolete, so it will have a zero salvage value at that time. Current depreciation allowances for 5-year class property are 0.20, 0.32, 0.19, 0.12, 0.11, and 0.06 in Years 1-6, respectively.

This system would replace a valve system which has been used for about 20 years and which has been fully depreciated. The costs for removing the current system are about equal to its scrap value, so its current net market value is zero. The advantages of the new system are greater reliability and lower human monitoring and maintenance requirements. In total, the new system would save Lone Star $60,000 annually in pre-tax operating costs. For capital budgeting, Lone Star uses an 11 percent cost of capital, and its federal-plus-state tax rate is 40 percent.

Natasha Spurrier, Chicago Valve's marketing manager, gave Houston a free hand in structuring the analysis, but with one exception—she told Houston to be sure to include the modified IRR (MIRR) as one of the decision criteria. To calculate MIRR, all of the cash inflows are compounded to the terminal year, in this case Year 8, at the project's cost of capital, and then these compounded values are summed to produce the project's terminal value. Then, MIRR is found as the discount rate which causes the present value of the terminal value to equal the net cost of the equipment. Spurrier had recently attended a seminar on capital budgeting and, according to the seminar leader, the MIRR method has significant advantages over the regular IRR. For that reason, it is rapidly replacing IRR as a primary capital budgeting method.

Now put yourself in Houston's position, and develop a capital budgeting analysis for the valve system. As you go through the analysis, keep in mind that the purpose of the analysis is to help Chicago Valve's sales representatives sell equipment to other nonfinancial people, so the analysis must be as clear as possible, yet technically correct. In other words, the analysis must not only be right, it must also be understandable to decision makers, and the presenter—Harrison, in this case—must be able to answer any and all questions, ranging from the performance characteristics of the equipment to the assumptions underlying the capital budgeting decision criteria.

Questions

1. Table 1 contains the complete cash flow analysis. Examine it carefully and be prepared to answer any questions which might be posed.

Table 1
Project Net Cash Flows

Year	Net Cost	Depreciation Tax Savings	After-Tax Cost Savings	Net Cash Flow
0	($212,500)			($212,500)
1		$17,000	$36,000	53,000
2		27,200	36,000	63,200
3		16,150	36,000	52,150
4		10,200	36,000	46,200
5		9,350	36,000	45,350
6		5,100	36,000	41,100
7		0	36,000	36,000
8		0	36,000	36,000

2. What is the project's NPV? Explain the economic rationale behind the NPV. Could the NPV of this particular project be different for Lone Star Petroleum Company than for one of Chicago Valve's other potential customers? Explain.

3. Calculate the proposed project's IRR. Explain the rationale for using the IRR to evaluate capital investment projects. Could the IRR for this project differ for Lone Star versus for another customer?

4. Suppose one of Lone Star's executives typically uses the payback as a primary capital budgeting decision tool and wants some payback information.

   a. What is the project's payback period?

   b. What is the rationale behind the use of payback as a project evaluation tool?

   c. What deficiencies does payback have as a capital budgeting decision method?

    d.   Does payback provide any useful information regarding capital budgeting decisions?

    e.   Chicago Valve has a number of different types of products: Some that are relatively expensive, some that are inexpensive, some that have very long lives, and some with short lives. Strictly as a sales tool, without regard to the validity of the analysis, would the payback be of more help to the sales staff for some types of equipment than for others? Explain.

    f.   People occasionally use the payback's reciprocal as an estimate of the project's rate of return. Would this procedure be more appropriate for projects with very long or short lives? Explain.

5.   What is the project's MIRR? What is the difference between the IRR and the MIRR? Which is better? Why?

6.   Suppose a potential customer wants to know the project's profitability index (PI). What is the value of the PI for Lone Star, and what is the rationale behind this measure?

7.   Under what conditions do NPV, IRR, MIRR, and PI all lead to the same accept/reject decision? When can conflicts occur? If a conflict arises, which method should be used, and why?

8.   Suppose Congress reinstates the investment tax credit (ITC), which is a direct reduction of taxes equal to the prescribed ITC percentage times the cost of the asset. What would be the impact of a 10 percent ITC on the acceptability of the control system project? No calculations are necessary; just discuss the impact.

9.   Plot the project's NPV profile and explain how the graph can be used.

10.   Now suppose that Chicago Valve sells a low-quality, short-life valve system. In a typical installation, its cash flows are as follows:

Year	Net Cash Flow
0	($120,000)
1	150,000

Assuming an 11 percent cost of capital, what is this project's NPV and its IRR? Draw this project's NPV profile on the same graph with the earlier project and then discuss the complete graph. Be sure to talk about (1) mutually exclusive versus independent projects, (2) conflicts between projects, and (3) the effect of the cost of capital on the existence of conflicts. What conditions must exist with respect to timing of cash flows and project size for conflicts to arise?

11. Natasha Spurrier informed Houston that all sales reps have laptop computers, so they can perform capital budgeting analyses for their clients. For example, they could insert data for their client companies into the models and do both the basic analysis and also sensitivity analyses, in which they examine the effects of changes in such things as the annual cost savings, the cost of capital, and the tax rate. Therefore, Houston and Spurrier developed the following "sensitivity questions" which they plan to discuss with the sales reps:

   a. Suppose the annual cost savings differed from the projected level; how would this affect the various decision criteria? What is the minimum annual cost savings at which the system would be cost justified? Discuss what is happening and, if you are using the *Lotus* model, quantify your answers; otherwise, just discuss the nature of the effects.

   b. Repeat the type of analysis done in Part a, but now, vary the cost of capital. Again, quantify your answers if you are using the *Lotus* model.

   c. Repeat the type of analysis done in Part a, but now, vary the tax rate. Again, quantify your answers if you are using the *Lotus* model.

   d. Would the capability to do sensitivity analysis on a laptop computer be of much assistance to the sales staff? Can you anticipate any problems that might arise? Explain.

12. Now suppose that Chicago Valve sells another product that is used to speed the flow through pipelines. However, after a year of use, the pipeline must undergo expensive repairs. In a typical installation, the cash flows of this product might be as follows:

Year	Net Cash Flow
0	($30,000)
1	150,000
2	(120,000)

Assuming an 11 percent cost of capital, what is this project's NPV, IRR, and MIRR? Draw this new project's NPV profile on a new graph. Explain what is happening with the cash flows on this project.

12

Cash Flow Estimation

Indian River Citrus Company (A)

Indian River Citrus Company is a leading producer of fresh, frozen, and made-from-concentrate citrus drinks. The firm was founded in 1929 by Matthew Stewart, a navy veteran who settled in Miami after World War I and began selling real estate. Since real estate sales were booming, Stewart's fortunes soared. His investment philosophy, which he proudly displayed behind his desk, was "Buy land. They aren't making any more of it." He practiced what he preached, but instead of investing in residential property, which he knew was grossly overvalued, he invested most of his sales commissions in citrus land located in Florida's Indian River County. Originally, Stewart sold his oranges, lemons, and grapefruit to wholesalers for distribution to grocery stores. However, in 1965, when frozen juice sales were causing the industry to boom, he joined with several other growers to form Indian River Citrus Company, which processed its own juices. Today, its Indian River Citrus, Florida Sun, and Citrus Gold brands are sold throughout the United States.

Indian River's management is currently evaluating a new product—lite orange juice. Studies done by the firm's marketing department indicate that many people who like the taste of orange juice will not drink it because of its high calorie count. The new product would cost more, but it would offer consumers something that no other competing orange juice product offers—35 percent less calories. Lili Romero and Brent Gibbs, recent business school graduates who are now working at the firm as financial analysts, must analyze this project, along with two other potential investments, and then present their findings to the company's executive committee.

Production facilities for the lite orange juice product would be set up in an unused section of Indian River's main plant. Relatively inexpensive, used machinery with an estimated cost of only $500,000 would be purchased, but shipping costs to move the machinery to Indian River's plant would total $20,000, and installation charges would add another $50,000 to the total equipment cost. Further, Indian River's inventories (raw materials, work-in-process, and finished goods) would have to be increased by $10,000 at the time of the initial investment. The machinery has a remaining economic life of 4 years, and the company has obtained a special tax ruling that allows it to depreciate the equipment under the MACRS 3-year class. Under current tax law, the depreciation allowances are 0.33, 0.45, 0.15, and 0.07 in Years 1 through 4, respectively. The machinery is expected to have a salvage value of $100,000 after 4 years of use.

The section of the main plant where the lite orange juice production would occur has been unused for several years, and consequently it has suffered some deterioration. Last year, as part of a routine facilities improvement program, Indian River spent $100,000 to rehabilitate that section of the plant. Brent believes that this outlay, which has already been paid and expensed for tax purposes, should be charged to the lite orange juice project. His contention is that if the rehabilitation had not taken place, the firm would have to spend the $100,000 to make the site suitable for the orange juice production line.

Indian River's management expects to sell 425,000 16-ounce cartons of the new orange juice product in each of the next 4 years, at a price of $2.00 per carton, of which $1.50 per carton would be needed to cover fixed and variable cash operating costs. Since most of the costs are variable, the fixed and variable cost categories have been combined. Also, note that operating cost changes are a function of the number of units sold rather than unit price, so unit price changes have no effect on operating costs.

In examining the sales figures, Lili Romero noted a short memo from Indian River's sales manager which expressed concern that the lite orange juice project would cut into the firm's sales of regular orange juice—this type of effect is called *cannibalization*. Specifically, the sales manager estimated that regular orange juice sales would fall by 5 percent if lite orange juice were introduced. Lili then talked to both the sales and production managers and concluded that the new project would probably lower the firm's regular orange juice sales by $40,000 per year, but, at the same time, it would also reduce regular orange juice production costs by $20,000 per year, all on a pre-tax basis. Thus, the net cannibalization effect would be −$40,000 + $20,000 = −$20,000. Indian River's federal-plus-state tax rate is 40 percent, and its overall cost of capital is 10 percent, calculated as follows:

$$\text{WACC} = w_d k_d (1 - T) + w_s k_s$$
$$= 0.5(10\%)(0.6) + 0.5(14\%)$$
$$= 10.0\%.$$

Lili and Brent were asked to analyze this project, along with two other projects, and then to present their findings in a "tutorial" manner to Indian River's executive committee. The financial vice president, Lili and Brent's supervisor, wants them to educate some of the other executives, especially the marketing and sales managers, in the theory of capital budgeting so that these executives will have a better understanding of capital budgeting decisions. Therefore, Lili and Brent have decided to ask and then answer a series of questions as set forth below.

Specifics on the other two projects that must be analyzed are provided in Questions 9 and 10.

Questions

1.   Define the term "incremental cash flow." Since the project will be financed in part by debt, should the cash flow statement include interest expenses? Explain.

2.   Should the $100,000 that was spent to rehabilitate the plant be included in the analysis? Explain.

3.   Suppose another citrus producer had expressed an interest in leasing the lite orange juice production site for $25,000 a year. If this were true (in fact, it was not), how would that information be incorporated into the analysis?

4.   What is Indian River's Year 0 net investment outlay on this project? What is the expected nonoperating cash flow when the project is terminated at Year 4? (Hint: Use Table 1 as a guide.)

5.   Estimate the project's operating cash flows. (Hint: Again use Table 1 as a guide.) What are the project's NPV, IRR, modified IRR (MIRR), and payback?   Should the project be undertaken? [Remember: The MIRR is found in three steps: (1) compound all

cash inflows forward to the terminal year at the cost of capital, (2) sum the compounded cash inflows to obtain the *terminal value* of the inflows, and (3) find the discount rate which forces the present value of the terminal value to equal the present value of the net investment outlays. This discount rate is defined as the MIRR.]

6. Now suppose the project had involved replacement rather than expansion of existing facilities. Describe briefly how the analysis would have to be changed to deal with a replacement project.

7. Assume that inflation is expected to average 5 percent per year over the next 4 years.

   a. Does it appear that the project's cash flow estimates are real or nominal? That is, are the cash flows stated in constant (current year) dollars, or has inflation been built into the cash flow estimates? (Hint: Nominal cash flows include the effects of inflation, but real cash flows do not.)

   b. Is the 10 percent cost of capital a nominal or a real rate?

   c. Is the current NPV biased, and, if so, in what direction?

8. Now assume that the sales price will increase by the 5 percent inflation rate beginning after Year 0. However, assume that cash operating costs will increase by only 2 percent annually from the initial cost estimate, because over half of the costs are fixed by long-term contracts. For simplicity, assume that no other cash flows (net externality costs, salvage value, or net working capital) are affected by inflation. What are the project's NPV, IRR, MIRR, and payback now that inflation has been taken into account? (Hint: The Year 1 cash flows, as well as succeeding cash flows, must be adjusted for inflation because the original estimates are in Year 0 dollars.)

9. The second capital budgeting decision which Lili and Brent were asked to analyze involves choosing between two mutually exclusive projects, S and L, whose cash flows are set forth as follows:

Case 12 *Cash Flow Estimation*

Expected Net Cash Flow

Year	Project S	Project L
0	($100,000)	($100,000)
1	60,000	33,500
2	60,000	33,500
3	--	33,500
4	--	33,500

Both of these projects are in Indian River's main line of business, orange juice, and the investment which is chosen is expected to be repeated indefinitely into the future. Also, each project is of average risk, hence each is assigned the 10 percent corporate cost of capital.

a. What is each project's single-cycle NPV? Now apply the replacement chain approach and then repeat the analysis using the equivalent annual annuity approach. Which project should be chosen, S or L? Why?

b. Now assume that the cost to replicate Project S in 2 years is estimated to be $105,000 because of inflationary pressures. Similar investment cost increases will occur for both projects in Year 4 and beyond. How would this affect the analysis? Which project should be chosen under this assumption?

10. The third project to be considered involves a fleet of delivery trucks with an engineering life of 3 years (that is, each truck will be totally worn out after 3 years). However, if the trucks were taken out of service, or "abandoned," prior to the end of 3 years, they would have positive salvage values. Here are the estimated net cash flows for each truck:

Year	Initial Investment and Operating Cash Flow	End-of-Year Net Abandonment Cash Flow
0	($40,000)	$40,000
1	16,800	24,800
2	16,000	16,000
3	14,000	0

The relevant cost of capital is again 10 percent.

a. What would the NPV be if the trucks were operated for the full 3 years?

97

b. What if they were abandoned at the end of Year 2? What if they were abandoned at the end of Year 1?

c. What is the economic life of the truck project?

11. Refer back to the original lite orange juice project. In this and the remaining questions, if you are using the *Lotus 1-2-3* model, quantify your answer. Otherwise, just discuss the impact of the changes.

    a. What would happen to the project's profitability if inflation were neutral, that is, if both sales price and cash operating costs increase by the 5 percent annual inflation rate?

    b. Now suppose that Indian River is unable to pass along its inflationary input cost increases to its customers. For example, assume that cash operating costs increase by the 5 percent annual inflation rate, but that the sales price can be increased at only a 2 percent annual rate. What is the project's profitability under these conditions?

12. Return to the initial inflation assumptions (5 percent on price and 2 percent on cash operating costs).

    a. Assume that the sales quantity estimate remains at 425,000 units per year. What Year 0 unit price would the company have to set to cause the project to just break even, that is, to force NPV = $0?

    b. Now assume that the sales price remains at $2. What annual unit sales volume would be needed for the project to break even?

Table 1
Project Cash Flow Estimates

Net Investment Outlay: Depreciation Schedule:

Price	X	Basis =		X	
Freight	X				
Installation	X		**MACRS**	**Depr.**	**End-of-Year**
Change in NWC	X	**Year**	**Factor**	**Expense**	**Book Value**
	X	1	33%	$188,100	$381,900
		2	X	X	X
		3	X	X	X
		4	7	39,000	0
			1.00%	X	

Cash Flow Statements:

	Year 0	Year 1	Year 2	Year 3	Year 4
Unit price		$ 2	X	X	$ 2
Unit sales		425,000	X	X	425,000
Revenues		$850,000	X	X	$ 850,000
Operating costs		637,500	X	X	637,500
Depreciation		188,100	X	X	39,900
Other project effects		20,000	X	X	20,000
Before tax income		$ 4,400	X	X	$ 152,600
Taxes		1,760	X	X	61,040
Net income		$ 2,640	X	X	$ 91,560
Plus depreciation		188,100	X	X	39,900
Net op cash flow		$190,740	X	X	$ 131,460
Salvage value					$ 100,000
SV tax					X
Recovery of NWC					X
Termination CF					X
Project NCF	X	X	X	X	X

13

Risk Analysis in
Capital Budgeting

Indian River Citrus
Company (B)

In Case 12, Lili Romero and Brent Gibbs analyzed a lite orange juice project for the Indian River Citrus Company. The project required an initial investment of $570,000 in fixed assets (including shipping and installation charges), plus a $10,000 addition to net working capital. The machinery would be used for 4 years and be depreciated on the basis of a 3-year MACRS class life. The appropriate MACRS depreciation allowances are 0.33, 0.45, 0.15, and 0.07 in Years 1 through 4, respectively, and the machinery is expected to have a salvage value of $100,000. If the project is undertaken, the firm expects to sell 425,000 cartons of lite orange juice at a current dollar (Year 0) wholesale price of $2 per carton. However, the sales price will be adjusted for inflation, which is expected to average 5 percent annually, so the actual expected sales price at the end of the first year is $2.10, the expected price at the end of the second year is $2.205 and so on.

The lite orange juice project is expected to cannibalize the before-tax profit Indian River earns on its regular orange juice line by $20,000, because the two product lines are somewhat competitive. Further, the company expects cash operating costs to be $1.50 per unit in Time 0 dollars, and it expects these costs to increase by 2 percent per year. Therefore, total operating cash costs during the first year of operation (Year 1) are expected to be ($1.50) (1.02) (425,000) = $650,250. Indian River's tax rate is 40 percent, and its cost of capital is 10 percent. Cash flow data and other information, as developed by Lili and Brent using a *Lotus 1-2-3* model, are given in Table 1.

When Lili and Brent presented their initial (Case 12) analysis to Indian River's executive committee, things went well, and they were congratulated on both their analysis and their presentation. However, several questions were raised. In particular, the executive committee wanted to see some type of risk analysis on the project—it appeared to be profitable, but what were the chances that it might nevertheless turn out to be a loser, and how should risk be analyzed and worked into the decision process? As the meeting was winding down, Lili and Brent were asked to start with the base case situation they had developed and then to discuss risk analysis, both in general terms and as it should be applied to the lite orange juice project.

To begin, Lili and Brent met with the marketing and production managers to get a feel for the uncertainties involved in the cash flow estimates. After several sessions, they concluded that there was little uncertainty in any of the estimates except for unit sales—cost and sales price estimates were fairly well defined, but unit sales could vary widely. (In theory, unit sales price is also uncertain, but companies typically set sales prices on the basis of competitors' prices, so, at least initially, it can be treated as certain.) As estimated by the marketing staff, if product acceptance were normal, then sales quantity during Year 1 would be 425,000 units; if acceptance were poor, then only 200,000 units would be sold (the price would be kept at the forecasted level); and if consumer response were strong, then sales volume for Year 1 would be 650,000 units. In all cases, the price would increase at the inflation rate; hence, Year 1 revenues stated in Year 1 dollars, as they would appear on the cash flow statement, would be $892,500 under the expected conditions, they would be only $420,000 if things went badly, and they would amount to $1,365,000 if things went especially well. Cash costs per unit would remain at $1.50 before adjusting for inflation, so total cash operating costs in Year 1 would be approximately $650,250 under normal conditions, $306,000 in the worst-case scenario, and $994,500 in the best-case scenario. These costs would be expected to increase in each successive year at a 2 percent rate.

Lili and Brent also discussed the scenarios' probabilities with the marketing staff. After considerable debate, they finally agreed on a "guesstimate" of 25 percent probability of poor acceptance, 50 percent probability of average acceptance, and 25 percent probability of excellent acceptance.

Lili and Brent also discussed with Victor Courtland, Indian River's director of capital budgeting, both the risk inherent in Indian River's average project and how the company typically adjusts for risk. Based on historical data, Indian River's average project has a coefficient of variation of NPV in the range of 0.50 to 1.00, and Courtland has been adding or subtracting 3 percentage points to the cost of capital to adjust for differential project risk. When Lili and Brent asked about the basis for the 3 percentage point adjustment, Courtland stated that the adjustment apparently had no basis except the subjective judgment of John Gerber, a former director of capital budgeting who was no longer with the company. Therefore, maybe the adjustment should be 2 percentage points, or maybe 5 points, or maybe some other number.

The discussion with Courtland raised another issue: Should the project's cost of capital be based on its stand-alone risk, on its risk as measured within the context of the firm's portfolio of assets (within-firm, or corporate, risk), or in a market risk context? Indian River's target capital structure calls for 50 percent debt and 50 percent common equity, and the before-tax marginal cost of debt is currently 10 percent. Lili and Brent also determined that the T-bond rate, which they use as the risk-free rate, is 8 percent, and that the market risk premium is 6 percent.

Since most members of Indian River's executive committee are unfamiliar with modern techniques of financial analysis, Lili and Brent planned to take a tutorial approach in the presentation. To structure the analysis, Lili and Brent developed the following set of questions, which they planned to ask and then answer as a method of presenting the analysis to the board. However, Lili and Brent contracted a contagious, though not fatal, viral infection. Neither will be able to attend the meeting. Therefore, you must make the presentation and answer any questions. Keep in mind that anyone on the board might interrupt you with a probing question at any time, so be sure you understand the logic, and the weaknesses, behind every technique you use and every statement you make.

Questions

1. a. Why should firms be concerned with the riskiness of individual projects?

   b. (1) What are the three types of risk that are normally considered in capital budgeting?

   (2) Which type of risk is most relevant?

   (3) Which type of risk is easiest to measure?

      (4)   Would you normally expect the three types of risk to be highly correlated? Would they be highly correlated in this specific instance?

2. a. What is sensitivity analysis?

    b. Complete Table 1, assuming initially that the project has average risk. Then develop a new table which shows a sensitivity analysis of NPV to sales quantity, salvage value, and the cost of capital. Assume that each of these variables can deviate from its base case, or expected value, by plus or minus 10 percent, 20 percent, and 30 percent. See Table 2 for partial results.

    c. Prepare a sensitivity diagram and discuss the results.

    d. What are the primary weaknesses of sensitivity analysis? What are its primary advantages?

3. Complete the scenario analysis initiated in Table 3. What is the worst case NPV? The best-case NPV? Use the worst-case, most likely, and best-case NPVs, and their probabilities of occurrence, to find the project's expected NPV, standard deviation, and coefficient of variation.

4. What are the primary advantages and disadvantages of scenario analysis?

5. What is Monte Carlo simulation, and what are simulation's advantages and disadvantages vis-a-vis scenario analysis?

6. a. Would the lite orange juice project be classified as high risk, average risk, or low risk by your analysis thus far? (Hint: Consider the project's coefficient of variation of NPV.) What type of risk have you been measuring?

    b. What do you think the project's corporate risk would be, and how could you measure it?

    c. How would it affect your risk assessment if you were told that the cash flows from this project were totally uncorrelated with Indian River's other cash flows? What if they were expected to be negatively correlated?

    d. How would the project's cash flows probably be correlated with the cash flows of most other firms, say the S&P 500, and hence with the stock market? What difference would that make in your capital budgeting analysis?

7. Calculate the project's differential risk-adjusted NPV. Should the project be accepted? What if it had a coefficient of variation (CV) of NPV of only 0.15 and was judged to be a low-risk project?

8. Lili and Brent thought long and hard about the lite orange juice project's market beta. They finally agreed, based on some data from the Florida Citrus Producers Association, to use 2.0 as their best estimate of the beta for the equity invested in the project.

   a. On the basis of market risk, what is the project's required rate of return?

   b. Describe briefly two methods that might possibly be used to estimate the project's beta. Do you think those methods would be feasible in this situation?

   c. What are the advantages and disadvantages of focusing on a project's market risk rather than on the other types of risk?

9. Indian River is also evaluating two different systems for disposing of wastes associated with another product, frozen grapefruit juice. Plan W requires more workers but less capital, while Plan C requires more capital but fewer workers. Both systems have an estimated 3-year life, but the one selected will probably be repeated at the end of its life into the foreseeable future. Since the waste-disposal choice has no impact on revenues, Lili and Brent think that the decision should be based on the relative costs of the two systems; these costs are set forth next (in thousands of dollars). The Year 0 costs represent the capital outlays.

	Expected Net Costs	
Year	Plan W	Plan C
0	($2,000)	($4,000)
1	(2,000)	(1,200)
2	(2,000)	(1,200)
3	(2,000)	(1,200)

   a. Assume initially that the two systems are both of average risk. Which one should be chosen?

   b. Now assume that the labor intensive Plan W is judged to be riskier than an average project, because future labor costs are very difficult to forecast, but Plan C is still of average risk, because most of its costs can be firmly established. When these risk differences are considered, which system should be chosen?

c. Suppose that during the presentation, you were asked what the two waste-disposal projects IRRs and NPVs were. How would you have answered that question?

Table 1

Selected Case Data

Net Investment Outlay:			*Depreciation Schedule:*		
Price	$500,000		**MACRS**	**Depr.**	**End-of-Year**
Freight	X	**Year**	**Factor**	**Expense**	**Book Value**
Installation	X	1	33%	$188,100	$381,900
Change in NWC	X	2	45	X	X
	X	3	15	X	X
		4	7	39,900	0
			100%	$570,000	

Cash Flows:					
	Year 0	**Year 1**	**Year 2**	**Year 3**	**Year 4**
Unit price		$ 2.10	X	X	$ 2.43
Unit sales		425,000	X	X	425,000
Revenues		$892,500	X	X	$1,033,180
Operating costs		650,250	X	X	690,051
Depreciation		188,100	X	X	39,900
Other project effects		20,000	X	X	20,000
Before tax income		$ 34,150	X	X	$ 283,230
Taxes		13,660	X	X	113,292
Net income		$ 20,490	X	X	$ 169,938
Plus depreciation		188,100	X	X	39,900
Net op cash flow		$208,590	X	X	$ 209,838
Salvage value					$ 100,000
SV tax					40,000
Recovery of NWC					10,000
Terminal CF					$ 70,000
Project NCF	($580,000)	$208,590	X	X	$ 279,838

Decision Measures:	
NPV	$ 166,719
IRR	X
MIRR	17.2%
Payback	2.6 years

Table 2

Sensitivity Analysis Results:
Lite Orange Juice Project

Variable Change from Base Level	NPV after Indicated Change		
	Quantity	Salvage Value	k
−30%	($ 2,572)	$154,425	$219,799
−20	X	X	X
−10	112,003	162,621	183,766
Base case	166,719	166,719	166,719
+10	X	X	X
+20	276,150	174,915	134,414
+30	X	X	X

Table 3

Scenario Analysis Results:
Lite Orange Juice Project

Scenario	Prob.	NPV	IRR	MIRR
Worst	25%	($122,952)	00.0%	3.6%
Most likely	50	166,719	22.2	17.2
Best	25	X	X	X
Expected value		$166,719	21.4%	X
Standard deviation		$204,829	14.6%	X
Coefficient of variation		1.2	0.7	X

14

Cash Flow Estimation

Robert Montoya, Inc. (A)

Robert Montoya, Inc., is a leading producer of wine in the United States. The firm was founded in 1950 by Robert Montoya, an Air Force veteran who had spent several years in France both before and after World War II. This experience convinced him that California could produce wines that were as good as or better than the best France had to offer. Originally, Robert Montoya sold his wine to wholesalers for distribution under their own brand names. Then in the early 1950s, when wine sales were expanding rapidly, he joined with his brother Marshall and several other producers to form Robert Montoya, Inc., which then began an aggressive promotion campaign. Today, its wines are sold throughout the world.

The table wine market has matured and Robert Montoya's wine cooler sales have been steadily decreasing. Consequently, to increase winery sales, management is currently considering a potential new product: a premium varietal red wine using the cabernet sauvignon grape. The new wine is designed to appeal to middle-to-upper-income professionals. The new product, Suavé Mauvé, would be positioned between the traditional table wines and super premium table wines. In market research samplings at the company's Napa Valley headquarters, it was judged superior to various competing products. Sarah Sharpe, the financial vice president, must analyze this project, along with two other potential investments, and then present her findings to the company's executive committee.

Production facilities for the new wine would be set up in an unused section of Robert Montoya's main plant. New machinery with an estimated cost of $2,200,000 would be purchased, but shipping costs to move the machinery to Robert Montoya's plant would total $80,000, and installation charges would add another $120,000 to the total equipment cost. Furthermore, Robert Montoya's inventories (the new product requires aging for 5 years in oak barrels made in France) would have to be increased by $100,000. This cash flow is assumed to occur at the time of the initial investment. The machinery has a remaining economic life of 4 years, and the company has obtained a special tax ruling that allows it to depreciate the equipment under the MACRS 3-year class life. Under current tax law, the depreciation allowances are 0.33, 0.45, 0.15, and 0.07 in Years 1 through 4, respectively. The machinery is expected to have a salvage value of $150,000 after 4 years of use.

The section of the plant in which production would occur had not been used for several years and, consequently, had suffered some deterioration. Last year, as part of a routine facilities improvement program, $300,000 was spent to rehabilitate that section of the main plant. Earnie Jones, the chief accountant, believes that this outlay, which has already been paid and expensed for tax purposes, should be charged to the wine project. His contention is that if the rehabilitation had not taken place, the firm would have had to spend the $300,000 to make the plant suitable for the wine project.

Robert Montoya's management expects to sell 100,000 bottles of the new wine in each of the next 4 years, at a wholesale price of $40 per bottle, but $32 per bottle would be needed to cover cash operating costs. In examining the sales figures, Sharpe noted a short memo from Robert Montoya's sales manager which expressed concern that the wine project would cut into the firm's sales of other wines—this type of effect is called *cannibalization*. Specifically, the sales manager estimated that existing wine sales would fall by 5 percent if the new wine were introduced. Sharpe then talked to both the sales and production managers and concluded that the new project would probably lower the firm's existing wine sales by $60,000 per year, but, at the same time, it would also reduce production costs by $40,000 per year, all on a pre-tax basis. Thus, the net externality effect would be –$60,000 + $40,000 = –$20,000. Robert Montoya's federal-plus-state tax rate is 40 percent, and its overall cost of capital is 10 percent, calculated as follows:

$$\text{WACC} = W_d k_d \, (1 - T) + W_s k_s$$

$$= 0.5(10\%) \, (0.6) + 0.5(14\%)$$

$$= 10\%.$$

Now assume that you are Sharpe's assistant and she has asked you to analyze this project, along with two other projects, and then to present your findings in a "tutorial" manner to Robert Montoya's executive committee. As financial vice president, Sharpe wants to educate some of the other executives, especially the marketing and sales managers, in the theory of capital budgeting so that these executives will have a better understanding of capital budgeting decisions. Therefore, Sharpe wants you to ask and then answer a series of questions as set forth next. Keep in mind that you will be questioned closely during your presentation, so you should understand every step of the analysis, including any assumptions and weaknesses that may be lurking in the background and that someone might spring on you in the meeting.

Specifics on the other two projects that must be analyzed are provided in Questions 9 and 10.

Questions

1. Define the term "incremental cash flow." Since the project will be financed in part by debt, should the cash flow statement include interest expenses? Explain.

2. Should the $300,000 that was spent to rehabilitate the plant be included in the analysis? Explain.

3. Suppose another winemaker had expressed an interest in leasing the wine production site for $30,000 a year. If this were true (in fact it was not), how would that information be incorporated into the analysis?

4. What is Robert Montoya's Year 0 net investment outlay on this project? What is the expected nonoperating cash flow when the project is terminated at Year 4? (Hint: Use Table 1 as a guide.)

5. Estimate the project's operating cash flows. (Hint: Again use Table 1 as a guide.) What are the project's NPV, IRR, modified IRR (MIRR), and payback? Should the project be undertaken? [Remember: The MIRR is found in three steps: (1) compound all cash inflows forward to the terminal year at the cost of capital, (2) sum the compounded cash inflows to obtain the *terminal value* of the inflows, and (3) find the discount rate which forces the present value of the terminal value to equal the present value of the net investment outlays. This discount rate is defined as the MIRR.]

6. Now suppose the project had involved replacement rather than expansion of existing facilities. Describe briefly how the analysis would have to be changed to deal with a replacement project.

7. a. Assume that inflation is expected to average 5 percent per year over the next 4 years. Does it appear that the project's cash flow estimates are real or nominal? That is, are they stated in constant (current year) dollars, or has inflation been built into the cash flow estimates? (Hint: Nominal cash flows include the effects of inflation, but real cash flows do not.)

   b. Is the 10 percent cost of capital a nominal or a real rate?

   c. Is the current NPV biased, and, if so, in what direction?

8. Now assume that the sales price will increase by the 5 percent inflation rate beginning after Year 0. However, assume that cash operating costs will increase by only 2 percent annually from the initial cost estimate, because over half of the costs are fixed by long-term contracts. For simplicity, assume that no other cash flows (net externality costs, salvage value, or net working capital) are affected by inflation. What are the project's NPV, IRR, MIRR, and payback now that inflation has been taken into account? (Hint: The Year 1, and succeeding cash flows, must be adjusted for inflation because the estimates are in Year 0 dollars.)

9. The second capital budgeting decision which Sharpe and you were asked to analyze involves choosing between two mutually exclusive projects, S and L, whose cash flows are set forth below:

	Expected Net Cash Flow	
Year	Project S	Project L
0	($400,000)	($400,000)
1	240,000	134,000
2	240,000	134,000
3	—	134,000
4	—	134,000

Both of these projects are in Robert Montoya's main line of business, table wine, and the investment which is chosen is expected to be repeated indefinitely into the future. Also, each project is of average risk, hence each is assigned the 10 percent corporate cost of capital.

a. What is each project's single-cycle NPV? Now apply the replacement chain approach and then repeat the analysis using the equivalent annual annuity approach. Which project should be chosen, S or L? Why?

b. Now assume that the cost to replicate Project S in 2 years is estimated to be $420,000 because of inflationary pressures. Similar investment cost increases will occur for both projects in Year 4 and beyond. How would this affect the analysis? Which project should be chosen under this assumption?

10. The third project to be considered involves a fleet of trucks with an engineering life of 3 years (that is, the trucks will be totally worn out after 3 years). However, if the trucks were taken out of service, or "abandoned," prior to the end of 3 years, they would have a positive salvage value. Here are the estimated net cash flows for each truck:

Year	Initial Investment and Operating Cash Flow	End-of-Year Net Abandonment Cash Flow
0	($60,000)	$60,000
1	25,200	37,200
2	24,000	24,000
3	21,000	0

The relevant cost of capital is again 10 percent.

a. What would the NPV be if the trucks were operated for the full 3 years?

b. What if they were abandoned at the end of Year 2? What if they were abandoned at the end of Year 1?

c. What is the economic life of the truck project?

11. Refer back to the original wine project. In this and the remaining questions, if you are using the *Lotus 1-2-3* model, quantify your answer. Otherwise, just discuss the impact of the changes.

a. What would happen to the project's profitability if inflation were neutral, that is, if both sales prices and cash costs increase by the 5 percent annual inflation rate?

b. Now suppose that Robert Montoya is unable to pass along its inflationary input cost increases to its customers. For example, assume that cash costs increase by the 5 percent annual inflation rate, but that the sales price can be increased at only a 2 percent

113

annual rate. What is the project's profitability under these conditions?

12. Return to the initial inflation assumptions (5 percent on price and 2 percent on cash costs).

   a. Assume that the sales quantity estimate remains at 100,000 units per year. What Year 0 unit price would the company have to set to cause the project to just break even, that is, to force NPV = $0?

   b. Now assume that the sales price remains at $40. What annual unit sales volume would be needed for the project to break even?

Table 1

Project Cash Flow Estimates

Net Investment Outlay: *Depreciation Schedule:*

Price	X	Basis =		X		
Freight	X		**MACRS**		**Depr.**	**End-of-Year**
Installation	X	**Year**	**Factor**		**Expense**	**Book Value**
Change in NWC	X	1	33%		$ 792,000	$1,608,000
	X	2	X		X	X
		3	X		X	X
		4	7		168,000	0
			100%		$2,400,000	

Cash Flow Statements:

	Year 0	Year 1	Year 2	Year 3	Year 4
Unit price		$ 40	X	X	$ 40
Unit sales		100,000	X	X	100,000
Revenues		$4,000,000	X	X	$4,000,000
Operating costs		3,200,000	X	X	3,200,000
Depreciation		792,000	X	X	168,000
Other project effects		20,000	X	X	20,000
Before tax income		($ 12,000)	X	X	$ 612,000
Taxes		(4,800)	X	X	244,800
Net income		($ 7,200)	X	X	$ 367,200
Plus depreciation		792,000	X	X	168,000
Net op cash flow		$ 784,800	X	X	$ 535,200
Salvage value					$ 150,000
SV tax					X
Recovery of NWC					X
Termination CF					X
Project NCF	($2,500,000)	X	X	X	X

114

15

Risk Analysis in Capital Budgeting

Robert Montoya, Inc. (B)

In Case 14, Sarah Sharpe, the financial vice president, analyzed a cabernet sauvignon red wine project for Robert Montoya, Inc. The project required an initial investment of $2,400,000 in fixed assets (including shipping and installation charges), plus a $100,000 addition to net working capital. The machinery would be used for 4 years and depreciated on the basis of a 3-year MACRS class life. The appropriate MACRS depreciation allowances are 0.33, 0.45, 0.15, and 0.07 in Years 1 through 4, respectively, and the machinery is expected to have a salvage value of $150,000. If the project is undertaken, the firm expects to sell 100,000 bottles of wine at a current dollar (Year 0) wholesale price of $40 per bottle. However, the sales price will be adjusted for inflation, which is expected to average 5 percent annually, so the actual expected sales price at the end of the first year is $42.00, the expected price at the end of the second year is $44.10 and so on.

The red wine project is expected to reduce the before-tax profit Robert Montoya currently earns on its other wines line by $20,000, because the product lines are somewhat competitive. Further, the company expects cash operating costs to be $32 per unit in Time 0 dollars, and it expects these costs to increase by 2 percent per year. Therefore, total variable costs during the first year of operation (Year 1) are expected to be ($32.00)(1.02)(100,000) = $3,264,000. Robert Montoya's tax rate is 40 percent, and its cost of capital is 10 percent. Cash flow data and other information, as developed by Sharpe using a *Lotus 1-2-3* model, are given in Table 1.

When Sharpe and her assistant presented their initial (Case 14) analysis to Robert Montoya's executive committee, things went well, and they were congratulated on both their analysis and their presentation. However, several questions were raised. In particular, the executive committee wanted to see some type of risk analysis on the project—it appeared to be profitable, but what were the chances that it might nevertheless turn out to be a loser, and how should risk be analyzed and worked into the decision process? As the meeting was winding down, Sharpe was asked to start with the base case situation she had developed and then to discuss risk analysis, both in general terms and as it should be applied to the red table-wine project.

To begin, Sharpe met with the marketing and production managers to get a feel for the uncertainties involved in the cash flow estimates. After several sessions, they concluded that there was little uncertainty in any of the estimates except for unit sales—cost and sales price estimates were fairly well defined, but unit sales could vary widely. As estimated by the marketing staff, if product acceptance were normal, then sales quantity during Year 1 would be 100,000 units; if acceptance were poor, then only 70,000 units would be sold (the price would be kept at the forecasted level); and if consumer response were strong, then sales volume for Year 1 would be 130,000 units. In all cases, the price would increase at the inflation rate; hence, Year 1 revenues stated in Year 1 dollars, as it would appear on the cash flow statement, would be $4,200,000 under the expected conditions, $2,940,000 if things went badly, and $5,460,000 if things went especially well. Cash costs per unit would remain at $32 before adjusting for inflation, so total cash operating costs in Year 1 would be approximately $3,264,000 under normal conditions, $2,284,800 in the worst-case scenario, and $4,243,200 in the best-case scenario. These costs would be expected to increase in each successive year at a 2 percent rate.

Sharpe also discussed the scenarios' probabilities with the marketing staff. After considerable debate, they finally agreed on a "guesstimate" of a 25 percent probability of poor acceptance, a 50 percent probability of average acceptance, and a 25 percent probability of excellent acceptance.

Sharpe also discussed with Art Maxwell, Robert Montoya's director of capital budgeting, both the risk inherent in Robert Montoya's average project and how the company typically adjusts for risk. Based on historical data, Robert Montoya's average project has a coefficient of variation of NPV in the range of 0.25 to 0.50, and Maxwell has been adding or subtracting 3 percentage points to the cost of capital to adjust for differential project risk. When Sharpe asked about the basis for the 3 percentage point adjustment, Maxwell stated that it apparently had no basis except the subjective judgment of David Cohn, a former director of capital budgeting who was no longer with the company. Therefore, maybe the adjustment should be 2 percentage points, or maybe 5 points, or maybe some other number.

The discussion with Maxwell raised another issue: Should the project's cost of capital be based on its stand-alone risk, on its risk as measured within the context of the firm's portfolio of assets (within-firm, or corporate, risk), or in a market risk context? Robert Montoya's target capital structure calls for 50 percent debt and 50 percent common equity, and the before-tax marginal cost of debt is currently 10 percent. Sharpe also determined that the T-bond rate, which she uses as the risk-free rate, is 8 percent, and that the market risk premium is 6 percent.

Since most members of Robert Montoya's executive committee are unfamiliar with modern techniques of financial analysis, Sharpe planned to take a tutorial approach in the presentation. To structure the analysis, Sharpe developed the following set of questions, which she planned to ask and then answer as a method of presenting the analysis to the board. However, Sharpe contracted laryngitis and will be unable to attend the meeting. As her assistant, you must make the presentation and answer any questions. Keep in mind that anyone on the board might interrupt you with a probing question at any time, so be sure you understand the logic, and the weaknesses, behind every technique you use and every statement you make.

Questions

1. a. Why should firms be concerned with the riskiness of individual projects?

    b. (1) What are the three types of risk that are normally considered in capital budgeting?

        (2) Which type of risk is most relevant?

        (3) Which type of risk is easiest to measure?

        (4) Would you normally expect the three types of risk to be highly correlated? Would they be highly correlated in this specific instance?

Part IV   *Capital Budgeting*

2. a.   What is sensitivity analysis?

   b.   Complete Table 1, assuming initially that the project has average risk.   Then develop a new table which shows a sensitivity analysis of NPV to sales quantity, salvage value, and the cost of capital. Assume that each of these variables can deviate from its base case, or expected value, by plus or minus 10 percent, 20 percent, and 30 percent. See Table 2 for partial results.

   c.   Prepare a sensitivity diagram and discuss the results.

   d.   What are the primary weaknesses of sensitivity analysis? What are its primary advantages?

3.   Complete the scenario analysis initiated in Table 3.   What is the worst-case NPV?   The best-case NPV?   Use the worst-case, most likely, and best-case NPVs, and their probabilities of occurrence, to find the project's expected NPV, standard deviation, and coefficient of variation.

4.   What are the primary advantages and disadvantages of scenario analysis?

5.   What is Monte Carlo simulation, and what are simulation's advantages and disadvantages vis-a-vis scenario analysis?

6. a.   Would the wine project be classified as high risk, average risk, or low risk by your analysis thus far?   (Hint: Consider the project's coefficient of variation of NPV.)   What type of risk have you been measuring?

   b.   What do you think the project's corporate risk would be, and how could you measure it?

   c.   How would it affect your risk assessment if you were told that the cash flows from this project were totally uncorrelated with Robert Montoya's other cash flows? What if they were expected to be negatively correlated?

   d.   How would the project's cash flows probably be correlated with the cash flows of most other firms, say the S&P 500, and hence with the stock market?   What difference would that make in your capital budgeting analysis?

7.   Calculate the project's differential risk-adjusted NPV.   Should the project be accepted? What if it had a coefficient of variation (CV) of NPV of only 0.15 and was judged to be a low-risk project?

8. Sharpe and her assistant thought long and hard about the red wine project's beta. They finally agreed, based on some data from the California Winegrowers Association, to use 2.0 as their best estimate of the beta for the equity invested in the project.

    a. On the basis of market risk, what is the project's required rate of return?

    b. Describe briefly two methods that might possibly be used to estimate the project's beta. Do you think those methods would be feasible in this case?

    c. What are the advantages and disadvantages of focusing on a project's market risk rather than on the other types of risk?

9. Robert Montoya is also evaluating two different systems for disposing of wastes associated with another product, grape juice. Plan W requires more workers but less capital, while Plan C requires more capital but fewer workers. Both systems have an estimated 3-year life, but the one selected will probably be repeated at the end of its life into the foreseeable future. Since the waste disposal choice has no impact on revenues, Sharpe thinks that the decision should be based on the relative costs of the two systems; these costs are set forth next (in thousands of dollars). The Year 0 costs represent the capital outlays.

	Expected Net Costs	
Year	Plan W	Plan C
0	($500)	($1,000)
1	(500)	(300)
2	(500)	(300)
3	(500)	(300)

    a. Assume initially that the two systems are both of average risk. Which one should be chosen?

    b. Now assume that the labor-intensive Plan W is judged to be riskier than an average project, because future labor costs are very difficult to forecast, but Plan C is still of average risk because most of its costs can be firmly established. When these risk differences are considered, which system should be chosen?

c. Suppose that during the presentation, you were asked what the two waste-disposal projects' IRRs and NPVs were. How would you have answered that question?

Table 1

Selected Case Data

Net Investment Outlay:

		Depreciation Schedule:			
Price	$2,200,000		**MACRS**	**Depr.**	**End-of-Year**
Freight	X	**Year**	**Factor**	**Expense**	**Book Value**
Installation	X	1	33%	$ 792,000	$1,608,000
Change in NWC	X	2	45	X	X
	X	3	15	X	X
		4	7	168,000	0
			100%	$2,400,000	

Cash Flows:

	Year 0	Year 1	Year 2	Year 3	Year 4
Unit price		$ 42.00	X	X	$ 48.62
Unit sales		100,000	X	X	100,000
Revenues		$4,200,000	X	X	4,862,025
Operating costs		3,264,000	X	X	3,463,783
Depreciation		792,000	X	X	168,000
Other project effects		20,000	X	X	20,000
Before tax income		$ 124,000	X	X	$1,210,242
Taxes		49,600	X	X	484,097
Net income		$ 74,400	X	X	$ 726,145
Plus depreciation		792,000	X	X	168,000
Net op cash flow		$ 866,400	X	X	$ 894,145
Salvage value					$ 150,000
SV tax					60,000
Recovery of NWC					100,000
Terminal CF					$ 190,000
Project NCF	($2,500,000)	$ 866,400	X	X	$1,084,145

Decision Measures:

NPV	$566,857
IRR	X
MIRR	15.8%
Payback	2.6 years

Table 2

Sensitivity Analysis Results:
Red Wine Project

Variable Change from Base Level	NPV after Indicated Change		
	Quantity	**Salvage Value**	**k**
−30%	($ 85,946)	$548,415	$782,468
−20	X	X	X
−10	349,256	560,710	636,123
Base case	566,857	566,857	566,857
+10	X	X	X
+20	1,002,059	579,151	435,541
+30	X	X	X

Table 3

Scenario Analysis Results:
Red Wine Project

Scenario	Prob.	NPV	IRR	MIRR
Worst	25%	($ 85,946)	8.4%	9.0%
Most likely	50	566,857	19.8	15.8
Best	25	X	X	X
Expected value		$566,857	19.6%	X
Standard deviation		$461,601	7.7%	X
Coefficient of variation		0.8	0.4	X

16

*Capital Budgeting
with Staged Entry*

New England Seafood Company

The senior executives of New England Seafood Company, a leading seafood harvester and processor, scheduled a meeting in early 1993 to consider a significant change in corporate strategy. New England Seafood's present strategy is to concentrate solely on harvesting and processing seafood from the Atlantic Ocean and the Gulf of Mexico. The company's products include a variety of saltwater fish, crab, lobster, shrimp, oysters, scallops, and clams. However, increased competition from low-cost, foreign producers, over-harvesting, and pollution have decreased the fish and shellfish population, resulting in significantly lower yields. Furthermore, the U. S. government has banned oyster harvesting along much of the Atlantic and Gulf coasts, following a number of cases where individuals became sick after eating oysters which were contaminated with toxins. These factors have prompted New England Seafood's management to reconsider the firm's strategic plan. Management is now thinking of making a major move into the freshwater catfish market.

New England Seafood was founded in 1958 in Bar Harbor, Maine, by a consortium of commercial fishermen, whose plan was to provide Americans throughout the country with fresh seafood. The company's seafood is regarded as being high quality, and the firm has the reputation of being the leader in its chosen line. However, it has never harvested or processed freshwater catfish. Until now, proposals to enter the catfish market were always rejected because (1) New England Seafood's operational and marketing advantages have always been in saltwater products, and (2) the company has never regarded the freshwater catfish market as having the profit potential necessary to make the investment worthwhile, since consumer demand for catfish has primarily been limited to only a few areas in the deep South.   Recently, though, consumer demand for catfish has been increasing throughout the United States. Further, by packaging the product under the New England Seafood name, which has an excellent reputation for quality and freshness, and by utilizing the company's marketing expertise, management believes that the effort will be financially successful.

New England Seafood's managers are examining a proposal for a two-step, strategic move into the catfish market.   Stage 1 calls for the construction of a number of catfish ponds and an unsophisticated, no-frills processing plant of limited capacity.   Stage 2 calls for the development of a major facility that would house the entire fresh-fish processing division— research and development (R&D), processing, marketing, and general management.   New England Seafood originally considered developing a major facility at this time that would have had an operational life of at least 10 years, but would have required a much larger capital investment than Stage 1.   However, this idea was abandoned in favor of the staged-entry plan.

To date, New England Seafood has spent $3 million on R&D, including both design and marketing studies, for the new facility.   Of this amount, $500,000 has been expensed for tax purposes, while the remaining $2.5 million has been capitalized and will be amortized over the 5-year operating life of Stage 1.   According to an IRS ruling specifically requested by New England Seafood, capitalized R&D expenditures could be immediately expensed if the catfish project is not undertaken.

If New England Seafood decides to build the facility, it would require a 50-acre site by December 31, 1993 (t = 0).   The firm has decided to locate the facility on the Gulf coast in Pascagoula, Mississippi, because a relatively warm, year-round climate is required so that the ponds will not freeze solid, which would prevent harvesting and kill the fish, and also because the largest growth in demand for catfish continues to be in the South.   The firm currently owns a suitable tract of land along the Pascagoula River, which empties into the Gulf of Mexico. The tract cost New England Seafood $500,000 several years ago, but it could be sold now for $1 million, net of realty fees and taxes. Other suitable sites could also be purchased for $1 million.   The site currently owned was purchased by the Gulf Shrimp Processing Division, which plans an expansion in 1999. If the site is used for the catfish project, New England Seafood would have to make other arrangements for the Gulf Shrimp Processing Division. New England Seafood can obtain an option on a similar site in the same area for $100,000 on December 31, 1993.   The option would give New England Seafood the right to purchase the site on December 31, 1998 (t = 5) for \$1.3 million. It is estimated that similar sites will then have a market value of \$1.5 million, so the purchase could always be made at that time for the Gulf Shrimp Processing Division, should the currently owned tract be used for the catfish project.

Most of 1994 would be spent obtaining state, county, and city approvals for the project. The costs incurred would not be material to the decision. Construction would take place during 1995 at a cost of \$4 million. For planning purposes, assume that the expenditure would occur on December 31, 1994 (t = 1). The building falls into the MACRS 31.5-year class, and New England Seafood could begin to depreciate it during 1997, the year the plant would go into service. Although its depreciable life is 31.5 years, the plant would actually be used for only 5 years, starting on January 1, 1997, with operating cash flows (end of year) occurring from December 31, 1997, through December 31, 2001 (t = 4 through t = 8). New England Seafood estimates that the land would have a market value of \$2 million at the end of 2001, at which time the building would have a market value of \$3 million.

The required processing equipment would be obtained and installed during 1996 at a cost of \$6 million. (Assume that payment would be made on December 31, 1995, or at t = 2.) The equipment falls into the MACRS 7-year class. As with the building, tax depreciation would begin when operations commence, in 1997. At the end of 5 years, the wear and tear, along with technological obsolescence, would cause the equipment to be worth very little. The best estimate is only \$500,000. Table 1 contains the depreciation schedules as developed by the firm's tax accountants.

If New England Seafood builds the Stage 1 plant, the initial investment in net working capital would equal 25 percent of the estimated first-year sales. (Assume that this investment would be made on December 31, 1996, at t = 3.) Additions to net working capital in each subsequent year would be 25 percent of the dollar sales increase expected in the following year. For example, any additional net working capital required to support the projected increase in 1998 sales over 1997 sales would be paid for on December 31, 1997.

Table 1

MACRS Depreciation Rates

	Recovery Year				
MACRS Class	**1**	**2**	**3**	**4**	**5**
7-year	14.3%	24.5%	17.5%	12.5%	8.9%
31.5-year	3.2	3.2	3.2	3.2	3.2

Notes:

(a) For simplicity, these allowances were rounded to the nearest one-tenth percent. In actual applications, the allowances would not be rounded.

(b) Since the plant is entering service on January 1, a full year's depreciation can be taken on the building in the first year. In most situations, the first year's depreciation allowance on the building would be reduced because the allowance is based on the month that the property is placed in service. The first year's depreciation on the equipment follows the half-year convention, regardless of when during the year the equipment is placed into service.

New England Seafood's marketing department has projected wholesale sales of the catfish at 10,000 units (one unit equals one ton) for 1997. The sales price is expected to be set at $2,000 per unit. The processing department has estimated variable costs to be 60 percent of sales. Fixed costs, excluding depreciation, are estimated to be $6 million annually.

Fixed costs, which include such things as managerial salaries and property taxes, but not depreciation, are expected to increase after 1997 at the expected rate of general inflation—4 percent. Unit sales are expected to increase at an annual rate of 10 percent as catfish gains more and more market recognition and acceptance. The sales price, however, is expected to remain flat because of increasing competition in the catfish market. Variable costs will remain at 60 percent of dollar sales, and hence will increase at the same rate as dollar sales, or 10 percent.

If the company decides to go forward with the project, Stage 2 would begin on December 31, 1999 (t = 6), when New England Seafood would have to spend $12.5 million on land, buildings, and equipment. Capital investment would continue for two more years, and the operating cash flows (end of year) would begin the year following the shutdown of the Stage 1 plant. The Stage 2 net cash flows are forecasted as follows:

End of Year	t	High Demand	Low Demand
		Net Cash Flow	
1999	6	($12,500,000)	($12,500,000)
2000	7	(1,150,000)	(1,150,000)
2001	8	(400,000)	(400,000)
2002	9	5,000,000	4,250,000
2003	10	5,500,000	4,000,000
2004	11	6,000,000	3,750,000
2005	12	37,500,000	18,750,000

The net working capital from Stage 1 would be transferred to Stage 2 if it is undertaken. Stage 2 is projected to last beyond 2005; but cash flow estimation is so difficult when looking that far ahead that a terminal value, which incorporates the present value of all cash flows beyond 2005, including salvage values, has been included in the 2005 cash flow.

New England Seafood's current federal-plus-state tax rate is 40 percent, and this rate is projected to remain fairly constant into the future. The firm's weighted average cost of capital is 10.0 percent, but New England Seafood adjusts this amount up or down by 3 percentage points for projects with substantially more or less risk than average.

Assume that you are the financial analyst charged with analyzing the catfish project. Accordingly, it is your job to evaluate the project and to prepare a recommendation for New England Seafood's executive committee. In developing your recommendations, answer the following questions, which were posed by the financial vice president, your boss.

Questions

1. Consider the land acquisition for Stage 1.

    a. What cost, if any, should be attributed to the catfish project?

    b. Assuming that the currently owned site is used for this project, how should the Gulf Shrimp Processing Division obtain a site? What discount rate should be used in analyzing the option alternative?

2. Now think about the other cash flows associated with Stage 1.

    a. If Stage 1 is undertaken, what would the R&D cash flows be for 1997 through 2001? Should any R&D cash flow for 1993 be included in the Stage 1 analysis? Explain.

b. Describe how salvage values are taxed. Use the building's salvage value to illustrate your answer.

c. Complete the project's cash flow statement by filling in the blanks in Table 2.

3. Assume that the Stage 1 project is judged to be of average risk. What are its stand-alone NPV, IRR, MIRR, and payback?[1]

4. Now consider the expansion (Stage 2) project. What are its stand-alone NPV, IRR, and MIRR as of December 31, 1999 (t = 6) under each demand scenario? What are today's (t = 0) NPVs? What is Stage 2's expected NPV, assuming there is a 70 percent probability that demand will be high during Stage 2, but a 30 percent chance that demand will be low? Again, assume that Stage 2 is an average-risk project. (Hint: Remember that acceptance of Stage 2 requires the firm to forego the Stage 1 net working capital recovery. This represents an opportunity cost to Stage 2 that is not reflected in the cash flows shown on the previous page.)

5. New England Seafood estimates that there is an 80 percent chance that Stage 1 will meet all expectations and, consequently, that Stage 2 will be undertaken. What is the expected NPV of New England Seafood's catfish project? Using Figure 1 as a guide, construct a decision tree to help in the analysis.

6. Use the decision-tree data to find the project's standard deviation and coefficient of variation of NPV. Suppose that New England Seafood's average project has a coefficient of variation of NPV in the range of 0.5 to 1.5. Would this project be classified as a high-, average-, or low-risk project?

7. What is the overall project's risk-adjusted NPV?

8. What do you think New England Seafood should do? Carefully justify your final conclusions.

9. Your boss, the financial vice president, is concerned that the variable cost percentage used (60%) might be too low, and that variable costs might actually amount to 70 percent of dollar sales. If variable costs do amount to 70 or even 75 percent, how would this affect the NPV of Stage 1? Of the total project? If you are using the *Lotus* model,

---

[1]The modified IRR (MIRR) is similar to the IRR except that the MIRR assumes reinvestment at the project's cost of capital, while the IRR assumes reinvestment at the IRR rate.

calculate the NPV of Stage 1 at several higher variable cost percentages. Use a 10 percent cost of capital.

10. The marketing vice president thinks the salvage value estimate included in the Year 2005 high-demand scenario cash flow is inaccurate, so she asked you to use $30,000,000 instead of $37,500,000. She also asks you to assume that there is only a 60 percent chance that demand will be high during Stage 2 and a 40 percent chance that demand will be low. What would be the general effect of these changes on the expected NPV of the total catfish project? Again, if you are using the *Lotus* model, what is the specific effect of these changes on NPV?

Table 2

Stage 1 Cash Flow Statement

(In Thousands of Dollars)

End of Year	1993	1994	1995	1996	1997	1998	1999	2000	2001
Land	X				X	X	X	X	X
R&D expense	X	($4,000)							X
Building			($6,000)						
Equipment cost									
Working capital				X	X	X	X	X	X
Total capital	X	($4,000)	($6,000)	X	X	X	X	X	X
Sales					$20,000	$22,000	$24,200	$26,620	$29,282
Variable cost					12,000	13,200	14,520	15,972	17,569
Fixed cost					6,000	6,240	6,490	6,749	7,019
Depreciation					986	1,598	1,178	878	662
Op income	$0	$ 0	$ 0	$0	$ 1,014	$ 962	$ 2,012	$ 3,021	$ 4,032
Tax	0	0	0	0	406	385	805	1,208	1,613
Net income	$0	$ 0	$ 0	$0	$ 608	$ 577	$ 1,207	$ 1,812	$ 2,419
Depreciation	0	0	0	0	986	1,598	1,178	878	662
Op cash flow	$0	$ 0	$ 0	$0	$ 1,594	$ 2,175	$ 2,385	$ 2,690	$ 3,081
Cap cash flow	X	(4,000)	(6,000)	X	X	X	X	X	X
Land SV									X
Land SV tax									X
Bldg SV									X
Bldg SV tax									X
Equip SV									X
Equip SV tax									X
Net Cash Flow	X	($4,000)	($6,000)	X	X	X	X	X	X

Figure 1
Catfish Project Decision Tree

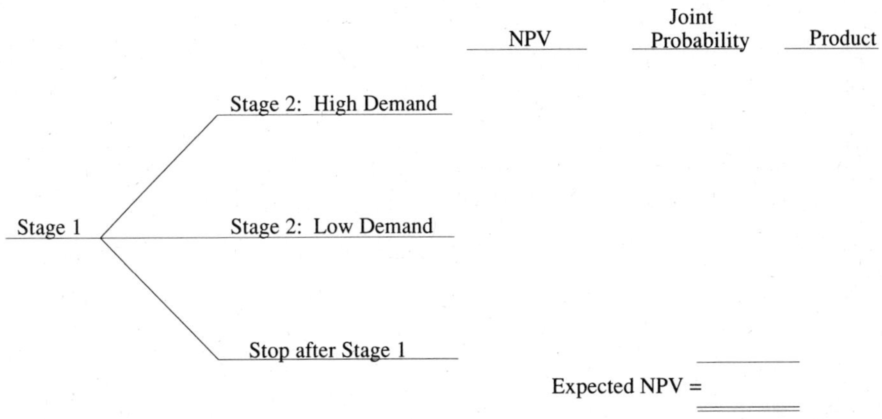

	NPV	Joint Probability	Product

Stage 2: High Demand

Stage 1

Stage 2: Low Demand

Stop after Stage 1

Expected NPV =

17

Establishing the Optimal Capital Budget

Lawn Depot, Inc.

Lawn Depot, Inc., is a nationwide retailer of lawn and garden supplies and equipment. The company operates a chain of 380 retail outlets located throughout the United States. Lawn Depot sells all types of lawn and garden supplies and equipment, including pesticides, fertilizers, seed, sod, hand tools, and heavy-duty equipment. Each outlet also offers lawn care and maintenance services and equipment repair services as well.

Lawn Depot began operations as a small, family-owned lawn care center in Champaign, Illinois. The company carries a large inventory of supplies and equipment to meet almost any customer's needs. In addition, the stores are open when customers most often need them—namely, on Saturdays and Sundays and until 9 P.M. on weeknights—and competent employees are available to advise customers and to provide first-rate service. As the firm's reputation for service and convenience grew, Lawn Depot began to expand within the state of Illinois and, later, throughout the country.

The high standards and business acumen of Michael Jaegar, the founder of the company, were responsible for the firm's success. Lawn Depot remained privately held by the Jaegar family until 1983, when 70 percent of the outstanding stock was sold in a public offering to raise funds for expansion. The firm continued to be managed by members of the Jaegar family. After Michael Jaegar retired early in 1993, his nephew, Jeff Jaegar, was unanimously elected to the company's top post by the board of directors. Jeff Jaegar's background was in marketing, so he decided to bring in Eric Kresser, who has an MBA in finance, to be his assistant and to provide expertise in the areas of finance and operations. Kresser would be responsible for looking for problems in Lawn Depot's operations and then determining how they could be eliminated.

As he began to familiarize himself with the activities of the various departments and the company's operations, Kresser became aware of the fairly haphazard way capital-investment decisions were made. Mike Doyle, the company's financial vice president, is responsible for capital budgeting at Lawn Depot. He usually approves all capital investment requests as they come in from the district managers. Recently, however, Doyle has begun to calculate the return on investment (ROI) for each district and to let managers know if their districts' ROIs are below the company average. Kresser noticed that with this procedure, managers in districts with low returns on investment typically do not make substantial capital investment requests until they are able to pull up their district's ROI to that of the overall company. Thus, funds for projects are simply allotted to those districts that have had above-average ROIs in the past.

In addition, in those years in which there were many project requests, or in which funds for capital expenditures were limited, Doyle had the finance department calculate the payback period on larger investments. Several potential capital investments whose payback periods were fairly long had been rejected in favor of projects with quicker returns.

Kresser sent a memorandum to Jeff Jaegar, recommending that a formal process be used to make capital budgeting decisions. When Kresser met with Jaegar to discuss the idea, he explained why a net present value approach would be best for the company. Jaegar agreed and was eager to put the new procedures into effect. Therefore, he asked Kresser to address this topic at the board of directors' meeting to be held the following week.

Kresser's presentation to the board went smoothly, and the other board members seemed to agree that a formal capital budgeting process should be implemented. Doyle, however, was skeptical about Kresser's plan, and he questioned him about the appropriate cost of capital to use in evaluating the company's projects. The other board members requested that Kresser estimate a discount rate to be used in generating Lawn Depot's 1993 capital budget.

Kresser's first step was to obtain the projected December 31, 1993, balance sheet (Table 1) and information on sales and earnings for each year from 1983 to 1993 (Table 2). Next, he met with several security analysts and investment bankers to find out about investor expectations for the firm and the costs to Lawn Depot of raising outside debt and equity capital. The analysts said that investors do not expect the company to experience the same high growth rates that it has enjoyed over the previous decade; indeed, the consensus of these experts was that the rate would be only half of that realized from 1983 to 1993.

Kresser also made an analysis of the firm's capital structure and decided that Lawn Depot's current mix of debt, preferred stock, and common stock was probably close to optimal. The capital structure, which is reflected in the balance sheet shown in Table 1, has been stable over the past five years. The company's accounting department estimates depreciation for 1993 to be $60 million, and since depreciation is not a cash charge, this amount will be available to Lawn Depot to finance new projects. In discussions with the firm's investment and commercial bankers, Kresser learned that costs as specified in the following sections would be incurred as the company sought to obtain additional capital.

Short-Term Debt

New short-term debt, which currently has an interest rate of 7 percent, could be issued in the form of bank notes payable and commercial paper.

Table 1

Lawn Depot, Inc.
Pro Forma Balance Sheet for December 31, 1993
(Millions of Dollars)

Cash & marketable securities	$ 42	Accounts payable[a]	$ 27
Accounts receivable	210	Short-term debt (7%)[b]	50
Inventories	279	Total current liabilities	$ 77
Total current assets	$531	Mortgage bonds[c]	310
Net fixed assets	384	Preferred stock[d]	145
		Common equity[e]	110
		Retained earnings	273
Total assets	$915	Total claims	$915

[a] Accounts payable are exceptionally low because the firm follows the practice of paying cash on delivery in return for substantial purchase discounts.

[b] Lawn Depot uses short-term debt as part of its permanent capital structure.

[c] The bonds outstanding have a par value of $1,000, a remaining life of 15 years, and a coupon rate of 7 percent. The current rate of interest for 15-year bonds with Lawn Depot's rating is 8 percent per year. The bonds pay annual interest.

[d] The preferred stock currently sells at its par value of $100 per share.

[e] There are 8 million shares outstanding, and the stock currently sells at a price of $60 per share.

Long-Term Debt

The company could obtain an additional long-term loan of up to $19.2 million from its commercial bank's trust department under its existing line of credit agreement at an interest rate of 8 percent. Because of regulatory constraints, however, this is the maximum additional amount the trust department can lend to Lawn Depot, so if the company needs more than $19.2 million in new long-term debt, it must issue subordinated debentures with a B rating which would carry an interest rate of 12.5 percent.

Preferred Stock

The company's perpetual preferred stock pays a $9 annual dividend, has a $100 par value, and is currently selling at par. Additional preferred stock can be sold to private investors, but the market for new preferred issues is poor, and the after-flotation cost on any new issues would be 10 percent.

Common Stock

Lawn Depot's investment bankers have estimated that they could sell new common stock to the public at the current market price, $60 per share, but the underwriting commission would be $12 per share. (If the amount of new stock sold increased too much, the market price of the stock would eventually decline. Because of difficulties in determining the exact effects of capital requirements on k_d, k_p, and k_e, Kresser did not think it worthwhile to attempt to precisely define the MCC schedule beyond the break point for retained earnings. Therefore, for purposes of this analysis, he decided to assume that Lawn Depot can sell any amount of new common stock at the $48 net price.)

Table 2

Lawn Depot, Inc.

Sales and Earnings

Year	Sales (Millions of Dollars)	Earnings after Taxes Available to Common Stock (Millions of Dollars)[a]	Earnings per Share of Common Stock
1993 (estimated)	$1,536	$80.00	$10.00
1992	1,278	73.76	9.22
1991	1,130	64.96	8.12
1990	1,066	63.68	7.96
1989	954	54.88	6.86
1988	890	51.36	6.42
1987	810	46.72	5.84
1986	746	43.04	5.38
1985	698	40.32	5.04
1984	635	37.76	4.72
1983	550	30.88	3.86

[a]The firm's marginal tax rate is 40 percent.

Finally, the analysts noted that investors expect Lawn Depot's 60 percent dividend payout ratio to hold steady for some time into the future. Indeed, in his last annual report to the stockholders, Jeff Jaegar had emphasized that the company's policy of paying out cash dividends equal to at least 60 percent of earnings would be continued.

The board also asked Kresser to estimate the amount of funds that would be required for capital projects during 1993. Kresser decided that the best way to do this would be to calculate the company's investment opportunity schedule and to superimpose this schedule over the firm's marginal cost of capital schedule. In order to find out what projects are under consideration, Kresser interviewed each division manager. From his conversations with the operating managers, Kresser discovered that there were a large number of relatively minor projects (replacement decisions and the like) that could be grouped into three broad categories based on their expected profitability—high, average, or low. The total costs and expected average internal rates of return for each group are shown in Table 3.

Table 3

Investment Project Groups
(Millions of Dollars)

Project Group	Total Cost	Average IRR
Group 1	$32	15%
Group 2	48	12
Group 3	40	10

Kresser also learned that there were three special projects being considered in addition to the projects listed above. (See Table 4.) Two of these projects, Projects A and A*, are mutually exclusive. Project B in Table 4 is a potential major strategic investment. If Project B is accepted, the company would begin to manufacture its own line of heavy-duty lawn care equipment. Obviously, the cost of Project B would be quite high (approximately 17.5 percent of the company's total assets), but members of the Lawn Depot board believe the project would give the company a major competitive advantage in the market. None of the projects in Table 4, or the three project groups in Table 3, are divisible, hence each must be accepted or rejected in its entirety. As Kresser's special assistant, you have been asked to answer the following questions.

Table 4

Investment Opportunities
(Millions of Dollars)

Project Identification	Cost of Project	Estimated Annual Cash Inflows	Estimated Life (Years)	Estimated Internal Rate of Return on Project
A	$ 30.0	$ 6.26	12	18%
A*	30.0	7.81	8	x
B	160.0	27.36	15	15

Note: Projects A and A* are mutually exclusive; that is, only one or the other can be accepted. The IRR on A* must be calculated.

Questions

1. Kresser concluded that Lawn Depot's present capital structure minimizes the firm's weighted average cost of capital and maximizes the stock's price. Ignoring the spontaneously generated accounts payable, calculate Lawn Depot's *market value* capital structure. Be sure to include notes payable in your answer, because Lawn Depot uses notes as a source of permanent financing. Also, round your numbers to the nearest whole percentage.

2. Where will the break point(s) in the marginal cost of capital curve occur? Assume that the current capital structure is held constant, the dividend payout ratio is set at 60 percent, depreciation charges are $60 million, and earnings of $80 million are available to common shareholders in 1993.

3. Find the weighted average cost of capital (WACC) on each side of the breakpoint and graph the marginal cost of capital schedule. Recall that Lawn Depot's marginal tax rate is 40 percent and use 60 percent of estimated 1993 EPS for D_1 and the current price of the stock as P_0.

4. a. Based on the information given in Table 4, what is the internal rate of return for Project A*? Graph the investment opportunity schedule, along with the marginal cost of capital schedule, and determine which projects should be accepted.

    b. Discuss the accept/reject decision for the mutually exclusive projects A and A*.

5. Your calculations reflect Lawn Depot's best estimates as of the beginning of 1993; however, activities such as issuing securities and investing in capital assets will occur over the entire year. How should the company respond if (a) more "good" projects become available, or (b) if the cost of capital to Lawn Depot changes, causing the MCC schedule to be raised or lowered?

6. Is Kresser more likely to have doubts about the estimated MCC or IOS schedule? Explain.

7. Thus far in the analysis, no assumptions have been made about the riskiness of the projects as compared either to each other or to the firm's existing capital assets. Discuss how the analysis might be revised to take risk into account.

8. In Question 1, we indicated that spontaneously generated "free capital" can be ignored. Why is this a reasonable procedure?

9. Kresser actually believes that the modified internal rate of return (MIRR) approach is superior to the traditional IRR as an evaluation criteria for capital investment projects. Therefore, he plans to use the regular IRR to establish a first-approximation value for the firm's marginal cost of capital, then to use this value to calculate MIRR for each project, and finally to recalculate the optimal capital budget based on MIRR. How would this procedure affect the IOS developed using the traditional IRR approach? (Hint: To answer this question, no calculations are necessary—just think about how the IOS would shift if MIRR is used.)

10. Assume now that Jeff Jaegar and other members of the Jaegar family own 70 percent of Lawn Depot's stock and are in the highest state-plus-federal tax bracket. Would this change the analysis?

11. a. Use the Security Market Line equation, $k_s = k_{RF} + (k_M - k_{RF})b$, to calculate the company's cost of equity at its existing capital structure. Assume that the firm's beta coefficient is 1.4, the risk-free rate is 6.0 percent, and the market return is 12 percent.

    b. Compare the cost of equity estimate found in Question 3 to that calculated in Part a. Which, if either, do you think is more correct? Explain.

18

Multinational Capital Budgeting

Alaska Oil Corporation

David Fay, Alaska Oil's financial vice president, is preparing a report for the monthly directors' meeting. An important issue is on the agenda, a project which some of the directors have called "the foreign aid project." The government of Russia has agreed to give Alaska Oil Exploration, the oil drilling subsidiary of Alaska Oil, some important offshore oil concessions, provided Alaska Oil agrees to undertake at least one of the four investment projects listed in Table 1. Project A involves the development and construction of a power plant which, although it will not be completed and thus not produce any income for ten years, is expected to be worth approximately $594.45 million at the end of the tenth year. Project B, the construction of a deepwater seaport facility, has expected revenues of $22.945 million per year. Project C calls for the construction and operation of an airport facility from which revenues should increase as Russia's economic development progresses. Finally, Project D involves the development of a gold mining operation in central Siberia. D's revenues will be highest in the first year, but the ore body will be completely exhausted after four years.

The projects' cash flows, standard deviations, and correlation coefficients as set forth in Table 1 were all developed by the World Bank, an organization supported by the United States and other industrialized nations to finance economic development in Third-World countries. The World Bank economists, who took the potential oil resources into consideration when they made their study, judged all four projects to be economically feasible. Although the projects admittedly carry a high degree of risk, the Bank is willing to finance any of them. However, the Bank's funds are sufficient to lend the Russian government the amounts necessary to complete only three of the four projects. Russia has therefore tied the granting of its oil concessions to Alaska Oil's taking on one or more of the listed projects.

Table 1

Estimated Cash Flows for the "Foreign Aid Projects"

Project Return in Year	Project A: Power Plant (Cost = $75 Million)	Project B: Deepwater Seaport (Cost = $75 Million)	Project C: Airport Facility (Cost = $75 Million)	Project D: Gold Mine (Cost = $75 Million)
1	$ 0	$22.945	$19	$51.3
2	0	22.945	20	34.7
3	0	22.945	21	17.0
4	0	22.945	22	9.9
5	0	22.945	23	0
6	0	22.945	25	0
7	0	22.945	27	0
8	0	22.945	29	0
9	0	22.945	31	0
10	594.45	22.945	33	0

Notes:

1. As estimated by the World Bank, the standard deviation (SD) of each cash flow listed above, including the project costs, is estimated to be 20 percent of the cash flow itself. For example, the SD of Project B's cash flows is $22.945 \times 0.2 = 4.589 million, while the SDs of the costs are each $15 million.

2. Projects A's and D's cash flows are thought to be relatively uncorrelated with cash flows of B and D ($r = 0.0$). Also, D's cash flows are probably negatively correlated with cash flows on Alaska Oil's other assets ($r \approx -0.8$), but A's cash flows are probably positively correlated ($r \approx 0.8$) because electricity prices will probably be high if oil prices are high.

3. The intertemporal cash flows on Projects B and C (i.e., CF_t versus CF_{t+1}) are thought to be relatively uncorrelated ($r = 0.1$), but D's intertemporal cash flows are thought to be highly correlated ($r = 0.9$).

4. C's and D's cash flows are both fairly highly correlated with the oil project's cash flows ($r = 0.5$).

As noted above, some of Alaska Oil's directors consider the four projects to amount to foreign aid. They think that the costs are probably underestimated and the projected cash flows overestimated, with the result being that Alaska Oil would lose heavily on any project it undertakes. However, other directors are impressed with the research done by the World Bank's economists, whose report hinted that the projects' costs are very conservatively estimated and that revenues may well run double those shown in the table.

Fay has tentatively concluded (1) that the projects all carry considerable risk, and (2) that no one of them is obviously better than any other. Some board members would prefer not to undertake any of the projects and, therefore, not to accept the oil concessions. A majority of the board, however, tentatively favor taking on one of the projects in order to obtain the concessions. Several board members have even suggested that all of the projects look interesting, and, given Alaska Oil's excess cash flows and unused debt capacity, will probably suggest that Alaska Oil take on more than one of the projects. A spokesman for this group recently sent Fay a memorandum indicating that, according to some rough estimates, each of the listed projects has a rate of return in excess of the 16 percent cutoff rate Alaska Oil uses in capital budgeting. He also pointed out that, due to the benefits of international diversification, the cutoff rate on international (as opposed to domestic U.S.) investments should be even less than 16 percent.

The capital budgeting hurdle rate is almost sure to be brought up at the forthcoming directors' meeting. Using 16 percent as the cutoff rate, or "hurdle rate," for all projects has been criticized by some directors on the grounds that less-risky projects should be evaluated at a lower cutoff rate, while higher-risk projects should have to pass a higher hurdle rate. Tom Dickerson, president of a major bank and a long-term member of Alaska Oil's board, advocates the use of different discount rates to account for differential project risk. He recently sent Fay the figures shown in Table 2. According to Dickerson, these figures support his contention that projects with differing degrees of risk should be capitalized at different rates of return. Fay believes that, while the four projects may not be equally risky, they are all about as risky as the riskiest industries on Dickerson's list.

Table 2

Cost of Equity Estimates for Selected
Domestic Industries

	Required Rate of Return on Equity
Large public utilities	11%
Grocery chains	12
Major chemical producers	14
Large computer corporations	15
International oil companies	16
Smaller computer companies	21
Small oil exploration companies	26
Major industrial company stocks	17
Small industrial company stocks	23

Note: Estimates based on Justice Department Studies.

The riskiness of international as opposed to domestic (U.S.) investments has also been questioned. One group of directors has argued that international diversification lowers risk; hence, foreign projects should be evaluated with a *lower* cost of capital. However, another group takes the opposite view, arguing that the combination of exchange-rate risk and the risk of expropriation makes foreign investments far riskier. Fay himself thinks that the location of the investment is the key factor—investments in Western Europe may well be less risky because of the diversification factor, but those in Russia are, in his view, quite another thing.

Alaska Oil uses 40 percent debt in its capital structure, but it finances Alaska Oil Exploration only with equity because of the risks inherent in wildcat oil drilling. Fay believes that the exploration company's equity risk is similar to that of the parent company, because the parent's equity is leveraged, but the exploration company's equity is not. Thus, 16 percent is the estimated cost of equity to the parent, but that same number is both the cost of equity and the WACC to the subsidiary. This rate is used to evaluate average-risk projects; higher or lower rates are used for more or less risky investments.

Another recommendation Fay must consider as he completes his report came in a telephone call from his boss, Doug Cauldwell, president of Alaska Oil. Cauldwell suggested that, assuming Alaska Oil does undertake one of the projects in order to obtain the oil concessions, the project should be either B, the deepwater seaport, or C, the airport installation. Cauldwell's argument is that these two projects tie-in quite well with the oil concession, because if the oil exploration project turns out to be successful, the economy of Russia will boom. In this event, both the seaport and the airport should be highly profitable. Thus, Alaska Oil's earnings would be improved substantially by a major strike in the oil drilling operations. Earnings would flow in from the oil itself, and the resultant economic boom would cause the seaport or airport investment to turn out even better than anticipated. These higher earnings would naturally be reflected in the price of Alaska Oil's common stock. Fay himself wonders how the standard deviation information and the correlations given in the notes to Table 1 should be taken into account, if at all.

Alaska Oil has already spent (and expensed for tax purposes) $25 million on geologic surveys for the offshore oil concessions. These expenditures include seismographic work and the drilling of one exploratory well. The seismographic data indicate a high probability of a sizable oil strike, and the one well that was drilled did produce a substantial flow of oil. Assuming that Alaska Oil goes ahead with the project, it must spend an additional $20 million on exploratory wells to determine the size of the oil field. This drilling will take about one year to complete, and the cash outlay can be delayed until drilling is completed. Depending on the size of the field, the project may or may not be commercially feasible. The probability is 70 percent that the exploratory drilling will reveal that the field is commercially profitable. However, there is a 30 percent probability that additional drilling will indicate that the field cannot be developed commercially and, hence, that Alaska Oil should not go on with the project.

Assuming the field can be developed, an additional $60 million must be spent to provide storage facilities, transportation facilities, and development wells. The $60 million will have to be paid out in advance, at the time the "go" decision is made and simultaneously with payment for the drilling costs. If Alaska Oil does undertake the oil exploration project, expected cash inflows, which would commence one year after the drilling and development costs had been incurred, are as follows:

Probability	Net Cash Flow (Millions of Dollars)
.10	$10.00
.20	17.50
.40	27.50
.20	42.50
.10	60.00

Alaska Oil is not sure how long the annual flows would continue, but Fay's probability estimates are as follows:

Probability	Life of the Offshore Oil Project (in Years)
0.15	5
0.20	10
0.30	20
0.20	30
0.15	35

Because of the obvious uncertainties in the offshore venture, Fay regards this project as being more risky than the average project taken on by the company. Also, the oil project's cash flows will be positively correlated with Alaska Oil's other cash flows ($r = 0.7$).

Alaska Oil must commit itself to a "foreign aid" project before it can go ahead with the additional exploratory wells—it cannot wait until the results of the exploratory drilling are available before deciding on the "foreign aid" project. Therefore, if the company is to continue with the offshore oil concession project, it must commit itself to at least one of the four projects at this time.

Fay is concerned about a technical issue. Alaska Oil's financial staff has been debating the merits of the modified internal rate of return (MIRR) vis-a-vis the regular IRR and the period used to calculate MIRR. Fay regards the issue as pretty well settled that MIRR is generally superior to IRR, but he is concerned about what to do when two projects being compared have different lives, as is true for Project D versus the other projects. Should the calculated MIRR for the shorter-life project be based on its own life, or should the analysis be extended out to the end of the longer-life projects' lives? To illustrate the problem, Fay had been looking at a simple project with a cost of $10 and cash flows of $7 per year for two years, evaluated at a 10 percent cost of capital. The MIRR for the project is 21.24 percent based on its two-year life. However, if the project were being compared with a 10-year project, one *could* calculate the 2-year project's MIRR based on a 10 year time horizon; in this case, MIRR = 12.16%. Some of the staff argued for one procedure, while others argued for the alternative. The issue is relevant to the current decision, because Project D's life is shorter than those of the other projects.

As he was starting to analyze the available information, Fay recalled an experience he had with another World Bank project last year—the Bank had provided a lot of information, but some of it was contradictory. This had forced Fay to decide which of the "facts" were correct. Fay wondered if that same situation might not exist in the present case, either with regard to World Bank data or to other data in the case.

Questions

1. How should Alaska Oil use the information in Table 2 when deciding whether or not to select a project?

2. Calculate the expected internal rate of return and modified internal rate of return (MIRR) on the offshore oil project using both 16 percent and 26 percent as the appropriate cost of capital for the project. Should the $25 million spent on geologic surveys be included in the analysis? Assume for simplicity that all outlays are made immediately and that inflows begin one year from now.

3. Assuming Alaska Oil undertakes one of the four projects, calculate both the regular internal rates of return and the modified internal rates of return for Projects B and D. The regular IRRs are 23 and 27 percent for Projects A and C, respectively, and their MIRRs are 23 percent and 20.8 percent when compounded at 16 percent and, 23 percent and 26.4 percent when compounded at 26 percent. For these projects, are the regular or the modified IRRs more meaningful, or does it matter given that the projects are not mutually exclusive? Should D's MIRR be based on its own 4-year life or on the longer lives of the comparison projects? Based on your answers to this point, which foreign aid project, if any, should Alaska Oil accept?

4. How do (a) the timing patterns, (b) the correlations of the cash flows across projects, (c) the intertemporal correlations, and (d) the country in which the investments are located affect the relative riskiness of the projects?

5. Calculate the expected rate of return to Alaska Oil if it accepts either Project B or Project D, in combination with the oil drilling project. Undertaking Project A and the oil project yields a combined IRR of 26.25 percent, and for Project C plus the oil venture, this value is 30.21 percent. Based on these calculations, which project, if any, should Alaska Oil accept?

6. Fay thinks that while the data in Table 2 may be relevant for industries in the United States, the values do not adequately reflect the degree of risk inherent in international projects. Accordingly, he plans to use the capital asset pricing model (CAPM) to adjust for differential risk:[1]

$$k_i = k_{RF} + (k_M - k_{RF})b_i$$
$$= 8\% + (15\% - 8\%)b_i = 8\% + (7\%)b_i.$$

Here,

k_i = risk-adjusted discount rate appropriate for ith project

k_{RF} = risk-free rate of interest; Fay uses 8 percent based on U.S. Treasury bond yields.

k_M = expected return on "the market." Fay uses an historical figure of 15 percent.

b_i = beta coefficient of the ith project; these values must be subjectively estimated.

The World Bank analysts estimated the beta coefficients for each project as follows:

Project	Beta Coefficient
A	2.50
B	3.25
C	3.00
D	2.75
Oil Project	3.00

Alaska Oil's overall beta (with the market) is 1.143. Given this information, calculate the risk-adjusted discount rates for Alaska Oil, the oil exploration project, and Projects B and D. For Projects A and C, the values are 25.5 and 29 percent, respectively. Note that Alaska Oil's own beta was calculated without regard to the effects of any of these projects.

---

[1] The Security Market Line of the CAPM is used to estimate the required rate of return on equity. Since the cash flows developed in Table 1 represent only those flows that can be repatriated to the parent firm, all expenses, including interest costs on World Bank debt, have been deducted. Thus, the net cash flows are cash flows to equity holders and the appropriate hurdle rate is the cost of equity rather than the weighted average cost of capital.

7. Alicia Fernandez, president of Friends of Russia (a UN-sponsored organization) and a director of Alaska Oil, has called Fay's attention to the hurdle rate of 16 percent (the cost of capital currently used for all projects). Since the IRRs of all five projects exceed 16 percent, she asks why, especially in view of Alaska Oil's ample cash flows and funds available for investment, all of the projects should not be accepted? Fay, like Dickerson, disagrees with this thinking, contending that none of the "foreign aid" projects gives Alaska Oil an adequate return for the amount of risk the company would be taking. Fay plans to support his position by referring to Figure 1, which shows that while all four projects' returns lie above the line representing the subsidiary's weighted average cost of capital they are below the Security Market Line (SML), which represents the minimum rate of return that a firm should require for a specified amount of risk. For example, Project A's beta coefficient is 2.50, so the minimum expected return that would make the project acceptable is 25.5 percent. Since the project's expected return is only 23 percent, the firm is not receiving adequate compensation for the amount of risk inherent in the investment, and, if accepted, the project would raise the firm's cost of capital.

    On the other hand, the oil project has a beta of 3.0, a required return of 29 percent, and an expected return of 33.77 percent. Since the expected return exceeds the risk-adjusted required rate of return (the project's own cost of equity), it apparently should be accepted. Of course, the oil project cannot be accepted unless one of the "foreign aid" projects is accepted in conjunction with it.

    Therefore, calculate for Fay the weighted average beta coefficients for Projects B and D in conjunction with the oil drilling project. For Projects A and C, each combined with the oil project, the weighted beta coefficients are 2.73 and 3.00, respectively. Which combination of projects should be accepted? (Hint: plot these values, along with those found in Question 5, on Figure 1 to better illustrate the relative positions of the investment proposals.)

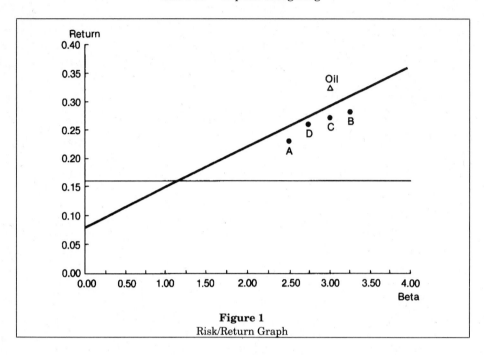

Figure 1
Risk/Return Graph

8. Often, due to its ample operating cash flows, Alaska Oil has excess
    cash on hand over and above the amount required for daily
    operations. Fay invests these excesses in marketable securities
    rather than holding them as cash. Fay has thoroughly investigated
    one such potential investment (not previously discussed in the case).
    Nockahoma Electronics Corporation, a Japanese company with a
    tight cash position due to its recent expansion program, requires a
    loan of $50 million. Nockahoma recently contacted Fay in hopes of
    borrowing the funds from Alaska Oil.

    After determining that his company has sufficient funds to meet
    the loan request, Fay estimated that this investment would have a
    beta coefficient of 0.5, while it would earn a return of 15 percent. He
    felt that the beta of 0.5 was appropriate for several reasons: (1) Fay
    has had a long history of successful dealings with Nockahoma; (2)
    Nockahoma is a very stable, profitable firm; (3) the loan can be called
    for repayment any time rates indicate a deteriorating situation, and
    (4) the loan will be secured by some liquid, safe assets owned by

Nockahoma. In combination, these factors make the loan a very low-risk investment proposal.

The problem Fay faces is that, although the Nockahoma proposal has a very small amount of risk and a return in excess of that required by the SML, the percentage return lies below the average cost of capital (or hurdle rate) of 16 percent that Alaska Oil Exploration presently employs. Fay sees this as an excellent opportunity to illustrate the desirability of using risk-adjusted discount rates rather than a constant discount rate for project selection.

Fay plans to point out that none of the individual "foreign aid" projects should be accepted, as their returns are not sufficient for the high degree of risk involved. Only when these individual projects are combined with the oil drilling project do some of them offer sufficient return to compensate for their risk. With the same argument, Fay contends that the Nockahoma loan should be accepted, as its return is in excess of the required rate of 11.5 percent read from the SML.

Should Alaska Oil make the $50 million loan to Nockahoma? Plot the loan, along with the oil project and the "foreign aid" projects, in Figure 1.

9. Using the risk-adjusted discount rates found in Question 6, calculate the NPVs of Projects B (the seaport) and D (the mine). On the basis of these calculations, should Alaska Oil accept any of the projects? The NPVs for Projects A and C are negative—$13,669,000 and $4,619,000, respectively.

10. Evaluate Doug Cauldwell's argument that either Project B (the deepwater seaport) or Project C (the airport) should be accepted along with the oil project.

11. What other factors should Alaska Oil take into consideration before making a final decision?

12. Which project(s), if any, would you recommend to Alaska Oil's board of directors?

V

Dividend Policy

19

Dividend Policy

Georgia Atlantic Company

During the depression of the 1930s, Ben Jenkins, Sr., a wealthy, expansion-oriented lumberman whose family had been in the lumber business in the southeastern United States for several generations, began to acquire small, depressed sawmills and wholesale lumber companies. These businesses prospered during World War II. After the war, Jenkins anticipated that the demand for lumber would surge, so he aggressively sought new timberlands to supply his sawmills. In 1954, all of Jenkins's companies were consolidated, along with some other independent lumber and milling companies, into a single corporation, the Georgia Atlantic Company.

By the end of 1992, Georgia Atlantic was a major force in the lumber industry, though not one of the giants. Still, it possessed more timber and timberlands in relation to its use of timber than any other lumber company. Worldwide demand for lumber was strong in spite of a soft world economy, and its timber supply should have put Georgia Atlantic in a good position. With its assured supply of pulpwood, the company could run its mills at a steady rate and, thus, at a low per-unit production cost. However, the company does not have sufficient manufacturing capacity to fully utilize its timber supplies; so it has been forced to sell raw timber to other lumber companies to generate cash flow, losing potential profits in the process.

Georgia Atlantic has enjoyed rapid growth in both sales and assets. This rapid growth has, however, caused some financial problems as indicated in Table 1. The condensed balance sheets shown in the table reveal that Georgia Atlantic's financial leverage has increased substantially in the past 10 years, while the firm's liquidity position markedly deteriorated over the same period. Remember, though, that the balance sheet figures reflect *historical* costs, and that the market values of the assets could be much higher than the values shown on the balance sheet. For example, Georgia Atlantic purchased 10,000 acres of cut timberland in southern Georgia in 1961 for $10 per acre, then planted trees which are now mature. The value of this acreage and its timber is estimated at $2,750 per acre, even though it is shown on the firm's balance sheet at $230 per acre, the original $10 plus capitalized planting costs. Note also that this particular asset and others like it have produced zero accounting income; indeed, expenses associated with this acreage have produced accounting losses.

Table 1

Georgia Atlantic Company
Condensed Balance Sheets for the Years Ended December 31
(In Millions of Dollars)

	1982	1992
Current assets	$ 125.2	$ 265.0
Fixed assets	241.5	813.4
Total assets	$ 366.7	$1,078.4
Accounts payable	$ 18.0	$ 55.9
Notes payable	6.7	98.3
Other current liabilities	18.6	23.6
Total current liabilities	$ 43.3	$ 177.8
Long-term debt	122.0	404.0
Common stock	25.0	50.0
Retained earnings	176.4	446.6
Total liabilities and net worth	$ 366.7	$1,078.4
Current ratio	2.9×	1.5×
Industry average	2.5×	2.4×
Debt ratio	45.1%	54.0%
Industry average	37.9%	40.2%

When Georgia Atlantic was originally organized, most of the outstanding stock was owned by the senior Jenkins and members of his family. Over time, however, the family's ownership position has gradually declined due to the sale of new common stock to fund expansion. In 1987, Ben Jenkins, Sr. died; the presidency of the firm was passed to his son, Ben Jenkins, Jr., who was 61 at the time. By the end of 1992, the Jenkins family held only about 35 percent of Georgia Atlantic's common stock, and this represented essentially their entire net worth.

The family has sought to finance the firm's growth with internally generated funds to the greatest extent possible. Hence, Georgia Atlantic has never declared a cash dividend, nor has it had a stock dividend or a stock split. Due to the plowback of earnings, the stock currently sells for almost $2,000 per share. The family has stated a strong belief that investors prefer low-payout stocks because of their tax advantages, and they also think that stock dividends and stock splits serve no useful purpose—they merely create more pieces of paper but no incremental value for shareholders. Finally, the family feels that higher-priced stocks are more attractive to investors because the percentage brokerage commissions on small purchases of higher-priced stocks are lower than on large purchases of lower-priced shares. They cite the example of Berkshire-Hathaway, whose stock price has risen phenomenally even though it now sells for over $8,000 per share and pays no dividends. (The family does acknowledge, though, that Warren Buffett, Berkshire's chairman, has done a superb job of managing the company's assets, and that the rise of its stock price reflects that factor as well as Buffett's financial policies.)

As the date for Georgia Atlantic's annual stockholders' meeting approached, Mary Goalshen, the corporate secretary, informed Ben Jenkins, Jr., who is commonly called "Junior" at the company, that an unusually low number of shareholders had sent in their proxies. Goalshen felt that this might be due to rising discontent over the firm's dividend policy. During the past two years, the average payout for firms in the paper and forest products industry has been about 35 percent; yet for the 39th straight year, Georgia Atlantic's board, under the Jenkins family's dominance, chose not to pay a dividend in 1992. The Jenkins family was also aware that several reports in the financial press in recent months indicated that Georgia Atlantic was a possible target of a takeover attempt. Since the family did not want to lose control of the company, they were anxious to keep the firm's stockholders as happy as possible. Accordingly, Junior announced that the directors would hold a special meeting immediately after the annual meeting to consider whether the firm's dividend policy should be changed.

Junior instructed Abe Markowitz, Georgia Atlantic's financial vice president, to identify and then evaluate alternative dividend policies in preparation for the special board meeting. He asked Markowitz to consider cash dividends, stock dividends, and stock splits. Markowitz then identified six proposals that he thought deserved further consideration:

(1) **No Cash Dividends, No Stock Dividend or Split.** This was the position Markowitz was certain that Junior and the family would support, both for the reasons given above and also because he thought the company, as evidenced by the balance sheet, was in no position to pay cash dividends.

(2) **Immediate Cash Dividend, but No Stock Dividend or Split.** This was simply the opposite of the no dividend policy. If a cash dividend policy were instituted, its size would still be an issue.

(3) **Immediate Cash Dividend plus a Large Stock Split.** The stock split would be designed to lower the price of the firm's stock from its current price of almost $2,000 per share to somewhere in the average price range of other large forest products stocks, or from $20 to $40 per share.

(4) **Immediate Cash Dividend plus a Large Stock Dividend.** The reasoning underlying this policy would be essentially the same as that of Alternative 3.

(5) **Cash Dividend, Stock Split, and Periodic Stock Dividends.** This policy would require the company to declare an immediate cash dividend and, simultaneously, to announce a sizable stock split. This policy would go further than Alternatives 3 and 4 in that, after the cash dividend and stock split or large stock dividend, the company would periodically declare smaller stock dividends equal in value to the earnings retained during the period. In effect, if the firm earned $3 per share in any given period—quarter, semi-annual period, and so on—and retained $1.50 per share, the company would also declare a stock dividend of a percentage amount equal to $1.50 divided by the market price of the stock. Thus, if the firm's shares were selling for $30 when the cash dividend was paid, a 5 percent stock dividend would be declared.

(6) **Share Repurchase Plan.** This plan is based on the premise that investors in the aggregate would like to see the company distribute some cash, but that some stockholders would not want to receive cash dividends because they want to minimize their taxes. Under the repurchase plan, individual stockholders could decide for themselves whether or not to sell some or all of their shares and thus to realize some cash and some capital gains, depending on their own situations.

To begin his evaluation, Markowitz collected the data shown in Tables 2 and 3. As he was looking over these figures, Markowitz wondered what effect, if any, Georgia Atlantic's dividend policy had on the company's stock price as compared to the prices of other stocks. Markowitz is also aware of one other issue, but it is one that neither he nor anyone else has had the nerve to bring up. Junior is now 66 years old, which is hardly ancient; but he is in poor health, and in recent years he has been almost obsessed with the idea of avoiding taxes. Further, the federal estate tax rate is currently 60 percent, and additional state estate taxes would be due; so well over half of Junior's net worth as of the date of his death will have to be paid out in estate taxes. Since estate taxes are based on the value of the estate on the date of death, to minimize his estate's taxes, Junior might not want the value of the company to be maximized until after his death. Markowitz does not know Junior's view of this, but he does know that his tax advisors have thought it through and have explained it to him.

Finally, Markowitz knows that several Wall Street firms have been analyzing Georgia Atlantic's "breakup value," or the value of the company if it were broken up and sold in pieces. He has heard breakup value estimates as high as $3,500 per share, primarily because other lumber companies, including Japanese and European companies, are eager to buy prime properties such as those owned by Georgia Atlantic. Of course, Georgia Atlantic could sell assets on its own, but Markowitz does not expect that to happen as long as Junior is in control.

Table 2

Georgia Atlantic Company
Selected Company and Industry Data

Year	Earnings per Share	Book Value per Share	Price per Share	Industry P/E Ratio	Industry M/B Ratio
1977	$100	$ 824	$1,253	16.8	2.5
1982	106	1,180	1,360	17.9	2.6
1987	109	1,769	1,597	19.1	2.9
1992	143	2,483	1,902	16.5	2.5

Industry Average Compound Annual Growth Rate in Earnings per Share	
1977-82	6.2%
1982-87	7.1
1987-92	7.9

Table 3
Selected Stock Market Data

	Average Payout	Average P/E
Boise Cascade	25%	7.1×
Chesapeake Corporation	31	9.2
Georgia-Pacific	40	9.0
Potlatch	35	10.2
Union Camp	44	10.5
Weyerhaeuser	42	10.0

Now assume that you are Abe Markowitz's assistant and that he has asked you to help him with the analysis by answering the following questions and then by discussing your answers with the executive committee. Junior is famous for asking tough questions and then crucifying the person being questioned if he or she has trouble responding, and that is probably why Markowitz wants you to make the presentation. So be sure that you thoroughly understand the questions and your answers and that you can handle any follow-up questions that you might receive.

Questions

1. For each of the years listed in Table 2, what is Georgia Atlantic's annual earnings per share growth rate, its P/E ratio, and its market/book ratio? Compare your answers with the industry averages shown in Table 2. What can be inferred about Georgia Atlantic's dividend policy from these data?

2. Do you think it is better for firms in general, and for Georgia Atlantic in particular, to have an announced dividend policy?

3. In general, how is a firm's growth rate in earnings affected by its dividend policy? What does this imply about Georgia Atlantic's historical rate of return on investment vis-a-vis that of the average lumber company? (Hint: Consider the retention growth model, $g = br$, where g = growth rate in EPS, b = retention ratio, and r = return on equity.)

4. Evaluate the family's argument that higher-priced stocks are more attractive to investors because the percentage transactions costs on such issues are lower. Is this a valid argument? Do you think Georgia Atlantic's current per-share price is "optimal" in the sense that the value of the shares to investors is maximized?

5. In general, and in this case, what impact should a firm's use of financial leverage have on its dividend policy?

6. Critique the alternative dividend policies that have been proposed. Discuss the implications of each of these policies for Georgia Atlantic Company.

7. Considering Georgia Atlantic's present financial condition, do you think the company is a likely target of a hostile takeover attempt? What effect would the firm's dividend policy have on its vulnerability to a takeover? How might the company use a restructuring that involved asset sales to reduce the threat of a takeover?

8. How should you deal with Junior's estate tax situation? Should you bring it up? If so, in what context and with what recommendation? If Junior does indeed want to hold down the price of the stock (but not hurt the long-run value of the corporation), should the other directors go along with him? How would "the market" be likely to deal with the situation, assuming that they have no information whatever regarding what is said or not said about it within the company?

9. What stockholder clientele do you believe currently owns most of Georgia Atlantic's stock? What impact does stockholder composition have on a firm's dividend policy?

10. What dividend policy do you think Georgia Atlantic should follow? First, should Georgia Atlantic declare a stock split and/or a stock dividend? If so, how large should it be? Second, should any assets be sold? If so, should the proceeds be used to pay dividends, to retire debt, to build new plants, or what? Finally, if you think cash dividends should be paid, how large should the initial payment be? What dividend growth rate should be targeted, and should the change in policy be announced? Explain your answers. If you do not think you have enough information to give a precise quantitative answer to any part of the question, explain how you would go about developing a quantitative answer if you had access to all the company's data and internal information.

20

Dividend Policy

Bessemer Steel Products, Inc.

For over 70 years, Bessemer Steel Products, Inc. has been a leading producer of various parts for automobiles, light trucks, and other vehicles. Its output is sold to the major automobile producers, auto supply companies, and repair shops. However, during the 1981 and 1982 recession, Bessemer's management concluded that the company should diversify in order to reduce risk and to enter markets with greater growth potential. Therefore, the decision was made to diversify into several totally new, but related, product lines.

Using substantial cash flows from profits and depreciation, and substantial unused debt capacity, Bessemer Steel's management resolved to seek only synergistic acquisitions, which meant either companies in high-growth industries whose operations could be improved by Bessemer's expertise or those whose expertise would help Bessemer in its core operations. This suggested that acquisitions be sought primarily in the newly developing fields of robotics and materials science. Thus, Bessemer acquired three robotics firms and two firms involved in metallurgical research and development.

These acquisitions produced the desired results—they strengthened Bessemer's research and development capabilities, helped it maintain and even expand its traditional businesses, and, most important, enabled the company to expand into several profitable new areas. To illustrate, in the early 1980s, virtually all of the company's assets were invested in traditional automobile and light-truck body production. However, as a result of the diversification program, by the end of 1992 these old product lines amounted to only 50 percent of assets, sales, and income, with the other 50 percent coming from new products and businesses, including a substantial amount of work in the space industry. The company is still interested in new acquisitions, and it is now investigating several potential candidates.

Other than during its first few years of operation, Bessemer has followed the practice of paying out approximately 60 percent of its earnings as cash dividends. Accordingly, dividends have fluctuated with earnings from year to year. In each annual report, the policy of paying out 60 percent of earnings has been reiterated, and this has given Bessemer a reputation for paying generous dividends. Because of its liberal dividend policy, Bessemer's stock is mainly owned by retired individuals, college endowment funds, income-oriented mutual funds, and other investors who are seeking high current income. The nature of its stockholders has been confirmed by several recent surveys conducted by the company—questionnaires completed by shareholders indicate clearly that they are income-oriented, and that, if anything, they would like to see the company increase its payout ratio.

The directors have always taken up plans for the coming year at the January board meeting. Until 1993, though, dividend policy was never discussed—it was simply assumed that the policy of a 60-percent payout would be maintained. However, at the 1993 meeting, Dennis Rite, the vice president in charge of the Materials Engineering Division who was brought in when the firm he founded was acquired by Bessemer, said that Bessemer's dividend policy should be examined. Rite argued that while a high dividend payout might have been a desirable policy for the company when it had poor internal growth potential, such a policy is totally inappropriate for a firm with growth opportunities as good as those now available to Bessemer. Rite also pointed out that capital limitations had recently forced the firm to turn down some expansion opportunities that promised relatively high rates of return, and he noted that he and several other directors who had large holdings of Bessemer stock had been paying approximately 40 percent of all dividends received to state and federal governments in the form of income taxes. Furthermore, it is likely that the Clinton administration will raise tax rates even higher. If the company revised its dividend policy and began to retain most of its earnings, this would, according to Rite, be reflected favorably in the price of the stock. Then, should he or any other stockholder desire to obtain cash, they could sell some of their shares and be taxed on the capital gains at that time, rather than be taxed each year on dividends.

Case 20 *Dividend Policy*

Amy Mashburn, who served as both corporate secretary and treasurer, strongly supported Rite's suggestion that dividends be reduced, but her argument was based on the company's financial position. Mashburn noted that the firm's current ratio had deteriorated from a level of about 5.5x in 1982 to only 1.71x in 1992 and that the debt ratio had risen from only 16.8 percent in 1982 to roughly 60 percent in 1992. The company's profits and cash flows for 1992, which would be reported in about a month, were sure to be at record levels, and 1993 levels were projected to break the 1992 records. Still, internal demands for capital would force Bessemer to turn to the debt markets again, hence increasing its debt ratio even more. Mashburn went on to report a reluctance on the part of banks, insurance companies, and other lenders to continue making funds available to Bessemer on attractive terms if the debt and liquidity ratios were not improved. She offered the figures shown in Table 1 to support her position.

Karl Brady, trustee of the endowment fund of Samford College and a long-time member of Bessemer's board of directors, took exception to Rite's and Mashburn's positions. Brady contended that the firm had followed a consistent dividend policy for many years and that its stockholders had bought their stock on the assumption that this policy would be continued. Moreover, he reminded the other directors that the questionnaire sent out the previous year revealed that Bessemer's stockholders showed an overwhelming preference for a policy of high dividends rather than a lower payout. Brady also said that because of its acute need for current income, his college's trust fund would be forced to sell its Bessemer stock if the dividend were cut significantly. He noted that his trust, like many others, was permitted to spend only income, not principal, so the trust would not have the option of selling stock and spending the proceeds in lieu of dividends, as Rite had suggested. For this trust, dividends and capital gains are not interchangeable, so it would basically be forced to sell and then reinvest in another company that did pay high dividends. Brady was sure that a number of other institutional holders were in the same position, and, based on the answers to the stockholder questionnaire, he believed that many individuals would also feel compelled to sell their stock in the event of a sizable dividend cut. Brady concluded by stating that the liquidation of Bessemer stock from so many portfolios could have a disastrous effect on the stock price.

Table 1

Bessemer Steel Products, Inc.

(Millions of Dollars)

	1982	1992
Current assets	$ 47.0	$ 615.0
Fixed assets	70.0	627.0
Total assets	$117.0	$1,242.0
Accounts payable	$ 1.8	$ 155.0
Notes payable	3.9	163.8
Other current liabilities	2.9	41.2
Total current liabilities	$ 8.6	$ 360.0
Long-term debt: nonconvertible	11.1	180.0
Long-term debt: convertible	--	215.0
Common stock ($1 par)	25.0	50.0
Retained earnings	72.3	437.0
Total liabilities and net worth	$117.0	$1,242.0
Current ratio	5.47×	1.71×
Industry average	3.22×	2.96×
Debt ratio	16.8%	60.8%
Industry average	26.9%	30.2%

Mashburn said she had to agree with Brady's arguments regarding shareholder preferences and the likelihood of liquidations if the payout ratio were lowered.   As corporate secretary, Mashburn handled correspondence with stockholders, and in this capacity she had gained the distinct impression that the majority of stockholders did indeed want dividends and would sell their holdings if dividends were eliminated or reduced significantly.   Mashburn also noted that Bessemer Steel, like most other companies, is concerned about the possibility of a hostile takeover, and she was asked by the board to keep up with who was acquiring large blocks of stock.   She pointed out that if a dividend reduction led to a sharp price decline, this could stimulate the raiders to take action, and the company might be "put into play."

Jerry Harris, manager of the Robotics Division, who was also brought into the company when his firm was acquired, joined the discussion in favor of the payout reduction.   Harris argued that the company's dividend policy is responsible for the type of stockholders the firm has.   He suggested that if the firm had always retained most of its earnings rather than paying out 60 percent in dividends, acquisitions could have been made for cash rather than by issuing new stock. With fewer shares of stock outstanding, earnings per share would be higher today, and the company would have enjoyed a higher growth rate over the past decade. This higher growth rate, according to Harris, would have induced growth-oriented institutions and individuals to purchase Bessemer Steel stock. He discounted the argument that the price of the stock would be depressed if the dividend were cut. Rather, Harris argued, aggressive investors would more than take up the slack caused by possible liquidations of income-seeking investors. Thus, the price of the stock would increase, not decrease, if dividends were cut. Harris concluded by saying that he believed the high-dividend policy of past years had been a mistake, but a mistake that could be rectified by changing the policy at the present time.

The discussion continued for almost an hour past the scheduled adjournment time. It terminated only because Rite had to catch a plane to Berlin, where he was to make a presentation to a German industry group about newly developed materials for building extremely strong, rigid, but lightweight automobile bodies. Before adjourning, though, the board directed Mary Dowd, vice president of finance, to have her staff study the dividend policy issue and to prepare a report for the next directors' meeting. Dowd was given explicit directions to consider the following alternative policies:

(1) Continue the present policy of paying out 60 percent of earnings.

(2) Lower the present payout to some percentage below 60 percent—for example, 20, 30, or 40 percent—and then keep the payout ratio constant at this new figure.

(3) Set a relatively low regular dividend, such as 50 cents per share and then supplement it periodically with an extra dividend whose size would depend on the availability of funds and the company's need for capital. The size of the regular dividend would have to be determined at the outset, but all subsequent dividend decisions could be deferred, on a quarter-by-quarter basis, and made on the basis of a knowledge of the company's cash flow position and prospects at the time of the dividend decision.

(4) Establish a fixed dollar amount of dividends—for example, $1 per share per year, payable 25 cents per quarter—and then, as earnings grow, increase the dividend. Under this plan, the payout ratio would fluctuate somewhat as earnings rose or fell in response to business cycle fluctuations, but the dividend would never be cut except in a dire emergency. If this policy were adopted, the question of the size of the initial dividend would also have to be settled. In addition, it would be useful to decide, at least tentatively, whether or not the company should plan to increase the dividend annually, and if so, at what rate? Eventually, management would have to determine how hard to strive to meet the growth target, because earnings will surely fall below the projected level in some future year.

The directors also asked Dowd to consider whether the dividend policy should be announced. Rite and Harris both expressed the opinion that the dividend policy should not be announced, citing the company's present position as an example of how an announced policy could cause the firm to feel "locked in" and thus force it to take actions that otherwise would be undesirable. Mashburn and Brady, on the other hand, argued that stockholders, as owners of the company, ought to be told what management planned to do.

As Dowd was leaving the meeting, Harris asked her to include in her report an analysis of the firm's past growth rate in sales, total earnings, and earnings per share, as well as a statement of how the earnings per share figures might have differed if the firm had followed a different payout policy (see Table 2). Finally, Harris also promised to send Dowd some figures on payout ratios and price/earnings ratios that he had seen in a brokerage house report a few days before. He subsequently sent the figures shown in Table 3.

Table 2

Selected Company Data

Year	Sales (Millions)	Earnings after Taxes (Millions)	Earnings per Share	Dividends per Share	Average Stock Price during Year
1977	$ 189	$ 7.6	$0.76	$0.46	$ 4.95
1982	543	31.2	1.25	0.75	6.75
1985	1,060	61.5	1.71	1.03	13.68
1992	1,890	104.3	2.09	1.25	14.62

Table 3

Selected Stock Market Data

	Average Payout	Average P/E
Blockbuster Entertainment	0%	27×
Wal-Mart Stores	12	21
Standard Motor Products	32	17
Motorola	17	13
Eaton Corporation	36	11
General Dynamics	23	8
General Motors	47	7

Note: Eaton Corporation and Standard Motor Parts manufacture automotive parts.

Assume that you are Mary Dowd's assistant, and that she has given you the task of conducting the dividend policy study. To help you structure the study, she drew up the following set of questions. You must now answer the questions and then present your answers at the next board meeting. Anticipate some tough questions at the board meeting and be prepared both to explain your answers in detail and to answer any related follow-up questions.

Questions

1. Discuss the advantages and disadvantages of each of the four alternative dividend policies, considering each policy both in general and as it applies to Bessemer Steel Products. Use a graph showing the relationship between the investment opportunity schedule and the cost of capital schedule to illustrate your analysis. Be sure to discuss the clientele effect and the signaling hypothesis in your evaluation.

2. Discuss the advantages and disadvantages of having an announced dividend policy.

3. What effect does the payout policy have on the growth rate of earnings per share? Explain in terms of the formula $g = br$, where g is the growth rate, b equals the percentage of earnings retained, and r equals the average rate of return on equity.

4. Could the figures in Table 3 be considered proof that firms with low payout ratios have high price/earnings ratios? Justify your answer.

5. How does a firm's debt position affect its dividend policy?

6. Evaluate Harris's argument that a reduction in the dividend payout rate would increase the price of the stock versus Brady's opinion that such a reduction would drastically reduce the price of the stock.

7. Would a stock dividend or a stock split be of use in this situation? Explain.

8. What specific dividend policy should Dowd recommend to the board of directors at its next meeting? Fully justify your answer.

9. Prior to 1986, federal tax laws gave preferential treatment to capital gains income relative to ordinary income. Under the pre-1986 system, the top federal tax rate on ordinary income (dividends) was 50 percent, and the top federal capital gains tax rate was 20 percent. However, the 1986 tax act drastically changed the tax treatment of capital gains and ordinary income. Under this system, capital gains and ordinary income were no longer given differential treatment, and the top federal tax rate on both types of income was 28 percent. In 1990, tax laws were again changed, and now capital gains are taxed at a top rate of 28 percent while dividends (ordinary income) are taxed at a 31 percent top rate. Finally, the latest Clinton administration tax proposal has the dividend rate going up to almost 40 percent, while the capital gains tax rate is capped at 28 percent. How would these different tax structures affect firms such as Bessemer Steel Products when making dividend policy decisions?

VI

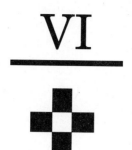

*Long-Term Financing
Decisions*

21

Going Public

Sun Coast Savings Bank

Sun Coast Savings Bank was founded in 1971 in Safety Harbor, Florida, which is just across the bay from Tampa. Safety Harbor is very popular with people who work in Tampa but do not wish to live within the city itself. Per-capita income in Safety Harbor is substantially above the national average; in fact, the town has a reputation for having the greatest population of BMWs and Mercedes Benzes per capita in the United States. The combination of an increasing population, high per capita income, and a huge demand for funds to finance new home construction has made Sun Coast the fastest-growing association in the state in terms of both assets and earnings.

Although Sun Coast is very profitable and has experienced rapid growth in earnings, the company's quick expansion has put it under severe financial strain. Even though all earnings have been retained, the net-worth-to-assets ratio has been declining to the extent that, by 1992, it was just above the minimum required by federal regulations (see Table 1).

Sun Coast now has the opportunity to open a branch office in a new shopping center. If the office is opened, it will bring in profitable new loans and deposits, further increasing the company's growth. However, an inflow of deposits at the present time would cause the net-worth-to-assets ratio to fall below the minimum requirements. Consequently, Sun Coast must raise additional equity funds of approximately $3 million if it is to open the new branch.

Table 1

Sun Coast Savings Bank
Balance Sheet for Year Ended
December 31, 1992

Assets

Cash and marketable securities	$ 83,441,700
Mortgage loans	815,235,000
Fixed assets	60,423,300
Total assets	$959,100,000

Liabilities

Savings accounts	
Other liabilities	$817,153,200
Capital stock ($100 par value)	83,077,000
Retained earnings	900,000
Total claims	57,969,800
	$959,100,000

Note: Federal law requires the ratio of capital plus retained earnings-to-assets to be at least 6 percent.

Even though Sun Coast has a ten-man board of directors, the company is completely dominated by the three founders and major stockholders: Jim Evans, chairman of the board and owner of 35 percent of the stock; Tony McCoy, president and owner of 35 percent of the stock; and Vincent Culverhouse, a builder serving as a director of the company and owner of 20 percent of the stock. The remaining 10 percent of the stock is owned by the other seven directors. Evans and Culverhouse both have substantial outside financial interests. Most of McCoy's net worth is represented by his stock in Sun Coast.

Evans, McCoy, and Culverhouse agree that Sun Coast should obtain the additional equity funds to make the branch expansion possible. They are not in complete agreement, however, as to how the additional funds should be raised. They could raise the additional capital by having Sun Coast sell newly issued shares to a few of their friends and associates. The other alternative is to sell shares to the general public. The three men themselves cannot put additional funds into the company at the present time.

Evans favors the private sale. He points out that he, McCoy, and Culverhouse have all been receiving substantial amounts of ancillary, or indirect, income from the savings bank operation. The three men jointly own a holding company which operates an insurance agency that writes insurance for many of the homes financed by Sun Coast and a title insurance corporation that deals with the association. Also, Culverhouse owns a construction company that obtains loans from the association. Evans maintains that these arrangements could be continued without serious problems if the new capital were raised by selling shares to a few individuals, but questions of conflict of interest would probably arise if the stock were sold to the general public. He also opposes a public offering on the grounds that the flotation cost would be high for a public sale, but would be virtually zero if the new stock were sold to a few individual investors.

McCoy disagrees with Evans. He feels that it would be preferable to sell the stock to the general public rather than to a limited number of investors. Acknowledging that flotation costs on the public offering are a consideration, and that conflict-of-interest problems may occur if shares of the company are sold to the general public, he argues that there would be several offsetting advantages if the stock were publicly traded: (1) the existence of a market-determined price would make it easier for the present stockholders to borrow money, using their shares in Sun Coast as collateral for loans; (2) the existence of a public market would make it possible for current shareholders to sell some of their shares on the market if they needed cash for any reason; (3) having the stock publicly traded would make executive stock-option plans more attractive to key employees of the company; (4) establishing a market price for the shares would simplify problems of estate tax valuation in the event of the death of one of the current stockholders; and (5) selling stock to the public at the present time would facilitate acquiring additional equity capital in the future.

Culverhouse, whose 20 percent ownership of the company gives him the power to cast the deciding vote, is unsure whether he should back the public sale or the private offering. He thinks that additional information is needed to help clarify the issues.

The board therefore instructed Madeline Brown, Sun Coast's chief financial officer, to study the issue and to report back in two weeks. As a first step, Brown obtained the data on Sun Coast's earnings given in Table 2. Brown then collected information on four publicly traded financial institutions; this data is shown in Table 3. She then set about the task of coming up with a recommendation for the board of directors.

Table 2

Sun Coast Savings Bank
Selected Information

Year	Net Profit	Earnings Per Share
1992	$8,562,780	$951.42
1991	7,476,390	830.71
1990	6,521,490	724.61
1989	5,231,610	581.29
1988	4,712,220	523.58
1987	3,905,550	433.95

Table 3

Data on Publicly-Traded
Financial Institutions

	Assets (Millions)	Net Worth (Millions)	Book Value per Share	Price	EPS 1992	EPS 1987
Virginia Federal	$14,000	$ 950	$30.30	$32.00	$5.25	$2.50
Southland Financial	30,500	2,020	16.15	17.00	2.00	0.83
Texas Federal	24,000	1,130	38.95	25.00	5.40	1.59
Great Southern Financial	27,000	1,400	56.50	28.00	6.25	3.94

Questions

1. Table 1 presents Sun Coast's balance sheet at the end of 1992. Using information contained in the balance sheet, calculate Sun Coast's net-worth-to-assets ratio, the number of shares of stock outstanding, and the book value per share of common stock.

2. Using the data in Table 2, calculate Sun Coast's average annual growth rate in earnings per share from 1987 to 1992. (Hint: In your calculations, use only the data for 1987 and 1992.)

3. For the four S&L's listed in Table 3, calculate the following:

   a. The net worth/assets ratios for 1992.

b. Compound annual growth rates in earnings per share for the five-year period 1987-1992.

c. The price/earnings ratios in 1992.

d. The market value/book value ratios for 1992.

4. Considering your answers to Questions 1 through 3, develop a range of values that you think would be reasonable for Sun Coast's market/book ratio if it were a publicly held company.

5. Regardless of your answer to Question 4, assume that 0.8× is an appropriate market value/book value ratio for Sun Coast. What would be the market value per share of the company?

6. Investment bankers generally like to offer the initial stock of companies that are going public at a price ranging from $10 to $30 per share. If Sun Coast stock were to be offered to the public at a price of $20 per share, how large a stock split would be required prior to the sale?

7. Assume that Sun Coast chooses to raise $3 million through the sale of stock to the public at $20 per share.

a. Approximately how large would the percentage flotation cost be for such an issue? Base your answer on available published statistics.

b. How many shares of stock would have to be sold in order for Sun Coast to pay the flotation cost and receive $3 million net proceeds from the offering?

8. Assume that each of the three major stockholders decided to sell half of his stock.

a. How many shares of stock and what total amount of money (assuming that the stock split occurred and that these shares were sold at a price of $20 per share) would be involved in this secondary offering? (A secondary offering is defined as the sale of stock that is already issued and outstanding. The proceeds of such offerings accrue to the individual owners of the stock, not to the company.)

b. Approximately what percentage flotation cost would be involved if the investment bankers were to combine the major stockholders' secondary offering with the sale by the company of sufficient stock to provide it with $3 million?

9. Assume that the major stockholders decide that Sun Coast should go public. Outline in detail the sequence of events from the first negotiations with an investment banker to Sun Coast's receipt of the proceeds from the offering.

10. Can you see why Evans and McCoy might have personal differences of opinion on the question of public ownership?

11. The analysis was based on the comparability of Sun Coast with four other savings institutions. What factors might tend to invalidate the comparison?

12. All things considered, do you feel that Sun Coast should go public? Fully justify your conclusion.

22

Investment Banking

Precision Tool Company

In late 1992, two executives of Workman Tool, Inc., the largest privately owned corporation in Ohio, decided to start a company of their own. There were two primary reasons for their decision. First, both men had the entrepreneurial spirit and longed to have a shot at their own business. Second, Workman's ownership structure precluded managers from receiving stock options as part of their compensation package. Thus, although the firm was generous in its salaries and bonuses, everything was subject to immediate taxation. Both men thought that a new business would give them the opportunity to defer taxes on a large part of their overall compensation.

The two men, Julio Rodriguez and Toby Fulton, found a medium-sized precision tool company that was on the market. The company, Precision Tool Company, is wholly owned by its founder, Nick Sanders. Although the company is in sound condition, Sanders, who is in his late 40s, recently suffered a heart attack and was advised by his doctor to sell the firm and relax—or else. Sanders is asking $8,250,000 for the firm, which works out to a Price/Earnings ratio of approximately 9x, and he has given Rodriguez and Fulton a 6-month purchase option to allow the pair time to arrange financing.

Rodriguez contacted Paul Van Buren, a partner in the New York City investment banking firm of Aberwald, Butler, Van Buren & Company, to help arrange the needed financing. Rodriguez and Fulton each have some savings to put into the purchase, but they need a substantial amount of outside capital to complete the deal. Although the funds could probably be borrowed, Van Buren is not enthusiastic about this alternative. For one thing, Precision Tool's debt ratio is currently at 30 percent, which is the industry average (see Table 1). Second, Rodriguez and Fulton envision using Precision Tool as a vehicle to acquire several smaller companies, and some reserve debt capacity would be needed if this strategy is pursued.

Van Buren proposes that the two partners obtain funds to purchase Precision Tool in accordance with the schedule shown in Table 2. Precision Tool would be restructured with 6 million common shares authorized—1,350,000 shares to be issued at the time of the sale and 4,650,000 shares to be held in reserve for future acquisitions. Rodriguez and Fulton would each purchase 180,000 shares at a price of $1 per share, the par value. Aberwald, Butler, Van Buren & Company would purchase 150,000 shares at a price of $8.50 and the remaining 840,000 shares would be sold to the public at the $8.50 price.

The underwriting fee to Aberwald, Butler, Van Buren & Company would be 5 percent of the proceeds from the public sale, or $357,000. Legal fees, accounting fees, and other charges would amount to $63,000, for total underwriting costs of $420,000. After deducting the under-writing charges and the payment to Sanders, the restructured Precision Tool would have an additional $105,000 in its cash account. Also as part of the agreement would be a provision which grants 1-year options to purchase additional shares. Rodriguez and Fulton could collectively purchase an additional 120,000 shares, while Parks, Van Buren & Company could purchase an additional 100,000 shares, all at $8.50.

A second financing alternative is also being considered, although Van Buren is less enthusiastic about this approach. Van Buren has made some preliminary inquiries to Silverman Sachs, a San Francisco investment banking house which specializes in junk-bond financing. It looks like $6 million of "high yield" bonds could be sold to help finance the acquisition. However, these bonds would require a coupon rate of 18 percent.

With the alternatives in mind, Rodriguez and Fulton must now make their financing decision. Van Buren believes that the financing could be obtained within 90 days once the decision is made. He also suggested that the partners develop some pro forma income statements for 1993 which reflect the impact of the two alternative financing plans. The partners believe that sales would grow by 10 percent under their leadership, and that cost of goods sold and general/administrative expenses would be about the same percentage of sales as in 1992. Lease and depreciation expenses would remain at their 1992 levels, while interest expense would be the 1992 level plus interest on any new debt issued. The firm's federal-plus-state tax rate is 40 percent.

Table 1

Selected Financial Statements

Balance Sheet as of December 31, 1992

Cash	$ 1,050,000	Accounts payable	$ 380,000
Accounts receivable	2,285,000	Notes payable	1,150,000
Inventories	1,777,000	Accruals	315,000
Current assets	$ 5,112,000	Current liabilities	$ 1,845,000
Net fixed assets	6,500,000	Long-term debt	1,639,000
		Total liabilities	$ 3,484,000
		Capital stock	$ 1,000,000
		Retained earnings	7,128,000
		Total equity	$ 8,128,000
Total assets	$11,612,000	Total capital	$11,612,000

Income Statement
for the Year Ended December 31, 1992

Sales	$12,850,000
Cost of goods sold	7,251,000
Gross margin	$ 5,599,000
General/administrative expenses	1,769,000
Lease expense	600,000
Depreciation	850,000
EBIT	$ 2,380,000
Interest expense	850,000
Earnings before taxes	$ 1,530,000
Taxes	612,000
Net income	$ 918,000

Table 2

Financing Proposal

Initial distribution of shares:

Rodriguez	180,000	shares at $1.00	180,000
Fulton	180,000	shares at $1.00	180,000
Parks, Van Buren & Co.	150,000	shares at $8.50	1,275,000
Public stockholders	840,000	shares at $8.50	7,140,000
	1,350,000		$8,775,000

Underwriting costs:

5% of $7,140,000	$357,000	
Other fees	63,000	
		420,000
		$8,355,000
Payment to Sanders		8,250,000
Net cash to Precision Tool		$ 105,000

Questions

1. Using the data in Table 2, calculate the total flotation costs as a percentage of external funds raised. How does this amount compare with published averages for the cost of selling new common stock? (For now, ignore the value of the options.)

2. Assume that Precision Tool's stock price one year from now has the following probability distribution:

Probability	Price
0.05	$ 3.50
0.10	7.00
0.35	12.50
0.35	13.90
0.10	19.40
0.05	22.90

   a. What is the additional expected dollar benefit to Aberwald, Butler, Van Buren & Company from the option package?

   b. Disregarding the time value of money, what would be the total underwriting expense expressed as a percentage of funds raised?

3. Considering that the public would be paying $8.50 per share, should Rodriguez and Fulton be allowed to purchase their shares for $1.00? Should the public be informed that the "insiders" are paying a lower price, and if so, how?

4. In light of your answer to Question 3, should Aberwald, Butler, Van Buren & Company be allowed to purchase its shares for $1.00 per share?

5. As stated at the beginning of the case, Rodriguez and Fulton are motivated partly by the urge to own and run their own firm. What would be the partners' ownership position under the proposal?

6. One goal of the proposal is to generate excess cash now that could potentially be used in the future for acquisitions. What are the pros and cons of raising the funds now rather than when needed?

7. Now consider the junk bond financing alternative.

    a. Construct pro forma income statements for 1993 for the two financing alternatives.

    b. What are the times-interest-earned, fixed charge coverage, and cash flow coverage ratios under each alternative?

8. What should Rodriguez and Fulton's final decision be?   Fully support your answer. Are there any other financing alternatives that should be considered?

9. Assume that another alternative would be to use only $3 million of debt financing. In this situation, the debt would be less risky and a 16 percent coupon would be sufficient. What would be the leverage ratios for this scenario?

10. Return to the $6 million debt scenario. What sales amount would result in a pro forma TIE of 1.0? A cash flow coverage of 1.0?

23

Rights Offerings

Art Deco Reproductions, Inc.

Art Deco Reproductions, Inc., is one of the largest manufacturers of Art Deco furniture in the United States. Organized in 1928, the company experienced a steady rate of growth in the post-World War II period, when the demand for housing was particularly strong. The Art Deco style of furniture has been popular for many years, and roughly 80 percent of all sales in this category are constructed from Western oak, the primary material used by Art Deco. The keynote of the Art Deco philosophy is value—excellence of design, pride in quality, craftsmanship, and fair prices. This tradition of giving full value for the money permeates the entire Art Deco organization, from the senior managers to the furniture craftsmen to the maintenance workers. Most Wall Street analysts point to this attitude of pride and to the "family" atmosphere of Art Deco Reproductions as the key elements of the company's outstanding market success.

In the early 1990s, the demand for Art Deco furniture increased even faster than in the past. The housing market started to show some life during this period after interest rates had fallen substantially, and many homeowners were willing to spend extra money to furnish their houses with long-lasting, high-quality furniture. Unlike the distant past, many young couples who were setting up households for the first time were dual wage earners, hence they had higher-than-average incomes. They were not averse to "upscale" consumption, including expensive furniture.

To meet the increased demand, Art Deco is undertaking a major capital expansion program. Approximately $40 million in new capital, over and above an expected $6 million of retained earnings, is required for the years 1993 and 1994. Of this $40 million, $20 million has already been borrowed as a long-term loan from a group of five pension funds. The loan agreement, which has already been finalized, calls for Art Deco to raise an additional $20 million through the sale of common stock.

Art Deco's board of directors is considering alternative ways to raise the $20 million in new equity funds. The firm's investment banker, Waugh & Company, has provided the board with the following proposals:

(1) Art Deco can sell shares of stock directly to the public, not specifically to its current stockholders, at a price of about $38 per share. The company would net $36 per share, with $2 per share going to the investment bankers as an underwriting commission. The actual offering price would be set at the market price the day before the issue is offered to the public. The current market price of the stock is $39, but the investment bankers feel that the price would decline temporarily to $38 as a result of the new shares coming on the market. The investment bankers would, of course, promote the new issue in an effort to stimulate demand and would assume all of the underwriting risk.

(2) The company can sell shares through a rights offering to its current stockholders at a price of $36 per share. An over-subscription plan giving stockholders the right to any stock not taken in the primary rights offering would be employed. Waugh & Company would guarantee the sale of the issue; the commission would be $1.25 per share for every share subscribed to by stockholders and $3 per share for any shares remaining after the oversubscription (which would be purchased by Waugh & Company). In other words, if its stockholders subscribed to the full amount of the rights offering, Art Deco would receive $36 per share less a $1.25 commission, or a total of $34.75 per share. The proceeds of any unsubscribed shares would be $36 minus a $3 commission, or $33 per share.

(3) Art Deco can sell stock through a rights offering at a price of $32 per share. Under this proposal, the underwriting cost would be $0.75 per share for each share subscribed to and $3 for each unsubscribed share purchased by the investment banker.

(4) Shares can be sold to current stockholders at a price of $20 per share. Under this arrangement, underwriting costs would be $0.25

per share for each share subscribed to by stockholders and $3 per share for each share taken by the investment banker.

(5) Shares can be sold to current stockholders at $5 per share. The assistance of investment bankers would not be necessary under this proposal, as the company could be quite sure that all shares offered would be taken.

After reviewing these proposals, the six members of Art Deco's board of directors had conflicting opinions about the alternatives.

Marcia Wagner, daughter of the original founder of Art Deco Furniture, thought that Proposal 2 was the best alternative. A rights offering at a high subscription price would result in the least amount of dilution of earnings per share while still giving loyal stockholders an opportunity to maintain their equity positions at a discount. Wagner opposed Proposal 1 because it would dilute proportional ownership and would give too much voting power to outsiders. She stated, "If we sell directly to the public, we will be going against the interests of our current stockholders. Furthermore, to choose any other alternative would cause serious dilution of the market price of the stock and this will hurt the company's hard-earned reputation."

Disagreeing with Marcia Wagner was David Paul, president of the Guilford Farmers and Merchants' Bank, Art Deco's primary bank. Paul argued, "Proposal 1 is the most favorable because it will allow for greater distribution of the stock throughout the market." He believed that this would expose the firm to a wider range of knowledgeable investors who would buy Art Deco's stock with genuine interest in the operations and objectives of the company. Paul also noted that selling the new issue at a minimal discount would alleviate any significant depressing effect on the current market price, and that, based on past rights offerings in related industries, 60 percent of the stockholders would be expected to sell their rights to outsiders anyway.

Debra Hastings represented the interests of an influential group of local professional business people who own a large block of Art Deco stock. She stated to the board, "Proposal 1 is clearly against the interests of my constituents, since present stockholders should have the right to maintain their proportionate holdings in the company with as little dilution as possible." Hastings also opposed Proposal 2 because of the high risk of unfavorable market price fluctuations. If the market price of the stock were to drop below $36 per share, the flotation costs of the issue would go up dramatically. Hastings contended that Proposal 3 is the best alternative because it provides an adequate margin of safety against downward market price fluctuations, protects the stockholders from the excessive equity dilution entailed in Proposals 4 and 5, and gives an appealing purchase discount.

Regis Filby, a representative of many small stockholders, argued that Proposal 5 is the only fair alternative. He said, "If a shareholder is given a privileged rights offering, he or she is almost forced to contribute additional capital or to accept an equity dilution as a consequence." He thought that the privilege of maintaining a proportionate share of the company is an important factor in upholding stockholder loyalty, and he argued that Proposals 2 and 3 cater to a small percentage of stockholders who may have immediate funds available for reinvestment, while leaving the larger percentage of stockholders no choice but to sell their rights. A subscription price of five dollars per share would appeal to a wider range of stockholders, and Art Deco Reproductions could be assured that all shares offered would be taken. Not only would this enhance stockholder relations, it would also eliminate the need for investment banking services. "I do realize the stock split effect of this proposal," Filby said, "but I believe the anticipated increase in future earnings will put the price of our stock within a more favorable trading range."

After listening to the various arguments, John Marcourt, board chairman, tentatively concluded that Proposal 4 is the best alternative, since it appears to contain favorable aspects of each of the other proposals. In his view, Proposal 1 fails to consider the importance of stockholder loyalty, while Proposal 5 goes to the opposite extreme and neglects the hard-earned reputation of Art Deco's stock price. He also argued against Proposal 2 by pointing out that the high risk of unfavorable market fluctuations, due to the small discount margin, could result in high flotation expenses. Proposal 3 has a reasonable safety margin between the subscription price and the market price of the stock, but he felt that the ex-rights price per share would be above the optimum trading range. Proposal 4 would, however, put the stock in a popular trading range; a subscription price of $20 would ensure a successful offering at a low flotation cost, and the resulting ex-rights price would appeal to a wider range of investors.

As the time for the board's adjournment approached, John Marcourt asked Kyle Macy, financial vice president, to prepare a report recommending which, if any, of the alternatives should be accepted. Tables 1 and 2 provide some of the data Macy will need to work on the report.

Table 1

Balance Sheet for the Year Ended
December 31, 1992
(Millions of Dollars)

Assets		Liabilities and Equities	
Cash and marketable securities	$ 4.75	Accounts payable	$ 13.20
Accounts receivable	30.90	Bank loans	18.75
Inventories	33.20	Total current liabilities	$ 31.95
Total current assets	$ 68.85	Long-term debt	$ 27.00
Net fixed assets	58.50	Capital stock (3 million	
		shares outstanding)	$ 18.00
		Retained earnings	50.40
		Total common equity	$ 68.40
Total assets	$127.35	Total claims on assets	$127.35

Table 2

Selected Financial Data

	1990	1991	1992
Net income (in millions)	$ 6.600	$ 7.088	$ 7.750
Total dividends paid (in millions)	1.000	1.375	1.875
Market price per share (year end)	30.250	34.125	39.000

Questions

1. Assuming all shares are subscribed, calculate the number of shares that would have to be issued under each of the alternative proposals. (Round your answers to the nearest 1,000 shares.)

2. Calculate the number of rights needed to buy one new share of common stock for each of the four rights proposals, Proposals 2 through 5.

3. For each of the four rights proposals, calculate the market value of the rights. Given these prices, would the average stockholder bother to sell or to exercise the rights? Use the rights formula to answer this question:

$$R = \frac{M_0 - S}{N + 1},$$

where

R	= value of one right
M_0	= rights-on market price of stock
S	= subscription price
N	= number of rights required to buy one new share

4. Use the formula $M_e = M_0 - R$ to calculate the price of Art Deco's common stock immediately after the issue of new shares for each of the rights proposals. Here, M_e = market value of the stock, ex-rights.

5. Because the subscription prices are set below the current market price of the firm's stock, the effect of issuing one of the four rights proposals will be essentially equivalent to that of a stock dividend or stock split. For each of the four proposals, calculate the equivalent percentage stock dividend that would result in the same final price per share. Use the following equation:

$$\text{Percent stock dividend} = \left[\frac{M_0}{M_e} - 1.0\right](100).$$

6. Calculate Art Deco's rate of return on net worth, earnings per share, and stock price for each of the five proposals, assuming the following:

    (1) The company increases its total assets by $20 million by issuing new common stock on January 1, 1993. (Note: the company's stock issue was sold to the market for more than $20 million, but the investment bankers retained the difference to cover underwriting charges. Therefore, capital stock increases by exactly $20 million.)

    (2) There are no other increases in assets in 1993, and the debt financing is deferred until 1994.

    (3) The company earns 8 percent after interest and taxes on beginning total assets in 1993.

    (4) Additions to retained earnings in 1993 are not employed until 1994.

(5) Current liabilities remain at their 1992 level.

(6) The company's price/earnings ratio is 15.

7. Explain the differences between the price-per-share figures obtained in Question 4 and those in Question 6. Which figures seem more realistic?

8. Assuming the following distribution of subscription percentages, calculate the maximum and minimum flotation costs for each of the alternative financing proposals.

	Proposal				
	1	2	3	4	5
Probability of no rights being exercised	—	0.25	0.15	0.05	0.00
Probability of 100% of the rights being exercised	—	0.75	0.85	0.95	1.00

For each proposal, calculate the expected flotation costs as a percentage of net funds raised (that is, $20 million). What factors could lead the company to incur the maximum flotation expense?

9. Would a rights offering have any incremental effect on "stockholder loyalty" relative to a stock offer to the general public?

10. Evaluate the advantages and disadvantages of each of the alternative proposals. Which alternative should be recommended to the board of directors?

11. Answer this question only if you are using the *Lotus* model. How would the value of the rights, the ex-rights stock price, and the percentage stock dividend change if Art Deco raises $40 million? Now assume commissions double in all cases (while new equity remains at $20 million). What are the value of the rights, the ex-rights price, and the percentage stock dividend change?

24

Bond Refunding

Bay Area Telephone Company

John Whiteck, financial vice president of Bay Area Telephone Company, has just begun reviewing the minutes of the company's November 1992 board of directors meeting. The major topic discussed at the meeting was whether Bay Area should refund any of its currently outstanding bond issues. Of particular interest is a $50 million, 30-year, 11.5 percent, first-mortgage bond (consisting of 50,000 $1,000 par value bonds) issued approximately five years ago. Four of the board members had taken markedly different positions on the question. At the conclusion of the meeting, Ronald Tire, chairman of the board, asked Whiteck to prepare a report analyzing the alternative points of view.

The bonds in question had been issued in January, 1988, when interest rates were still relatively high. It was necessary to issue the bonds at that time, despite the high interest rates, because the company needed to complete the modernization and expansion of its switching facilities outside San Francisco to meet rapidly growing demand for telephone services in its service area. At that time, Whiteck and the board strongly believed interest rates would decline in the future, but they were unsure of when rates would fall or by how much. Now, almost five years later, with lower rates, Bay Area can sell A-rated bonds at a coupon rate significantly less than 11.5 percent.

Since Whiteck had anticipated a decline in interest rates when he sold the $50 million issue, he had insisted that the bonds be made callable after five years. (If the bonds had not been callable, Bay Area would have had to pay an interest rate of only 11.0 percent, a full 50 basis points less than the actual 11.5 percent.) The bonds can be called after January 1, 1993, but an initial call premium of 11.5 percent, or

$115 per bond, would have to be paid. This premium declines by 11.5%/25 = 0.46 percentage points, or $4.60, each year. Thus, if the bonds were called in 1998, the call premium would be (0.115/25)(20) = 9.2%, or $92, where 20 represents the number of years remaining to maturity. The flotation costs on this issue amounted to 1.5 percent of the face amount, or $750,000. The firm's federal-plus-state tax rate is 40 percent.

Whiteck estimates that Bay Area can sell a new issue of 25-year bonds at an interest rate of 9.5 percent. The call of the old and the sale of the new bonds could take place five to seven weeks after the decision to refund has been made; this time is required to give legal notice to bondholders and to arrange the $50 million or more needed to pay them off. The flotation cost on the refunding issue would be one percent of the new issue's face amount, and funds from the new issue would be available from the underwriters the day they were needed to pay off the old bonds.

Whiteck had proposed at the last directors' meeting that the company call the 11.5 percent bonds and refund them with a new 9.5 percent issue. (The bonds could not have been called earlier because of the call protection provision in the indenture.) Although the refunding cost would be substantial, he believed the interest savings of 2 percent per year for 25 years on a $50 million issue would be well worth the cost. Whiteck did not anticipate adverse reactions from the other board members; however, four of them voiced strong doubts about the refunding proposal.

The first doubt was raised by Trish Esposito, a long-term member of Bay Area's board and president of Esposito, Arfaras, and Black, an investment banking house catering primarily to institutional clients such as insurance companies and pension funds. Esposito argued that calling the bonds for refunding would not be well received by the major financial institutions that hold the firm's outstanding bonds. According to Esposito, the institutional investors that hold the bonds purchased them with the expectation of receiving the 11.5 percent interest rate for at least 10 years, and these investors would be very disturbed by a call after only five years. Since most of the leading institutions hold some of Bay Area's bonds, and since the firm typically sells new bonds or common stock to finance its growth every two or three years, it would be most unfortunate if institutional investors developed a feeling of ill will toward the company.

A second director, Lee Chang, who was a relatively new member of the board and president of a local bank, also opposed the call, but for an entirely different reason. Chang believed that the decline in interest rates was not yet over. He said a study by his bank suggested that the long-term interest rate might fall to as low as 7.5 percent within the next six months. Under questioning from the other board members, however, Chang admitted that the interest rate decline could in fact be over and that interest rates might, very shortly, begin to rise. When pressed, Chang produced the following probability distribution that his economists had developed for interest rates on A-rated utility for January 1, 1994, one year from the pending refunding date:

Probability	Interest Rate on A-rated Telephone Company Issues
0.1	7.5%
0.2	9.0
0.4	10.0
0.2	11.0
0.1	12.5

The third director, Pete Koulianis, requested more information on the refunding. Koulianis suggested that a formal analysis using discounted cash flow (DCF) techniques be employed to determine the profitability of the refunding. As he reflected on Koulianis's proposal, Whiteck wondered whether it would be better to use Bay Area's cost of debt or its weighted average cost of capital as the discount rate in the analysis. Further, if the cost of debt were used, he wondered whether a before- or after-tax figure should be employed.

The fourth director, Tammy Malloy, Bay Area's treasurer, stated that she was not against the refunding, but wondered whether it was wise to sell the new bonds and call the old bonds at essentially the same time. Malloy was worried that something might go wrong, keeping the company from obtaining the cash generated by the sale of the new bonds in time to pay for the repurchase of the old bonds. Therefore, she suggested that the firm issue the new bonds two to three weeks before the refunding of the old bonds to ensure that sufficient cash is on hand when the old bonds are repurchased. Malloy also pointed out that the funds generated by the sale of the new bonds could be invested in short-term treasury securities yielding 6 percent during this overlap period. Finally, she noted that interest rates had been quite volatile lately and that if rates rose before the new issue could be sold, but after the firm had committed to the refunding, the refunding would be a disaster. Therefore, she wondered if the firm could "lock in a profit" and thus protect itself against rising interest rates by assuming a position in the futures market.

Assume that you have just joined the company as a financial analyst, and for the first six weeks you have been assigned as Whiteck's assistant to get an overview of the financial management function at a major telephone utility. One of your first assignments is to draft responses to the following set of questions, posed by Whiteck, concerning the bond refunding. Since you touted your analytical skills at the job interview, you wonder whether this assignment might be to test whether you've got the skills you claimed to have.

Questions

1. What discount rate should be used to perform the refunding analysis? Discuss the relative merits of using the current after-tax bond rate as opposed to the weighted average cost of capital. (Hint: Think about the probability distributions of cash flows from the refunding operation versus cash flows from a "typical" project.)

2. Calculate the net present value of the refunding if the firm goes ahead with the new bond issue on January 1, 1993. Use Table 1 as a guide for your analysis.

3. Give a critique of each of the positions taken by the various board members. As a part of your answer, calculate the expected NPV of refunding next year based on Chang's probability distribution of interest rates. Remember, however, that if Bay Area refunds next year, the old bonds will have 24 years left to maturity. Assume for the purposes of this question that the firm could issue the new bonds with a 24-year maturity. Also, remember that Bay Area would not act next year if the refunding had a negative NPV at that time.

4. Should the firm refund the old bonds now, refund the old bonds in one year, or not refund the bonds at all?

5. How would the nature of the probability distribution of expected future interest rates affect the decision to refund now or to wait? Draw two probability distribution curves on the same chart, with one curve suggesting that the refunding be deferred, and the other suggesting that the refunding take place immediately. (Hint: There is no single correct answer. Think about the expected values and shapes of the distributions.)

6. Suppose the major bond rating agencies downgraded Bay Area's credit rating from A to triple B before the firm could initiate the refunding, so that selected data given in the case changed as follows:

(1) The coupon rate on the new bond is 10.5 percent.

(2) The flotation cost on the new bonds is 1.5 percent of the issue's face value, or $750,000.

How would these factors affect the refunding decision?

7. If the yield curve had been downward sloping, and if Whiteck felt that "the market knows more than I do" about the future course of interest rates, how might this affect his decision to recommend immediate refunding versus deferring the refunding?

8. How would Bay Area's position as a regulated public utility affect the accept/reject decision on the bond refunding? Would Bay Area have more or less incentive to refund than an unregulated company? (Hint: Regulators set rates so that utilities just earn their costs of capital; that is, all projects, including bond refundings, have zero NPVs.)

9. Another bond that Bay Area is considering refunding is a $25 million, 30-year issue sold 25 years ago in January 1968. At the time this bond was issued, the firm was in poor financial condition and was considered to be a high credit risk. To raise the $25 million, the firm was forced to issue subordinated debentures with a B rating and a coupon rate of 10.3 percent, which was quite high at the time. The flotation cost on this issue was two percent of the face amount, or $500,000. The old bond had 5 years of call protection, and the call premium at first call was $103 per $1,000 par value bond. The call premium is reduced proportionally over the remaining life of the old issue. John Whiteck estimates that the firm could also refund this $25 million issue with a 25-year, 9.5 percent coupon bond that would require a flotation cost of $250,000. Assume that this $25 million of capital will be needed into the indefinite future; so whether the bond is refunded now or in five years, it will subsequently be refunded every 25 years with a 25-year, 9.5 percent bond, with each successive replacement bond remaining outstanding to its maturity. Is the refunding analysis you used in Question 2 appropriate for this bond? Explain how the analysis could be modified to make it better. If you are using the *Lotus* model, complete the numerical analysis. (Hint: Use Table 2 as a guide.)

10. Describe how Bay Area could use the futures market to protect against a possible interest rate increase between the time the decision is made to refund the old issue and the time the refunding

actually takes place. If you are using the *Lotus* model, calculate how much interest rates can increase before the refunding becomes unprofitable.

11. Do you think that a lower tax rate, say 20 percent, would make the refunding more or less attractive? If you are using the *Lotus* model, determine the relationship between refunding NPV and tax rate.

12. If you are using the *Lotus* model, run the refunding analysis at a range of interest rates, and then create a graph that shows the relationship between the refunding interest rate and NPV.

13. What impact will the refunding have on Bay Area's capital structure? (Hint: Think in terms of both book value and market value structures.)

Table 1

Bond Refunding Analysis

Cost of refunding at t=0:	Amount before Tax	Amount after Tax	Present Value
Call premium on old issue	($5,750,000)	($3,450,000)	($3,450,000)
Flotation cost on new issue			X
Tax saving on old flotation costs	625,000	X	X
Net investment outlay			X
Flotation cost tax effects:			
New issue tax benefit			
Tax benefit lost on old issue	$20,000	$8,000	$ 105,248
Net PV of flotation cost tax effects	(25,000)	X	X
			X
Interest savings due to refunding:			
Annual payment (old bond)	$5,750,000	$3,450,000	
Annual payment (new bond)	(4,750,000)	X	
Net annual savings and PV		X	X
NPV of the refunding decision:			X

Table 2

Replacement Chain Analysis

	After-Tax Cash Flow (Interest Expense + Flotation Cost)	
Year	Delay Refund	Refund Now
0	$ 0	($ 525,667)[a]
1	(1,538,333)	(1,421,000)
2	X	X
3	(1,538,333)	(1,421,000)
4	(1,538,333)	(1,421,000)
5	(1,788,333)[a]	(1,421,000)
6	(1,421,000)	(1,421,000)
7	(1,421,000)	(1,421,000)
8	(1,421,000)	(1,421,000)
9	(1,421,000)	(1,421,000)
10	(1,421,000)	(1,421,000)
11	(1,421,000)	(1,421,000)
12	(1,421,000)	(1,421,000)
13	(1,421,000)	(1,421,000)
14	(1,421,000)	(1,421,000)
15	(1,421,000)	(1,421,000)
16	(1,421,000)	(1,421,000)
17	(1,421,000)	(1,421,000)
18	(1,421,000)	(1,421,000)
19	(1,421,000)	(1,421,000)
20	(1,421,000)	(1,421,000)
21	(1,421,000)	(1,421,000)
22	(1,421,000)	(1,421,000)
23	(1,421,000)	(1,421,000)
24	(1,421,000)	(1,421,000)
25	(1,421,000)	X[a]
26	(1,421,000)	(1,421,000)
27	(1,421,000)	(1,421,000)
28	(1,421,000)	(1,421,000)
29	(1,421,000)	(1,421,000)
30	X[a]	(1,421,000)
31	(1,421,000)	(1,421,000)
32	(1,421,000)	(1,421,000)

[a] Indicates a refunding year.

25

Lease Analysis

Environmental Sciences, Inc.

Over the past few years, officials in Florida and other states that rely primarily on deep wells for drinking water have become aware of a potentially serious problem—the pollution of aquifers by the unrestrained use of fertilizers and pesticides. The results of a study conducted by the United States Geological Survey showed that while the primary aquifer underlying Florida is not yet contaminated, one chemical commonly found in agricultural pesticides has caused extensive contamination of wells that tap water-bearing strata near the surface. To combat this potentially widespread problem, officials in Florida and elsewhere are lobbying for strict environmental regulation of commercial fertilizers and pesticides. As a result, companies specializing in agricultural chemicals have been working furiously to supply new products that will not be banned under the proposed regulations.

Environmental Sciences, Inc., a regional producer of agricultural chemicals based in Orlando, recently developed a pesticide that meets the new regulations. Now the firm must acquire the necessary equipment to begin production. The estimated internal rate of return (IRR) of this project is 24 percent and the project is judged to have low risk. Environmental Sciences uses an after-tax cost of capital of 11 percent for relatively low-risk projects, 13 percent for those of average risk, and 15 percent for high-risk projects; so this low-risk project passed the hurdle rate with flying colors.

The production-line equipment has an invoice price of $1,375,000, including delivery and installation charges. It falls into the modified accelerated cost recovery system (MACRS) five-year class, with current allowances of 0.20, 0.32, 0.19, 0.12, 0.11, and 0.06 in Years 1-6, respectively. Environmental's effective tax rate is 40 percent. The manufacturer of the equipment will provide a contract for maintenance and service for $75,000 per year, payable at the beginning of each year, if Environmental Sciences buys the equipment.

Regardless of whether the equipment is purchased or leased, Susan Baker, the firm's financial manager, does not think it will be used for more than four years, at which time Environmental's current building lease will expire. Land on which to construct a larger facility has already been acquired, and the building should be ready for occupancy at that time. The new facility will be designed to enable Environmental to use several new production processes that are currently unavailable to it, including one that will duplicate all processes of the equipment now being considered. Hence, the current project is viewed as a "bridge" to serve only until the permanent equipment can become operational in the new facility four years from now. The expected useful life of the equipment is eight years, at which time it should have a zero market value, but the residual value at the end of the fourth year should be well above zero. Susan generally assumes that assets' salvage values will be equal to their tax book values at any point in time, but she is concerned about that assumption in this instance.

Currently, the company has sufficient capital, in the form of temporary investments in marketable securities, to pay cash for the equipment and the first year's maintenance. Susan estimates that the interest rate on a 4-year secured loan to buy the equipment would be 11 percent, but she has decided to draw down the securities portfolio and pay cash for the equipment if it is purchased.

Oceanside Capital, Inc. (OSC), the leasing subsidiary of a major regional bank, has offered to lease the equipment to Environmental for annual payments of $435,000, with the first payment due upon delivery and installation and additional payments due at the beginning of each succeeding year of the 4-year lease term. This price includes a service contract under which the equipment would be maintained in good working order. OSC would buy the equipment from the manufacturer under the same terms that were offered to Environmental, including the maintenance and service contract. Like Environmental, OSC generally assumes that the most likely residual value for equipment of this type is the tax book value at the end of the lease term. Some OSC executives think, however, that the residual value in this case will be much higher because of the expanding nature of the business. OSC is not expected to pay any taxes over the next 4 years, because the firm has an abundance of tax credits to carry forward. Finally, OSC views lease investments such as this as an alternative to lending, so if it does not write the lease, it will lend the $1,375,000 that would have been invested in the lease to some other party in the form of a term loan that would earn 11 percent before taxes.

Susan Baker has always had the final say on all of Environmental's lease-versus-purchase decisions, but the actual analysis of the relevant data is conducted by Environmental's assistant treasurer, Tom Linenberger. Traditionally, Environmental's method of evaluating lease decisions has been to calculate the "present value cost" of the lease payments versus the present value of the total charges if the equipment is purchased. However, in a recent evaluation, Susan and Tom got into a heated discussion about the appropriate discount rate to use in determining the present value costs of leasing and of purchasing. The following points of view were expressed:

(1)   Susan argued that the discount rate should be the firm's weighted average cost of capital. She believes that a lease-versus-purchase decision is in effect a capital budgeting decision, and as such it should be evaluated at the company's cost of capital. In other words, one method or the other will provide a net cash savings in any year, and the dollars saved using the most advantageous method will be invested to yield the firm's cost of capital. Therefore, the weighted average cost of capital is the appropriate opportunity rate to use in evaluating lease-versus-purchase decisions.

(2)   Tom, on the other hand, believes that the cash flows generated in a lease-versus-purchase situation are more certain than are the cash flows generated by the firm's average project. Consequently, these cash flows should be discounted at a lower rate because of their lower risk. At the present time, the firm's cost of secured debt reflects the lowest risk rate to Environmental Sciences. Therefore, 11 percent should be used as the discount rate in the lease-versus-purchase decision.

To settle the debate, Susan and Tom asked Environmental's CPA firm to review the situation and to advise them on which discount rate was appropriate. This led to even more confusion because the firm's accountants, Michelle Nobelitt and Bill Orr, were also unable to reach agreement on which rate to use. Michelle agreed with Susan that the discount rate should be based on the firm's cost of capital, but on the grounds that leasing is simply an alternative to other means of financing. Leasing is a substitute for "financing," which is a mix of debt and equity, and it saves the cost of raising capital; this cost is the firm's weighted average cost of capital. Bill, however, thought that none of the discount rates mentioned so far adequately accounted for the tax effects inherent in any capital budgeting decision, and he suggested using the after-tax cost of secured debt.

In the last lease-versus-purchase decision, the firm's weighted average cost of capital (13 percent) was used, but now Susan is uncertain about the validity of this procedure. She is beginning to lean toward Bill's alternative, but she wonders if it would be appropriate to use a low-risk discount rate for evaluating all the cash flows in the analysis. Susan is particularly concerned about the risk of the expected residual value. While the company is almost certain of the other cash flows and the tax shelters, the salvage value at the end of the fourth year is relatively uncertain, having a distribution of possible outcomes that makes its risk comparable to that of the average capital budgeting project undertaken by the firm. She is also concerned that using a discount rate based on the after-tax cost of a secured loan might be inappropriate when the funds used to purchase the equipment would come from internal sources. Perhaps the cost of equity capital also deserves consideration, because the funds could be used to increase the next quarterly dividend payment.

To settle all the disputes, the parties to the lease-versus-buy analysis agreed that an outside consultant should be hired to conduct the analysis. Assume you are that consultant and the firm has provided you with the following list of questions.

Questions

PART A: Lessee's Analysis

1. The conventional format for analyzing lease-versus-purchase decisions assumes that the money to buy the equipment will be obtained by borrowing. In this case, however, Environmental has sufficient internally generated capital, held in the form of marketable securities, to buy the equipment outright. What impact does this fact have on the analysis?

2. Should Environmental lease or purchase the equipment? Assume that if the decision is made to purchase the equipment, it will be sold for its book value on the first day of Year 5, hence the full Year 4 depreciation can be taken. Further, use the 11.0 percent before-tax (6.6 percent after-tax) cost of debt as the residual value discount rate. (Hint: Use Part A of Table 1 as a guide.)

3. Justify the discount rate you used in the calculation process. Now assume that Susan wants you to adjust the analysis to reflect differential residual value risk. What impact does this have on Environmental's lease-versus-purchase decision? (Hint: The 13 percent wighted average cost of capital used to evaluate average-risk projects is an *after-tax* cost.)

4. a. Based on the information given in the case, would you classify this lease as a financial lease or as an operating lease? For accounting purposes, a lease is classified as a financial lease, hence must be capitalized and shown directly on the balance sheet, if the lease contract meets any one of the following conditions:

   (1) The lessee can buy the asset at the end of the lease term for a bargain price.

   (2) The lease transfers ownership to the lessee before the lease expires.

   (3) The lease lasts for 75 percent or more of the asset's estimated useful life.

   (4) The present value of the lease payments is 90 percent or more of the asset's value.

   b. Does the differential accounting treatment of operating versus financial leases make comparative financial statement analysis more difficult for outside financial analysts? If so, how might analysts overcome the problem?

5. In some instances, a company might be able to lease assets at a cost less than the cost the firm would incur if it financed the purchase with a loan. If the equipment represented a significant addition to the lessee's assets, could this affect its overall cost of capital, hence the capital budgeting decision that preceded the lease analysis? Would this affect capital budgeting decisions related to other assets? Explain.

6. Now assume that Susan estimates the residual value could be as low as $0 or as high as $467,500. Further, she subjectively assigns a probability of occurrence of 0.25 to the extreme values and 0.50 to the base case value, $233,750. Describe how Susan's estimates could be incorporated into the analysis. If you are using the *Lotus* model, calculate Environmental's net advantage to leasing (NAL) at each residual value. What is the expected NAL? (For

this analysis, assume a 6.6 percent after-tax discount rate on all cash flows.)

PART B: Lessor's Analysis

7. Now evaluate the proposed lease from the point of view of the lessor, Oceanside Capital, Inc. Assume that the residual value is equal to the book value at the end of the fourth year, and use an 11 percent after-tax discount rate for all cash flows. Are the current terms favorable to OSC? (Hint: Use Part B of Table 1 as a guide.)

PART C: Combined Analysis

8. Based on a 4-year use of the asset, a 6.6 percent after-tax discount rate on the cash flows of the lessee, and an 11 percent after-tax discount rate on the cash flows of the lessor (that is, the original conditions), you should have found that the lease is advantageous to both Environmental Sciences and OSC. Is there a range of lease payments that would be acceptable to both the lessor and the lessee? At which end of the range do you think the actual payment would be set? If you are using the *Lotus* model, specify the actual range of payments.

9. There is a possibility that Environmental will move to its new production facility earlier than anticipated, hence prior to the expiration of the lease. Thus, Susan is considering asking OSC to include a cancellation clause in the lease contract. What impact would a cancellation clause have on the riskiness of the lease to Environmental? How would it affect the risk to OSC? If you were OSC's leasing manager, would you change the lease terms if a cancellation clause were added? If so, what changes might be made?

10. Leases are sometimes written so that the lessee makes payments at the end of each year rather than in advance. If the lessor structured the analysis with deferred payments, how would this affect (a) the NAL from the lessee's standpoint and (b) the rate of return earned by the lessor? Could the lease payments be adjusted, if they were made on a deferred basis, to produce the same NAL as existed when the payments were made in advance?

11. Assume now that OSC has no tax credits to carry forward, hence is in the 40-percent tax bracket. Also assume that both parties to the lease estimate a $233,750 residual value and discount it at a 6.6 percent after-tax discount rate. What do you think would happen

to OSC's NPV under these conditions? If you are using the *Lotus* model, do the calculation.

12. What effect do you think Environmental's tax rate has on its lease-versus-purchase decision? If you are using the *Lotus* model, find Environmental's NAL at tax rates of 0, 10, 20, 30, 40, 50, and 60 percent. Explain your results.

Table 1

Selected Cash Flow Data

(In Thousands of Dollars)

MACRS Depreciation Table:

Year	MACRS Rate	Depr Basis	Annual Depr	Ending Book Value
1	20%	$1,375.00	$ 275.00	$1,100.00
2	32	X	X	X
3	19	1,375.00	X	X
4	12	1,375.00	165.00	233.75
5	11	1,375.00	151.25	82.50
6	6	1,375.00	82.50	0.00
			$1,375.00	

PART A: Lessee's Analysis:

Cost of Owning:

	Year 0	Year 1	Year 2	Year 3	Year 4
Equipment cost	($1,375.00)				
Maintenance	(75.00)	($ 75.00)	X	($ 75.00)	
Maintenance tax savings	30.00	30.00	X	30.00	
Depreciation shield		110.00	X	104.50	$ 66.00
Residual value					233.75
RV tax					0.00
Net owning CF	($1,420.00)	$ 65.00	X	$ 59.50	$299.75

Cost of Leasing:

	Year 0	Year 1	Year 2	Year 3	Year 4
Lease payment	($ 435.00)	($435.00)	X	($435.00)	
Payment tax savings	174.00	174.00	X	174.00	
Net leasing CF	($ 261.00)	($261.00)	X	($261.00)	$ 0.00

PART B: Lessor's Analysis:

	Year 0	Year 1	Year 2	Year 3	Year 4
Equipment cost	($1,375.00)				
Maintenance	(75.00)	($ 75.00)	X	($ 75.00)	
Maintenance tax savings	0.00	0.00	X	0.00	
Depreciation shield		0.00	X	0.00	$ 0.00
Residual value					233.75
RV tax					0.00
Lease payment	435.00	435.00	X	435.00	
Lease payment tax	0.00	0.00	X	0.00	
Net CF	($1,015.00)	$360.00	X	$360.00	$233.75

26

Lease Analysis

Prudent Solutions, Inc.

For the past 25 years, nuclear power companies have been storing spent fuel rods underwater in pools located at the plant sites, awaiting the opening of a permanent federal high-level nuclear waste storage facility. Unfortunately, the government's final decision on a suitable location for this facility has been long delayed. Furthermore, environmental concerns from special interest groups and ever-increasing design and construction requirements for new government nuclear storage facilities greatly lessen the chance of opening the facility for storage within the next 10 to 15 years. Thus, nuclear power companies are now facing serious storage problems at their plant sites as spent fuel continues to accumulate.

Recently, rumors have been circulating that Prudent Solutions, Inc., a firm devoted to finding solutions to the nuclear waste storage problem, has made a significant breakthrough in this area. Prudent Solutions, Inc. was formed by several nuclear physics professors from North Carolina, North Carolina State, and Duke Universities—the schools which make up the "Research Triangle" in North Carolina. The company recently discovered a process which makes spent nuclear fuel inert and thus harmless. The firm must now move from research and development to commercial production. The estimated internal rate of return (IRR) on this project is 24 percent, and the project is judged to have low risk. Prudent uses an after-tax cost of capital of 11 percent for low-risk projects, 13 percent for those of average risk, and 15 percent for high-risk projects. Thus, this low-risk project was easily approved by the firm's management.

Among the equipment required to move this process to commercial production is a sophisticated computerized data acquisition system, which is needed to monitor closely the entire fuel conversion process to ensure spent fuel is rendered safe upon completion.   The required data acquisition system has a cost of $41.25 million, including delivery and installation charges, and it falls into the modified accelerated cost recovery system (MACRS) 5-year class, with current allowances of 0.20, 0.32, 0.19, 0.12, 0.11, and 0.06 in Years 1 through 6, respectively. Prudent's federal-plus-state tax rate is 40 percent.   The manufacturer of the equipment will provide a contract for maintenance and service for $2.25 million per year, payable at the beginning of each year, if Prudent decides to buy the equipment.

Regardless of whether the system is purchased or leased, Suzanne Terrell, the firm's financial manager, does not think that it will be used for more than 4 years, at which time Prudent's current building lease will expire.   Land on which to construct a larger facility has already been acquired, and the building should be ready for occupancy at that time. The new facility will be designed to enable Prudent to use several new production processes that are currently unavailable to it, including the spent-fuel conversion process.   At that time, Prudent will procure a new data acquisition and control system.   This system will provide for enhanced capabilities, allowing Prudent both to monitor and to control three different processes simultaneously.   Hence, the current system is viewed as a "bridge" to serve only until the permanent data acquisition and control system can become operational in the new facility 4 years from now.   The expected useful life of the equipment is 8 years, at which time it should have a zero market value, but the residual value at the end of the fourth year should be well above zero.   Terrell generally assumes that assets' salvage values will be equal to their tax book values at any point in time, but she is concerned about that assumption in this instance.

Currently, the company has sufficient capital in the form of temporary investments in marketable securities to pay cash for the equipment.   Terrell estimates that the interest rate on a 4-year secured loan for $41.25 million would be 10 percent, but she has decided to draw down the marketable securities portfolio and to pay cash for the data acquisition system if it is purchased.

Commercial Capital Corporation, the leasing subsidiary of a major regional bank, has offered to lease the required data acquisition system to Prudent for annual payments of $12.75 million, with the first payment due upon delivery and installation, and additional payments due at the beginning of each succeeding year of the 4-year lease term.   This price includes a service contract under which the system would be maintained in good working order.   Commercial would buy the system from the manufacturer under the same terms offered to Prudent, including the maintenance and service contract.   Like Prudent, Commercial generally assumes that the most likely residual value for equipment of this type is the tax book value at the end of the lease term. Some Commercial executives think, however, that the residual value in this case may be much higher given the capabilities of this system. Commercial is not expected to pay any taxes over the next 4 years, because the firm has an abundance of tax credits to carry forward. Finally, Commercial views lease investments such as this as an alternative to lending, so if it does not write the lease, it will lend the $41.25 million that would have been invested in the lease to some other party in the form of a term loan which would earn 10 percent before taxes.

Suzanne Terrell has always had the final say on all of Prudent's lease decisions, but the actual analysis of the relevant data is conducted by the firm's assistant treasurer, Tony Davis. Traditionally, Prudent's method of evaluating lease decisions has been to calculate the "present value cost" of the lease payments versus the present value of the cash flows if the equipment is purchased. However, in a recent evaluation, Terrell and Davis got into a heated discussion about the appropriate discount rate to use in the analysis. The following opinions were expressed:

(1) Terrell argued that the discount rate should be the firm's weighted average cost of capital. She believed that a lease-versus-purchase decision was, in effect, a capital budgeting decision. Accordingly, it should be evaluated at the company's cost of capital. In other words, one method or the other will provide a net cash savings in any year, and the dollars saved using the most advantageous method will be invested to yield the firm's cost of capital. Therefore, the weighted average cost of capital is the appropriate opportunity rate to use in evaluating lease-versus-purchase decisions.

(2) Davis, on the other hand, said that the cash flows generated in a lease-versus-purchase situation are more certain than are the cash flows generated by the firm's average projects. Consequently, these cash flows should be discounted at a lower rate because of their lower risk. At the present time, the firm's cost of secured debt reflects the lowest risk rate to Prudent. Therefore, 10 percent should be used as the discount rate in the lease-versus-purchase decision.

To settle the debate, Terrell and Davis asked Prudent's auditing firm to review the situation and to advise them on which discount rate was appropriate. This led to even more confusion, because the firm's accountants, Pat Parker and Don Monroe, were also unable to reach agreement on which rate to use. Parker agreed with Terrell that the discount rate should be based on the firm's cost of capital, but on the grounds that leasing is simply an alternative to other means of financing. Leasing is a substitute for "financing," which is a mix of debt and equity, and it thus saves the cost of raising capital; this cost is the firm's weighted average cost of capital. Monroe, however, thought that none of the discount rates mentioned so far adequately accounted for the tax effects inherent in any capital budgeting decision, and he suggested using the after-tax cost of secured debt.

In Prudent's last lease-versus-purchase decision, the firm's weighted average cost of capital (13 percent) was used, but now Terrell is uncertain about the validity of this procedure. She is beginning to lean toward Don Monroe's alternative, but she wonders if it would be appropriate to use the same low discount rate for evaluating all the cash flows in the analysis. Terrell is particularly concerned about the risk of the expected residual value. While the company is almost certain of the other cash flows and the tax shelters, the salvage value at the end of the fourth year is relatively uncertain, having a distribution of possible outcomes that makes its risk comparable to that of an average-risk capital project undertaken by the firm. She is also concerned that using a discount rate based on the after-tax cost of a secured loan might be inappropriate when the funds used to purchase the equipment would come from internal sources. Perhaps the cost of equity capital also deserves consideration, because the funds could be used to increase the next quarterly dividend payment.

Assume that you are Tony Davis's assistant and that he has asked you to conduct the lease analysis. As a guide, he has provided you with the following questions.

Questions

PART A: Lessee's Analysis

1. The conventional format for analyzing lease-versus-purchase decisions assumes that the money to buy the data acquisition system will be obtained by borrowing. In this case, however, Prudent has sufficient internally generated capital, held in the form of marketable securities, to buy the system outright. What impact does this fact have on the analysis?

2. Should Prudent lease or purchase the system? Assume that if the decision is made to purchase the system, it will be sold for its book value on the first day of Year 5, hence the full Year 4 depreciation can be taken. Further, use the 6 percent after-tax

cost of debt as the residual value discount rate. (Hint: Use Part A of Table 1 as a guide.)

3. Justify the discount rate you used in the calculation process. Now assume that Davis wants you to adjust the analysis to reflect the differential residual value risk. What impact does this have on Prudent's lease-versus-purchase decision? (Hint: The 13 percent cost of capital used to evaluate average-risk projects is an *after-tax* cost.)

4. a. Based on the information given in the case, would you classify this lease as a financial lease or as an operating lease? For accounting purposes, a lease is classified as a financial lease, hence must be capitalized and shown directly on the balance sheet, if the contract meets any one of the following conditions:

   (1) The lessee can buy the asset at the end of the lease term for a bargain price.

   (2) The lease transfers ownership to the lessee before the lease expires.

   (3) The lease lasts for 75 percent or more of the asset's estimated useful life.

   (4) The present value of the lease payments is 90 percent or more of the asset's value.

   b. Does the differential accounting treatment of operating versus financial leases make comparative financial statement analysis more difficult for outside financial analysts? If so, how might analysts overcome the problem?

5. In some instances, a company might be able to lease assets at a cost less than the cost the firm would incur if it financed the purchase with a loan. If the equipment represented a significant addition to the lessee's assets, could this affect its overall cost of capital, hence the capital budgeting decision that preceded the lease analysis? Would this affect capital budgeting decisions related to other assets? Explain.

6. Now assume Terrell estimates that the residual value could be as low as $0 or as high as $14.025 million. Further, she subjectively assigns a probability of occurrence of 0.25 to the extreme values and 0.50 to the base case value, $7.0125 million. Describe how Davis's estimates could be incorporated into the analysis. If you are using the *Lotus* model, calculate Prudent's net advantage to leasing (NAL) at each

residual value.   What is the expected NAL? (For this analysis, assume a 10 percent pre-tax discount rate on all cash flows.)

PART B: Lessor's Analysis

7. Now evaluate the proposed lease from the point of view of the lessor, Commercial Capital. Assume that the residual value is equal to the book value at the end of the fourth year and use a 10 percent discount rate for all cash flows. Are the current terms favorable to Commercial? (Hint: Use Part B of Table 1 as a guide.)

PART C: Combined Analysis

8. Based on a 4-year use of the asset and a 10 percent pre-tax discount rate for all cash flows (i.e., the original conditions), you should have found that the lease is advantageous to both Prudent and Commercial.   Is there a range of lease payments that would be acceptable to both the lessor and the lessee? At which end of the range do you think the actual payment would be set?   If you are using the *Lotus* model, specify the actual range of payments.

9. There is a possibility that Prudent will move to its new production facility earlier than anticipated, and hence prior to the expiration of the lease. Thus, Davis is considering asking Commercial to include a cancellation clause in the lease contract.   What impact would a cancellation clause have on the riskiness of the lease to Prudent? How would it affect the risk to Commercial?   If you were Commercial's leasing manager, would you change the lease terms if a cancellation clause were added? If so, what changes might be made?

10. Leases are sometimes written so that the lessee makes payments at the end of each year rather than in advance. If the lessor structured the analysis with deferred payments, how would this affect (a) the NAL from the lessee's standpoint and (b) the rate of return earned by the lessor? Could the lease payments be adjusted, if they were made on a deferred basis, to produce the same NAL as existed when the payments were made in advance?

11. Assume now that Commercial has no tax credits to carry forward, hence is in the 40 percent tax bracket. Also assume that both parties to the lease estimate a $7.0125 million residual value and discount it at a 6.0 percent after-tax discount rate. What do you think would happen to Commercial's NPV under these conditions? If you are using the *Lotus* model, do the calculation.

12. What effect do you think Prudent's tax rate has on its lease-versus-purchase decision? If you are using the *Lotus* model, find Prudent's NAL at tax rates of 0, 10, 20, 30, 40, and 50 percent. Explain your results.

Table 1

Selected Cash Flow Data

(in Millions of Dollars)

MACRS Depreciation Table:

Year	MACRS Rate	Depr Basis	Annual Depr	Ending Book Value
1	20%	$41.25	$ 8.25	$33.00
2	32	X	X	X
3	19	41.25	X	X
4	12	41.25	4.95	7.01
5	11	41.25	4.54	2.48
6	6	41.25	2.48	0.00
			$41.25	

PART A: Lessee's Analysis:

Cost of Owning:

	Year 0	Year 1	Year 2	Year 3	Year 4
Equipment cost	($41.25)				
Maintenance	(2.25)	($2.25)	X	($2.25)	
Maintenance tax savings	0.90	0.90	X	0.90	
Depreciation shield		3.30	X	3.14	$1.98
Residual value					7.01
RV tax					0.00
Net owning CF	($42.60)	$1.95	X	$1.79	$8.99

Cost of Leasing:

	Year 0	Year 1	Year 2	Year 3	Year 4
Lease payment	($12.75)	($12.75)	X	$12.75	
Lease payment tax	5.10	5.10	X	5.10	
Net leasing CF	($ 7.65)	$ 7.65	X	$ 7.65	$0.00

PART B: Lessor's Analysis:

	Year 0	Year 1	Year 2	Year 3	Year 4
Equipment cost	($41.25)				
Maintenance	(2.25)	($ 2.25)	X	($ 2.25)	
Maintenance tax savings	0.00	0.00	X	0.00	
Depreciation shield		0.00	X	0.00	$0.00
Residual value					7.01
RV tax					0.00
Lease payment	12.75	12.75	X	12.75	
Lease payment tax	0.00	0.00	X	0.00	
Net CF	($30.75)	$10.50	X	$10.50	$7.01

27

---

*Financing with
Convertibles and
Warrants*

Virginia May Chocolate Company

"Regardless of the reaction in the stock and bond markets," said Terry Barnhardt, treasurer of Virginia May Chocolate Company, "we must still raise $60 million of external capital next year. We've already contracted for the construction of the new plant, and penalty payments would be horrendous if we cancelled. Besides, if we are going to maintain our market position, we simply must continue our expansion program. I know money is expensive, but the investment bankers tell me we can cut our costs by issuing convertibles or bonds with warrants." Barnhardt's remarks were directed to Virginia May's board of directors. The topic under consideration was how Virginia May would raise $60 million in 1993 to finance a major plant expansion, which is a key element in the company's long-term modernization and expansion plan. Virginia May had already committed to the construction program, and the contracts for this phase had been signed several months ago.

Virginia May is one of the largest producers of chocolate goods in the world, with a product line including everything from candy bars to chocolate cake mixes and frostings. Most of its products are packaged for grocery chains and sold under the stores' labels, and the remainder are sold as generic products. Like many packaged foods companies, however, Virginia May's financial condition has deteriorated significantly over the past five years due to higher ingredient costs. In addition, the firm's use

---

of debt financing has been steadily rising in the face of declining earnings. These events have caused Virginia May's interest coverage ratio to fall to a dangerously low 2.7×, the firm's bonds to be downgraded from A to BBB, and the company's common stock to sell at roughly only 70 percent of book value. (See Table 1 for Virginia May's 1992 balance sheet.)

The company's deteriorating financial situation has reduced its flexibility in obtaining external capital. Virginia May had originally planned to issue first-mortgage bonds for the debt financing component and to meet its equity requirements for the expansion in 1993 by retaining earnings. However, given the firm's low interest coverage, a new long-term debt issue at this time would almost certainly cause Virginia May's credit rating to be downgraded again, which would relegate its bonds to the junk category. Additionally, the cost figures developed by the firm's investment bankers and shown in Table 2 are based on the capital structure currently employed by Virginia May. These data indicate that Virginia May could expect a significant increase in its weighted average cost of capital if management increased the use of leverage at this time.

Management is also unwilling to issue new common stock at this time, both because of the depressed share price and also because of the dilution in book value and earnings per share that would occur if it sold stock at a price below book value. Finally, Virginia May's board has always refused to issue preferred stock because (1) preferred dividends, which the board regards as being similar to interest payments, are nondeductible; (2) preferred stock is riskier to investors than debt, and thus preferred has a relatively high rate of return; and (3) the company would be unable to pay common stock dividends if the preferred dividends had to be passed (omitted).

Thus, Barnhardt felt that the only viable alternatives available to Virginia May were either convertible bonds or bonds with warrants. Based on several discussions with Virginia May's investment bankers, Barnhardt has tentatively concluded that the firm could raise the required $60 million by selling one of three alternative issues. First, the company could sell 9 percent, annual-payment convertible debentures with a par value of $1,000 and convertible into 50 shares of common stock. This issue would mature in 25 years and would be callable on any interest payment date after 2 years, with an initial call premium of $90 per bond that would decline by $90/23 = $3.91 per year thereafter. Alternatively, Virginia May could issue 11 percent, $1,000 par value, annual-payment debentures which would be convertible into 40 shares of common stock. This issue would also have a maturity of 25 years and would again be callable on any interest payment date after 2 years, with a call premium of $110 in Year 2 but declining by $4.78 per year after

Year 2.   Finally, Virginia May could issue 10 percent, annual-payment debentures carrying 80 detachable warrants, with each warrant giving the holder the right to buy a share of common stock at $20 each.   These bonds would have a par value of $1,000 and would mature in 25 years, and the warrants would expire in 6 years if they had not been exercised. Since Barnhardt does not regard these rates as firm, they might have to be adjusted on the basis of further analysis.

Table 1

Balance Sheet for Year Ended
December 31, 1992

Assets	
Cash	$ 5,600,000
Accounts receivable	17,840,000
Materials and supplies	36,680,000
Total current assets	$ 60,120,000
Plant and equipment (net)	433,432,000
Total assets	$ 493,552,000
Claims on Assets	
Accounts payable	$ 11,600,000
Accruals	7,664,000
Notes payable[a]	40,000,000
Total current liabilities	$ 59,264,000
Long-term debt[b]	220,000,000
Total liabilities	$ 279,264,000
Common stock[c]	$ 68,784,000
Retained earnings	145,504,000
Total common equity	$ 214,288,000
Total claims on assets	$ 493,552,000

[a]Unlike many companies, Virginia May uses short-term notes payable as a source of permanent financing. Virginia May's notes payable currently carry an interest cost of 8.5 percent and are valued at par.

[b]Virginia May's outstanding bonds have a par value of $1,000, a remaining life of 15 years, a coupon rate of 9 percent, and pay annual interest. These are first-mortgage bonds, and the current rate of interest for 15-year bonds with Virginia May's rating is 10.5 percent.

[c]The current price of the company's common stock is $17.45 per share, and there are 9 million shares outstanding.

Table 2

Assumed Relationships Between Leverage
and the Cost of Capital

Leverage (Long-Term Debt/Capital)	Short-Term Interest Rate	Long-Term Interest Rate	Cost of Retained Earnings	Cost of New Common Stock
0.0%	7.50%	9.50%	12.50%	13.30%
10.0	7.70	9.75	12.60	13.40
20.0	7.90	10.00	13.00	13.80
30.0	8.10	10.20	13.40	14.30
40.0	8.30	10.40	14.20	15.25
50.0 (Target)	8.50	10.50	16.10	17.30
60.0	9.50	12.50	18.50	20.30
70.0	12.00	15.00	21.60	23.40

Note: The numbers presented here assume that the short-term debt/total capitalization ratio remains constant at the predetermined optimal amount. Also, capital is defined here as notes payable plus long-term debt plus total equity.

Both of the convertible issues, and also the bonds with warrants, would be subordinated debentures, so they would stand behind the firm's existing mortgage bonds in the event of bankruptcy. Virginia May's outstanding mortgage bonds only have a BBB rating, so its convertibles or bonds with warrants would probably be rated BB. Currently, double-B bonds with a maturity similar to that of the convertibles or bonds with warrants yield, on average, 12 percent. Therefore, the "straight bond value" of either the convertibles or the bonds with warrants would be determined by discounting at 12 percent.

As the directors' meeting was winding to a close, Barnhardt was asked to evaluate thoroughly each of the financing alternatives and to develop a recommendation for the next board meeting. As part of his analysis, Barnhardt was asked to calculate the firm's weighted average cost of capital (WACC) under each of the financing choices. The WACC is found using the following equation:

The weights in the preceding equation are *market value* weights, not
$$\text{WACC} = w_{dST}k_{dST}(1-T) + w_{dLT}k_{dLT}(1-T) + w_s(k_s \text{ or } k_e).$$

Here,

w_{dST} = weight assigned to short-term debt

k_{dST} = cost of new short-term debt

w_{dLT} = weight assigned to long-term debt

k_{dLT} = cost of new long-term debt

T = marginal tax rate

w_s = weight assigned to equity

k_s = cost of retained earnings

k_e = cost of new common stock

220

book value weights. To include either of the convertible issues or the bonds with warrants in the analysis, the term $w_c k_c$ ($w_w k_w$) will have to be added to the equation. Here, w_c (w_w) is the proportion of capital obtained in the form of convertibles or warrants, and k_c (k_w) is the cost of convertible capital or the cost of capital with warrants. To determine the cost of convertible or warrant capital (k_c or k_w), Barnhardt will have to make an assumption about when the bonds will be converted or the warrants exercised. Note that Virginia May's marginal tax rate is 40 percent.

Your task is to assist Barnhardt in preparing his report by answering the following questions.

Questions

1. a. Calculate Virginia May's current market value capital structure. In your calculations, ignore the relatively minor amounts of spontaneously generated liabilities, but do include notes payable, because Virginia May uses them as a permanent source of capital.

    b. Determine Virginia May's current weighted average cost of capital based on the cost data and the WACC equation given in the case. In your calculations, use the cost of new common stock given in Table 2 for the cost of equity.

2. Complete Table 3 and use these data to construct a graph (that is, complete Figure 1) which shows the conversion value, straight bond value, call price, maturity value, and estimated market value of the 11 percent convertible issue over time. To answer this question, assume that Virginia May's stock price will grow at a rate of 5 percent per year for the foreseeable future.

3. Once a convertible becomes callable, what factors would influence a company's decision to call the issue as opposed to letting it remain outstanding? What factors would induce the holders of a convertible to convert voluntarily?

4. Assume that Virginia May would call the 11 percent convertible issue after the first interest payment date on which the conversion value of the bond is 40 percent greater than the bond's par value. Using the assumptions embodied in your completed Figure 1, in what year should the bond be called for conversion? (Hint: Set $C_t =$ par value × 1.4, and find the value of t which forces equality. Note:

The 9 percent convertible issue would be called in 10 years under the same set of assumptions.)

Table 3

Conversion and Bond Values

for 11 Percent Convertible Bonds

Year	Conversion Value[a]	Straight Bond Value[b]	Call Price[c]	Maturity Value	Estimated Market Value[d]
0	$ 698	$ 922	$1,110	$1,000	$1,000
5	891	925	1,096	1,000	1,132
10	1,137	932	1,072	1,000	1,282
15	X	X	X	1,000	1,451
20	1,852	964	1,024	1,000	1,852
25	2,364	1,000	1,000	1,000	2,364

[a]Conversion value = $C_t = P_0(1 + g)^t R$, where,

t =   years since issue date

P_0 =   initial stock price

g =   growth rate in stock price

R =   conversion ratio

Example for Year 5: $C_5 = \$17.45(1 + 0.05)^5 40 = \$22.27(40) = \$891$.

[b]Bond value

$$\text{Bond Value} = B_t = \sum_{j=1}^{n} \frac{I}{(1+k_d)^j} + \frac{M}{(1+k_d)^n} = I\,(\text{PVIFA}_{k_d, n}) + M\,(\text{PVIF}_{k_d, n}), \text{where}$$

n =   number of years remaining until maturity

j =   time subscript from 1 to n

k_d =   market rate of interest of equivalent risk, nonconvertible debt issue

I =   dollars of interest paid each year

M =   maturity value

Example for Year 5: $B_5 = \$110\,(\text{PVIFA}_{12\%,20}) + \$1,000\,(\text{PVIF}_{12\%,20}) = \$925$.

[c]The bond is not callable for the first two years. After Year 2, the call premium is reduced by a constant amount each year to result in a zero call premium at maturity; that is, the premium is reduced by $1/23(\$110) = \$4.78$ per year.

Example for Year 5: Call price in Year 5 = $\$1,110 - 3(\$4.78) = \$1,096$.

[d]The market value estimates were obtained by first determining the year in which conversion is expected to occur (see Question 4). At that time, and in subsequent years, the market value should be equal to the conversion value. For years prior to conversion, we found the growth rate which would equate the initial market value, $1,000, with the conversion value at the expected date of conversion. In this instance, the growth rate was found to be 2.51 percent.

Example for Year 5: MV = $\$1,000\,(1 + 0.0251)^5 = \$1,132$.

Figure 1

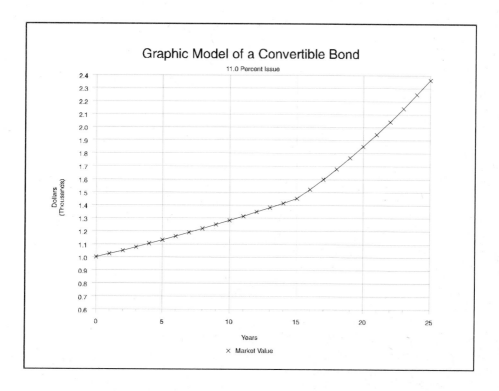

Graphic Model of a Convertible Bond

5. For this and the next question, assume that your answer to Question 4 was N = 15, the number of years to conversion, regardless of your actual answer. What is the after-tax cost to Virginia May of the 11 percent convertible issue? For the 9 percent issue, k_c is 8.27 percent if conversion occurs in Year 10; this value is calculated as follows:

$$M = \sum_{t=1}^{n} \frac{I(1-T)}{(1+k_c)^t} + \frac{P_N CR}{(1+k_c)^N} \; ,$$

where

  M = market value of bond = $1,000
  N = number of years to conversion = 10
  I = interest in dollars = $90
  T = tax rate = 0.40
  P_N = expected market price of stock at the end of period N,

$$= \$17.45(1.05)^{10} = \$28.42$$

$$CR = \text{conversion ratio} = 50$$

Then,

$$\$1,000 = \sum_{t=1}^{10} \frac{\$90\,(1-0.4)}{(1+k_c)^t} + \frac{\$28.42(50)}{(1+k_c)^{10}}$$

$$\$1,000 = \$54.00\,(\text{PVIFA}_{k_c,\,10}) + \$1,421.21\ (\text{PVI}$$

$k_c = 8.27\%$.

6. What is the expected before-tax rate of return to investors on the 11 percent convertible issue, assuming a call in Year 15? What accounts for the difference between the investor's return and the company's cost on the same issue? (Note: The expected before-tax rate of return on the 9 percent convertible issue is 11.46 percent, assuming a call in Year 10.)

7. What would Virginia May's weighted average cost of capital be if it issues $60 million of the 11 percent convertible bonds? In your calculation, assume that all new equity is raised as retained earnings. Even though the capital structure weights will necessarily change due to the addition of $60 million of convertibles, assume that the costs of notes payable, long-term debt, and common stock do not change; that is, use $k_{dST} = 8.5\%$, $k_{dLT} = 10.5\%$, and $k_s = 16.1\%$. (Note: WACC = 9.86 percent if the 9 percent convertibles are used.) Do you think it is reasonable to assume that the component costs would remain constant? If not, how would they be likely to change?

8. A graphic model of the market value of the convertible is shown in Figure 1. According to Table 3, the market value of the convertible in Year 10 is $1,282. Suppose you purchased ten bonds at $1,282, and then the next day the company called the bonds for conversion. How much would you gain or lose? What does this suggest about the market value line; that is, is the market value line in the graph consistent with the other data, and is it drawn correctly? Explain.

9. Calculate the after-tax cost to the company of the bonds with warrants. The before-tax yield to investors is 11.74 percent, calculated as follows:

(1) The straight-debt value of the bond is

$$V_B = \sum_{t=1}^{25} \frac{\$100}{(1.12)^t} + \frac{\$1,000}{(1.12)^{25}} = \$843.14.$$

(2)   Therefore, the value of the warrants must be

V_W = $1,000 – $843.14 = $156.86, or

$156.86/80 = $1.96 per warrant.

(3)   The expected stock price in 6 years is $17.45(1.05)^6 = $23.38. With an exercise price of $20, the expected value of the warrants in 6 years is $3.38, for a total value of $3.38(80) = $270.77 ≈ $271.

(4)   Thus an investor faces this cash flow stream:

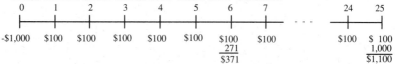

With a financial calculator, we find the IRR of this stream to be 1.74 percent, so k_w to investors = 11.74 percent before taxes.

10.   Do you think investors would be willing to pay par value for either the warrant or convertible issues? If you think that any of the securities would be overvalued or undervalued at an initial price of $1,000, how might the terms of the various issues be changed to make them "more reasonable"?

11.   Based on your analysis to this point, what recommendation should Barnhardt make to Virginia May's board of directors regarding the financing alternatives?

12.   Assume that Virginia May changes the coupon rate on the 11 percent convertible issue to 10.5 percent. Also, it changes the call premium in Year 2 to $105, and this premium will fall by $4.57 each year. If you are not using the *Lotus* model, discuss how these changes would affect the company's cost and the investors' return. If you are using the model, quantify the after-tax cost to the company and the before-tax return to investors for this issue. What would the company's weighted average cost of capital be with this issue? Again, assume that Virginia May would call the convertible in Year 15.

28

Financing
Alternatives

Julian Eastheimer and Company

While investment banking firms traditionally hire relatively few new graduates (especially those without advanced degrees), the positions they do fill are highly sought after and are extremely lucrative. Prime candidates not only need to have knowledge of the financial markets, but also must have the ability to sell their firm's services to some of the most successful members of the financial community. Quite often, knowledge of oenology, a person's ancestry, and a scratch golf game have just as much persuasive power in obtaining a client's business as do the actual services provided by a firm such as Julian Eastheimer and Company.

Through an old family contact pulling the right strings, Parker Z. Bentley III was fortunate enough to obtain the job of assistant to Maria Talbot, a senior partner and managing director at Julian Eastheimer. Bentley received his bachelor's degree in physical education from a very expensive and prestigious Ivy League school only two weeks ago, and this is his first day on the job. After a rather pleasant morning spent meeting various people around the office, Bentley was given his first task—he was asked to review the financing recommendations that Talbot had recently made for nine client firms.

The first thing Bentley did was to pull out the financial analyses and recommendations from the clients' folders and give them to one of the secretaries to type. When the secretary returned the typed reports, Bentley discovered that he did not know which recommendation belonged to which company! He had folders for nine different companies and financing recommendations for nine companies, but he could not match them up. Bentley's major was physical education, so he could not be expected to match the financing recommendations with the appropriate companies.

Questions

As a finance student, you should be able to help Bentley by telling him which companies in Section B should use the financing methods listed in Section A.

Section A

1. Leasing arrangement

2. Long-term bonds

3. Debt with warrants

4. Friends or relatives

5. Common stock: nonrights

6. Preferred stock (nonconvertible)

7. Common stock: rights offering

8. Convertible debentures

9. Factoring (Hint: Factoring is the selling of a firm's accounts receivable.)

Section B

A. **Boudoir's, Inc.:** This company, a retail clothing store with three suburban locations in Atlanta, Georgia, is incorporated, with each of the three Boudoir sisters owning one-third of the outstanding stock. The company is profitable, but rapid growth has put it under severe financial strain. The real estate is all under mortgage to an insurance company, the inventory is being used under a blanket chattel mortgage to secure a bank line of credit, and the accounts receivable are all being factored. With total assets of $7 million, the company now needs an additional $450,000 to finance a building and fixtures for a new outlet.

B. **Timberland Power & Light**: Since Timberland Power & Light, a major electric utility, is organized as a holding company, the Securities and Exchange Commission must approve all of its securities issues. Such approval is automatic if the company stays within conventional norms for the public utility industry. Reasonable norms call for long-term debt in the range of 45 percent to 65 percent, preferred stock in the range of 0 to 15 percent, and common equity in the range of 25 percent to 45 percent. Timberland currently has total assets of $1.5 billion financed as follows: $900 million debt, $75 million preferred stock, and $525 million common equity. The company plans to raise an additional $37 million at this time.

C. **Ripe and Fresh Canning Company**: Ripe and Fresh Canning Company is a large operation located in Valdosta, Georgia, that purchases peaches and other fruits from farmers in Georgia, Florida, South Carolina, Alabama, and Kentucky. These fruits are then canned and sold on 60-day credit terms, largely to food brokers and small retail grocers in the same five-state area. The company's plant and equipment have been financed in part by a mortgage loan, and this is the only long-term debt. Raw materials (fruits) are purchased on terms calling for payment within 30 days of receipt of goods, but no discounts are offered. Because of an increase in the popularity of vegetables and fruits, canned fruit sales have increased dramatically. To finance a higher level of output to take advantage of this increased demand, Ripe and Fresh will need approximately $550,000.

D. **Piper Pickle Company:** Piper Pickle Company is a major packer of pickles and pickled products (horseradish, pickled watermelon rinds, relishes, and peppers). The company's stock is widely held, actively traded, and listed on the New York Stock Exchange. Recently, it has been trading in the range of $18 to $22 a share. The latest 12 months' earnings were $1.70 per share. The current dividend rate is 64 cents a share, and earnings, dividends, and the price of the company's stock have been growing at a rate of about 7 percent over the last few years. Piper Pickle's debt ratio is currently 42 percent versus 25 percent for other large pickle packers. Other firms in the industry, on the average, have been growing at a rate of about 5 percent a year, and their stocks have been selling at a price/earnings ratio of about 10. Piper Pickle has an opportunity to begin growing its own cucumbers, which would result in a substantial cost savings and reduce the risk involved in having to compete for cucumbers in the open market. This vertical integration would require $20 million in cash for the necessary farms and equipment.

E. **Copper Mountain Mining Company:** Copper Mountain Mining needs $12 million to finance the acquisition of mineral rights to some land in south central New Mexico and to pay for some extensive surveys, core-borings, magnetic aerial surveys, and other types of analyses designed to determine whether the mineral deposits on this land warrant development. If the tests are favorable, the company will need an additional $12 million. Copper Mountain Mining's common stock is currently selling at $11, while the company is earning approximately $1 per share. Other firms in the industry sell at from 8 to 13 times earnings. Copper Mountain's debt ratio is 30 percent, compared to an industry average of 35 percent. Total assets at the last balance sheet date were $120 million.

F. **Bull Gator Saloon and Dance Hall:** Robert Radcliffe, a professor at the University of Florida, is an avid country-and-western music fan and a square dancer. He has just learned that a recently developed downtown shopping and entertainment center still has a lease available for the original, renovated building of the First National Bank of Gainesville. The bank outgrew the building in the late 1950s, and the large open spaces and high ceilings would be ideal for a country-and-western nightclub. Radcliffe knows the market well and has often noted the lack of a real "kicker bar" in Gainesville; the closest being in Starke, about 25 miles from Gainesville. Radcliffe believes that if he can obtain approximately $50,000 for a sound system and interior decorations, he can open a small but successful operation in the old bank building. His liquid savings total $15,000, so Radcliffe needs an additional $35,000 to open the proposed nightclub.

G. **Golden Gate Aircraft Corporation:** Golden Gate Aircraft is a medium-sized aircraft company located just outside San Francisco whose sales distribution is approximately 30 percent for defense contracts and 70 percent for nonmilitary uses. The company has been growing steadily in recent years, and projections based on current research-and-development prospects call for continued growth at a rate of 5 percent to 7 percent a year. Although recent reports of several brokerage firms suggest that the firm's rate of growth might be slowing down because of the high price of fuel and the softness of the business aircraft market, Golden Gate's management believes, based on internal information, that no decline is in sight. The company's stock, which is traded on the Pacific Stock Exchange, is selling at 15 times earnings. This is slightly below the 17 times ratio of Standard & Poor's aircraft industry average. The company has assets of $35 million and a debt ratio of 25 percent (the industry average is 23 percent). Golden Gate needs an additional $5 million over and above additions to retained earnings to support the projected level of growth during the next 12 months.

H. **Schooner Yachts:** Schooner Yachts is a closely held company that was founded in 1970 by Russ Breaker to build a top-quality line of sailboats. The company's debt ratio is 48 percent, compared to an average ratio of 36 percent for sailboat companies in general. The stock is owned in equal parts by ten individuals, none of whom is in a position to put additional funds into the business. Sales for the most recent year were $12 million, and earnings after taxes amounted to $720,000. Total assets, as of the latest balance sheet, were $9.6 million. Schooner Yachts needs an additional $4 million to finance expansion during the current fiscal year. Given the worldwide growth in leisure-time activities and interest in sailing in particular, the firm can anticipate additional outside capital needs in the years ahead.

I. **Teller Pen Corporation:** Teller Pen is engaged in the manufacture of mechanical pens and pencils, porous pens, and a recently developed line of disposable lighters. Since the firm sells to a great many distributors, and its products are all considered nondurable consumer goods, sales are relatively stable. The current price of the company's stock, which is listed on the New York Stock Exchange, is $25. The most recent earnings and dividends per share are $3.10 and $1.50, respectively. The rate of growth in sales, earnings, and dividends in the past few years has averaged 5 percent. Teller Pen has total assets of $400 million. Current liabilities, which consist primarily of accounts payable and accruals, are $28 million; long-term debt is $83 million; and common equity totals $289 million. An additional $33 million of external funds is required to build and equip a new disposable-lighter manufacturing complex in central Ohio and to supply the new facility with working capital.

VII

Working Capital
Decisions

29

*Working Capital
Policy and Financing*

Office Mates, Inc.

Office Mates, Inc. is a medium-sized manufacturer of metal file cabinets for home and office use. The company sells its office furniture through regular channels, but its home products are sold under the trade name "Office Friends" through mass merchandisers such as Wal-Mart. Sales of both lines have grown substantially over the past 20 years because of the ever increasing demand for storage containers. Because the demand for paper storage appears to be slowing, Office Mates has recently moved into the manufacture and distribution of computer CDs and diskette storage systems, which it believes to be the "hot" growth area of the future.

Although the firm has always been up to date in manufacturing and marketing, financial management has tended to take a back seat. In fact, the recently retired financial manager joined the company right out of high school and worked his way up from an initial position of mail clerk. To revitalize the finance function, the company brought in Bob Knight, who has an MBA and who had worked as treasurer for several years at a competing company, as chief financial officer (CFO).

After spending several weeks familiarizing himself with Office Mates' operations, Knight concluded that one of his first tasks should be the development of a rational working capital policy. With this in mind, he decided to examine three alternative policies: (1) an *aggressive* policy, which calls for minimizing the amount of cash and inventories held and for using only short-term debt, (2) a *conservative* policy, which calls for holding relatively large amounts of cash and inventories and for using only long-term debt, and (3) a *moderate* policy, which falls between the two extremes. The aggressive policy would result in the smallest investment in net working capital (current assets minus current liabilities).

Tentatively, Knight plans to hold the level of accounts receivable constant, i.e., it would be the same under each of the three policies. Brian King, the company's president, suggested that as a part of the aggressive policy, under which cash and inventories are minimized, the company could also minimize accounts receivable, and vice versa under the conservative policy. However, Knight is bothered by labeling a policy which allows accounts receivable to rise as "conservative." After all, the actions that would cause receivables to rise (while holding sales constant) would include lengthening credit terms and selling on credit to weaker customers, and neither of those actions seems "conservative." Still, Knight knows that King will bring this point up when they discuss the merits of the three policies, and in the board of directors' meeting, when the directors are asked to approve one of the policies.

Knight also concluded that the company's $5 million of net fixed assets is sufficient to accommodate a relatively wide range of sales, so fixed assets can remain constant regardless of what is done in the working capital area. As for current assets, Table 1 contains Knight's estimates of the firm's balance sheet under the three alternative working capital policies. Office Mates' stock sells at about its book value, and the company's target capital structure calls for a debt ratio in the range of 45 to 55 percent, so all three working capital policies are consistent with Office Mates' target debt/equity mix. In fact, all three alternatives have a 50/50 debt/equity mix, hence the decision does not affect the mix of debt and equity, but, rather, the level of the current assets and the maturity structure of the debt. Knight's best estimate of debt costs is 10 percent for short-term debt and 13 percent for long-term debt.

The choice of working capital policy will affect some of the company's costs. Thus, while variable costs are expected to be 50 percent of sales regardless of which working capital policy is adopted, fixed costs are likely to be a function of the level of current assets held—the greater the level of current assets, the greater are fixed costs. This situation results primarily because of the need to hold the larger inventories in high-cost, dehumidified warehouses, and because of higher insurance costs. Knight estimates annual fixed costs to be $4,000,000 under the aggressive policy, $4,500,000 under a moderate policy, and $5,000,000 with the conservative policy. Office Mates' federal-plus-state tax rate is 40 percent.

Table 1
Estimated Balance Sheets

	Alternative Working Capital Policies		
	Aggressive	Moderate	Conservative
Current assets	$4,000,000	$ 5,000,000	$ 6,000,000
Net fixed assets	5,000,000	5,000,000	5,000,000
Total assets	$9,000,000	$10,000,000	$11,000,000
Short-term debt	$4,500,000	$ 2,500,000	$ 0
Long-term debt	0	2,500,000	5,500,000
Total equity	4,500,000	5,000,000	5,500,000
Total Claims	$9,000,000	$10,000,000	$11,000,000

   Working capital policy will also affect the firm's ability to respond to varying economic conditions. In an average economy, Office Mates' sales would be highest if the firm used a conservative policy. Here the firm's inventories would be the highest, so it could respond immediately to incoming orders and not risk losing sales because of stockouts. Office Mates' cash and marketable securities would also be highest under a conservative policy. Furthermore, if higher sales occurred because of the conservative policy, then accounts receivable would also be higher, even if credit standards and credit terms were not changed.[1] Conversely, expected sales are lowest under an aggressive policy. Here the firm would have low cash and inventory levels, hence some sales would be lost, which would depress the level of receivables.
   The different policies would also cause sales to react differently to changing economic conditions. In a strong economy, the conservative approach with its higher inventories would be best for generating increased sales. On the other hand, an aggressive policy would inhibit the firm from responding to increased demand. Table 2 contains Knight's best estimates of the sales levels under the alternative policies for three different states of the economy.

---

[1]   Note that working capital policy actually consists of two independent decisions: (1) the level of current assets, and (2) the way in which the current assets are financed. In this case, to simplify the numerical analysis, the two independent decisions are treated as dependent. Thus, a conservative policy implies a conservative financing policy, along with large holdings of current assets. Similarly, an aggressive policy signifies a heavy use of short-term debt along with relatively small holdings of current assets.

Table 2
Estimated Sales Under Each Working Capital Policy

	Working Capital Policy		
Economy	Aggressive	Moderate	Conservative
Weak	$ 9,000,000	$11,000,000	$13,000,000
Average	12,000,000	13,000,000	14,000,000
Strong	13,000,000	14,500,000	16,000,000

With these estimates in mind, Knight must now draft a report to present to Brian King and Office Mates' board of directors. Assume that you are Knight's assistant, and he has asked you to help him prepare the report. To help you get started, Knight has generated the following list of questions. Your task now is to answer them, after which you must help Knight prepare the final report. Since you were hired by the previous CFO, you know that Knight does not have much confidence in your knowledge or ability. This assignment will give you a chance to prove your worth—in effect, your performance will start you on the path to the top, or out the door, so you really need to get it right.

Questions

1. The two most basic decisions when establishing a working capital policy relate to the level of current assets and the manner in which current assets are financed. Explain the differences between aggressive, moderate, and conservative working capital policies.

2. Bob Knight expresses some doubts as to how to characterize accounts receivable in terms of conservative, moderate, or aggressive working capital policies. Obviously, the higher the level of sales, the higher the level of accounts receivable. On the other hand, if the firm takes deliberate actions which raise the level of receivables as a percentage of sales, would you characterize that action as "aggressive" or "conservative"? Clearly, if the company takes the action of keeping more cash or inventories on hand, that is a conservative action, but is an action which raises receivables "conservative"? Explain.

3. Construct pro forma income statements for each working capital policy, assuming an average economy, a weak economy, and a strong economy. Then, use these data to calculate ROEs and basic earning power ratios (EBIT/Total assets). (Hint: Use Table 3 as a guide.) How could these data be used to help decide on the optimal working

capital policy? Could you choose a working capital policy on the basis of the information generated thus far?

4. Assume that there is a 50 percent chance of an average economy, a 25 percent chance of a weak economy, and a 25 percent chance of a strong economy. What is the expected ROE under each policy? How do the policies compare in terms of relative riskiness? (Hint: Riskiness can be expressed in terms of standard deviation and coefficient of variation.)

5. Now assume that the Federal Reserve, reacting to increasing inflationary pressures, tightens monetary policy shortly after Office Mates has made its working capital policy decision. Any long-term debt outstanding would be locked in at 13 percent, but Office Mates would have to roll over any short-term debt outstanding at the new rate, which has skyrocketed to 15 percent. Assuming an average economy, what would be the resulting ROE under each policy? Do these results affect your previous conclusions about the relative riskiness of the three alternatives?

6. Like most companies of its size, Office Mates has two primary sources of short-term debt: trade credit and bank loans. One supplier, which furnishes Office Mates with $500,000 (gross) of materials a year, offers terms of 3/10, net 60.

   a. What are Office Mates' net daily purchases from this supplier? (Use a 360-day year.)

   b. What is the average level of Office Mates' accounts payable to this supplier, assuming the discount is taken? What is the average payables balance if the discount is not taken? What are the dollar amounts of free credit and costly credit from this supplier?

   c. What is the approximate percentage cost of the costly credit? What is the effective annual percentage cost?

   d. What conclusions do you reach from this analysis?

7. In discussing a possible loan with the firm's banker, Knight learned that the bank would be willing to lend Office Mates up to $5,000,000 for one year at a 10 percent nominal, or stated, rate. However, Knight failed to ask the banker about the specific terms of the loan. Assume that Office Mates will borrow $2,500,000.

a. What would the effective interest rate be on the loan if it was a simple interest loan? If the banker offered to lend the money for 6 months, but with a guaranteed renewal at the same 10 percent simple interest rate, would this be as good, better, or worse than a straight one-year loan at 10 percent simple interest? Explain.

b. What would be the effective interest rate if the loan was a discount loan? What face amount would be needed to provide Office Mates with $2,500,000 of available funds?

c. Assume now that the loan terms call for an installment loan with add-on interest and 12 equal monthly payments with the first payment due at the end of the first month. What would be Office Mates' monthly payments? What would be the approximate percentage cost of this loan? What would be its effective annual rate? Would this type of loan be suitable if Office Mates needs all of the money for the entire year? What type of asset is most suitably financed by an installment-type loan?

d. Now assume that the bank charges simple interest, but it requires a 20 percent compensating balance.

    (1) Suppose Office Mates does not carry any cash balances at that bank. How much would the firm have to borrow to obtain the needed $2,500,000 while meeting its compensating balance requirement? What is the effective annual percentage rate on this loan?

    (2) Now suppose Office Mates currently carries an average cash balance of $75,000 at the bank and that those funds can be used as a part of the compensating balance requirement. What effect does this have on the amount borrowed and on the cost of the loan?

    (3) Return to the scenario in which Office Mates currently maintains its working cash balances in another bank. Now assume that the bank from which Office Mates would borrow pays 5 percent simple interest on all checking account balances. What would the effective percentage cost of the loan be in this situation?

e. Finally, assume that the bank charges discount interest and also requires a 20 percent compensating balance. How much would Office Mates have to borrow, and what would be the effective interest rate under these conditions?

8. Assume now that you have had some additional discussions with Bob Knight in which he told you that he would like more information on the ROE and the riskiness of the alternative working capital policies under different sets of assumptions. He asked you, first, to assume that sales are independent of working capital policy and then to determine the expected ROE and standard deviation of ROE under each policy if the sales estimates are $11,000,000 for a weak economy, $13,000,000 for an average economy, and $14,500,000 for a strong economy. Similarly, he asked you to assume that a different manufacturing process is used, causing the mix of fixed and variable costs to change. Using the original sales estimate, he wants to know what the expected ROE and standard deviation of ROE would be under the three policies if variable costs increased to 70 percent of sales (in all cases), and fixed costs decreased to $1,000,000 under an aggressive policy, to $1,500,000 under the moderate policy, and to $2,000,000 under the conservative policy. How would your answers to these questions, and similar questions, be used by top managers as they actually make the working capital policy decision? Quantify your answer if you have access to the *Lotus 1-2-3* model, but just discuss the situation in words if you do not have access to the model.

9. What is your recommendation regarding a working capital policy for Office Mates, and in what form should the company raise short-term debt? You really do not have enough information to make a definitive statement when answering this question, but assume that Knight wants you to at least make a preliminary recommendation which can be modified later if necessary.

Table 3
Pro Forma Income Statements

Average Economy	Aggressive	Moderate	Conservative
Sales	$ 12,000	$ 13,000	$ 14,000
Cost of goods sold	10,000	X	12,000
EBIT	$ 2,000	$ 2,000	$ 2,000
Interest on debt	450	X	715
EBT	$ 1,550	X	$ 1,285
Taxes	620	X	514
Net income	$ 930	X	$ 771
Basic Earning Power			
(EBIT/Assets)	22.2%	X	18.2%
Return on equity	20.7%	X	14.0%
Weak Economy			
Sales	$ 9,000	X	$ 13,000
Cost of goods sold	8,500	X	11,500
EBIT	$ 500	X	$ 1,500
Interest on debt	450	X	715
EBT	$ 50	X	$ 785
Taxes	20	X	314
Net income	$ 30	X	$ 471
Basic Earning Power			
(EBIT/Assets)	5.6%	X	13.6%
Return on equity	0.7%	X	8.6%
Strong Economy			
Sales	$ 13,000	X	$ 16,000
Cost of goods sold	10,500	X	13,000
EBIT	$ 2,500	X	$ 3,000
Interest on debt	450	X	715
EBT	$ 2,050	X	$ 2,285
Taxes	820	X	914
Net income	$ 1,230	X	$ 1,371
Basic Earning Power			
(EBIT/Assets)	27.8%	X	27.3%
Return on equity	27.3%	X	24.9%

30

Inventory Management

Narragansett Yacht Corporation

Narragansett Yacht manufactures fiberglass sailboats which range from 18-foot day sailors to 50-foot ocean racing yachts. The company was founded in Newport, Rhode Island, a hotbed of sailing activity, but high labor costs forced it to move its manufacturing operations to Corpus Christi, Texas, in 1990. The boat-building industry is very competitive and highly labor intensive, and profitability depends on getting the maximum efficiency out of the labor force. Narragansett has managed to keep its workforce nonunionized; this means that all of its employees can be shifted from task to task, and Narragansett can thus maintain flexibility. However, the price for this freedom has been a relatively high basic wage rate and a no-layoff policy. The no-layoff policy, in turn, makes it essential that the workforce is kept productively employed; this means that Narragansett simply must not run out of the various parts that go into the assembly of a boat. Therefore, a good inventory management system, which must track a large and varied inventory of parts ranging from inboard diesel engines and masts costing thousands of dollars each to screws and rivets costing only pennies each, is essential.

Sailboats are built in sequential steps. First, the major fiberglass components are laid up in molds. To begin, each mold is cleaned and inspected, and if no damage is found, the mold is waxed with an agent which facilitates lift-out of the finished work. Then gelcoat, the cosmetic outer layer, is sprayed into the mold and left to dry. If the gelcoat layer shows any imperfections, it must be destroyed, resulting in losses to Narragansett of $50 to $500, depending on the size of the mold. If the gelcoat layer is good, fiberglass strips are hand-laid on top of the gelcoat and bonded with liquid resin until the desired thickness is reached. Some sections on the hulls of the large racing yachts have sections which exceed one inch in thickness, but most of the sections are only about 1/4-inch thick. Finally, the sections which do not require significant strength are formed by a "chopper gun" which sprays fiberglass strands into the mold rather than using hand-laid strips.

After drying, the sections from the molding room are trimmed and brought to the assembly line. Here, the decks and hulls are joined, and the inboard engines, electrical wiring, steering systems, and plumbing fixtures are installed. After the structural work has been completed, the woodwork is done. Finally, the deck hardware (winches, cleats, running lights, and so on) and the interior upholstery are installed.

After a last inspection, the boat is taken to a water testing facility where the engines and transmissions are tested, and the boat is checked for leaks. Finally, the boat is cleaned, installed on a shipping cradle, and placed on a truck for delivery to a dealer located somewhere in the United States or Canada.

It should be obvious why efficient inventory control is so important to Narragansett Yacht. If stocks of gelcoat, fiberglass, or resin were to run out, the molding room would be forced to shut down, and input to the assembly line would be curtailed. Without engines, wiring harnesses, and steering systems, the boats could not progress to the finishing work stage. Any disruption in production would slow shipments to dealers and, possibly, result in missed sales. Furthermore, since selling prices are fixed, any increase in production costs due to poor inventory control must be borne by the company, and the intense competition and resulting low profit margins makes this an almost intolerable situation.

Narragansett carries more than 10,000 different items in inventory, and these items vary widely in price, ordering lead times, and stockout costs. (Stockout costs are all the costs, from higher production costs to lost profits, that result from running out of stock of a particular item.) Narragansett uses the ABC method of inventory classification, along with a variety of inventory control methods, to manage its different inventory items. The ABC inventory classification system works like this: Narragansett maintains data on the average annual usage and cost of each item. Based on these data, plus the multiplier values given in Table 1, Narragansett assigns a numerical *inventory importance value* to each item using the following formula:

$$
\begin{array}{c} \text{Inventory} \\ \text{importance} = \\ \text{value} \end{array}
\begin{bmatrix} \text{Average} \\ \text{annual} \\ \text{usage} \end{bmatrix}
\times
\begin{bmatrix} \text{Cost} \\ \text{per} \\ \text{unit} \end{bmatrix}
\times
\begin{bmatrix} \text{Lead} & \text{Stock-} \\ \text{time} & + & \text{out} \\ \text{multiplier} & \text{multiplier} \end{bmatrix}.
$$

Table 1

Inventory Multiplier Values

Order Lead Time Multipliers:		Stockout Consequence Multiplier:	
Lead Time Class	Lead Time Multiplier	Consequence Class	Stockout Multiplier
0–2 days	0	Unimportant	1
3–7 days	1	Average	3
8–30 days	2	Critical	5
1–3 months	4		
4–6 months	8		
7–12 months	12		

For example, a customized 5-inch chrome-plated winch costs Narragansett $300, and the firm uses 1,500 units per year. The winches require an order lead time of 10 days, and they are in the average consequence class. Thus, the inventory importance value of the winches is $2,250,000:

Inventory importance value = (1,500)($300)(2 + 3) = $2,250,000.

No particular significance can be attached to the $2,250,000—it is just a number that is used to compare the importance of this item with other inventory items.

Each of Narragansett's inventory items is analyzed similarly, the inventory importance values for the various items are arrayed from highest to lowest, each item's percentage of the total importance value is calculated, and then the *cumulative* percentage values are plotted as shown in Figure 1. Finally, the items are separated into three classes, labeled A, B, and C. Note that only 10 percent of the inventory items—those in the A class—account for 50 percent of the total importance value, while 60 percent of the number of items is in the C class, but these items constitute only 18 percent of the total importance value.

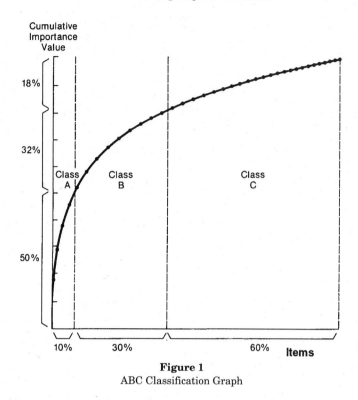

Figure 1
ABC Classification Graph

To better utilize its managerial time, Narragansett focuses most of its attention on the Class A items. For items in this class, Narragansett's financial manager reviews recent usage rates, stock position, and delivery time on a monthly basis and adjusts the control and ordering system as necessary. Class B items are reviewed every quarter, while Class C items are only reviewed annually.

Even though this process has served Narragansett well, Kevin Hayes, the firm's newly hired financial manager, thinks the company is carrying excess inventories. He notes that Narragansett has never come close to having a stockout, even when boat orders required around-the-clock production and when supplier backlogs led to significant shipping delays. Hayes believes that a thorough review should be undertaken of all Class-A items and that it might be possible to increase inventory turnover 25 percent by trimming current stocks. To convince Narragansett's president and CEO, Hayes plans to focus initially on a single item, the 5-inch chrome-plated winch. Table 2 contains inventory cost and delivery data on this item.

246

Case 30 *Inventory Management*

Narragansett currently uses a single source for this item, Sea Supply, Inc. (Supplier A). Supplier A requires an $800 set-up fee on each order, in addition to the basic cost per unit, and it delivers in 10 days. Although the winches are basically standard items, Narragansett, as a top-of-the-line producer, customizes the winches with an imprint of the firm's logo. Narragansett is considering another supplier, Mariner Winch (Supplier B), which charges only a $300 set-up fee, but which takes 20 days to deliver. It costs Narragansett another $200 to process each order and to customize the winches, regardless of which supplier is used. Thus, the total order cost is $1,000 for Supplier A and $500 for Supplier B.

Assume that you are Hayes's assistant and that he has asked you to look into the inventory situation. To give you direction, he prepared the following list of questions. Answer them and then be prepared to discuss Narragansett's inventory situation with Hayes and the management team.

Table 2

Cost and Usage Data:
Customized 5-Inch Chrome-Plated Winch

Expected annual usage	1,500 units
Cost per unit	$300
Inventory carrying costs:	
Depreciation	1%
Storage and Handling	8
Interest expense (bank loans)	10
Property taxes	2
Insurance	2
Total carrying costs	23%
Inventory ordering costs:	
Supplier A	$1,000
Supplier B	$500
Delivery lead times:	
Supplier A	10 days
Supplier B	20 days

Questions

1. What is the economic ordering quantity for standard 5-inch winches if they are ordered from (a) Supplier A, and (b) Supplier B? Round your answers up to the next whole unit, because Narragansett cannot order a fraction of a winch.

2. What assumptions are implied in the EOQ model? Do these assumptions appear reasonable when applied to Narragansett Yacht?

3. a. How many orders should be placed each year if Narragansett buys from Supplier A? If the firm buys from Supplier B?

    b. What is the reorder point (in units) for each supplier? Assume for now that no safety stocks are held and use a 360-day year.

4. Calculate the total inventory cost (the cost of ordering plus the cost of carrying inventories) that Narragansett would incur from each supplier. On the basis of the information developed thus far, which supplier should Narragansett use?

5. Narragansett currently carries a safety stock of 75 winches to protect itself against stockouts due to delivery delays and/or an increase in its usage rate. However, if it decides to switch to Supplier B, Narragansett would need to increase the safety stock to 150 units to reflect Supplier B's longer lead time.

    a. Assuming that the desired safety stock is currently on hand, what is the total cost of ordering and carrying inventories, including the safety stock, using Supplier A? What is the cost of using Supplier B?

    b. How does the introduction of safety stocks affect the reorder points as calculated in Question 3?

    c. Assume that there is a shipping delay. How many days after an order is placed could Narragansett continue to operate, at its expected usage rate, before its entire stock of 5-inch winches is reduced to zero? Compute this figure for both Supplier A and Supplier B.

6. The cost of carrying inventories has been calculated using the current cost of bank loans (see Table 2). Do you think this is the appropriate rate? Explain, and in your answer consider both the WACC and tax effects.

7. Narragansett's production is relatively constant throughout the year, but if its sales and production were highly seasonal, could the EOQ model still be used? If so, would modifications be required? Explain.

8. Suppose Supplier A, the current supplier, offers a 2 percent discount on the $300 per-unit purchase price on orders of 250 or more units. In an attempt to win the contreact, Supplier B is also offering a 2 percent discount on orders of 250 or more. Should Narragansett take the quantity discount from Supplier A? (In answering this question, assume that Narragansett holds a 75-unit safety stock.)

9. What are some methods that Narragansett might use to control the inventory of 5-inch winches? That is, how can it keep track of the number of units in stock and then be sure an order is placed when the order point is reached?

10. How much difference does it make in terms of total costs if the EOQ is followed exactly as opposed to letting orders vary 10 to 20 percent on either side of the EOQ? If you are using the *Lotus* model, provide some data to support your answer.

11. a. There is some question as to the proper cost of capital to be applied to estimate carrying costs. How sensitive is the EOQ to carrying costs if Supplier A is used? Put another way, does the cost of capital used to obtain the EOQ make a great deal of difference or only a little difference in terms of the resulting EOQ? If you are using the *Lotus* model, provide some data to support your answer and show the effect of the changed EOQ and carrying costs on total costs.

    b. How sensitive is EOQ to ordering costs, assuming a carrying cost of 23 percent is used? Again, if you are using the *Lotus* model, show the effect on total costs.

12. In many situations, companies are using just-in-time inventory procedures with good results. What is involved in the JIT approach, and what factors would need to be considered before you could recommend that Narragansett adopt or not adopt a JIT system?

31

Setting the Target Cash Balance

Elite Manufacturing Company

Debby Brennen and Denisa Cawley had just stepped off the racquetball court after their weekly game. Normally they are closely matched, but that day Cawley beat Brennen badly. Brennen, who had recently been promoted to vice-president of the Elite Manufacturing Company, admitted that she had been preoccupied with a business problem. Her primary responsibility is in the area of finance, and her predecessor had been forced to resign from the firm because the president of the company, Henry Zunker, was dissatisfied with the way the finance department was being run. That morning, Zunker had called Brennen in to tell her that the firm's total asset turnover has been going down, yet he had received no report from the unit. Consequently, he was concerned that she was not on top of the situation.

Elite manufactures and distributes uniforms and professional equipment for such fields as law enforcement, health care, and other public service professions. Henry Zunker founded the firm in 1960, and under his direction it has grown into the largest uniform company in the state. The operation has always been very profitable, reflecting Zunker's general business acumen and careful attention to detail. The problem that he brought up with Debby Brennen related to a slight deterioration in the total assets turnover ratio, from 2.77× in 1991 to 2.70× in 1992. Zunker actually has a great deal of confidence in Brennen's abilities, but it is his style to "keep the pressure on." Also, when he does lose confidence in someone, Zunker is quick to call in an outside consultant, often from one of the major national consulting companies, and to come down hard on his employees if they are not following the best business practices.

Denisa Cawley, Brennen's racquetball opponent, is a senior commercial lending officer with the bank that handles the Elite account. Cawley knows Brennen well and realizes that her friend is unsure of her ability to handle the new position, which she has held for less than two weeks. Brennen's primary training, and most of her job experience, has been in marketing. Although she has worked for Elite for over six years, understands the operations, and has the ability to learn quickly the details of the financial end of the business, Brennen is a bit uncertain of where to start in tackling the current problem. To help her overcome this temporary lack of confidence, Cawley offered to help her analyze the financial statements and to show her what needs to be done. Brennen gladly accepted Cawley's offer of assistance.

The next day, Brennen gathered up some documents, including the financial statements shown in Tables 1 and 2, and went to see Cawley. Upon careful examination of the data, the two executives discovered several things about the asset turnover. First, the company's days sales outstanding is approximately 20 days. Elite sells on terms of 2/10, net 30, so this number is reasonable. Cawley checked the figures from previous years and discovered that there has actually been a slight improvement in the days sales outstanding over the past few years. The inventory turnover (based on the cost of goods sold) is 8.7×, exactly the same figure it has been over the past few years, and it is above the industry average. Similarly, the fixed assets turnover is roughly the same as it has been since 1990 and is superior to the industry average. However, it appears that there may be some difficulties with the cash turnover. Historically, the cash turnover has been between 55× and 70×, but in 1992 cash turnover was only 46.6×. In 1990, it had been 60×; in 1991, it was 51.3×. Thus, there is a clear downward trend in this ratio. Cawley suspected that the cause of the decline was Brennen's predecessor's lack of attention to good cash management practices, and that this is the source of Zunker's concern.

Brennen's session with Cawley was helpful, and when she left she had more confidence in her ability to deal with the working capital situation. When she got back to her office, Brennen asked her assistant, John Pettingill, whom she had personally promoted, to explore the cash management practices of the company. Pettingill had been with Elite for two years and has a financial background. It is his opinion that the cash management activities are operating smoothly and that there are no problems. The decreased turnover, he believes, is a natural consequence of expanded sales. Brennen, however, questions why the level of cash needed to support sales increased more than proportionally as the sales level went up—it seemed to her that, if anything, it should increase less than proportionally because of economies of scale.

Table 1

Balance Sheet at Year-End 1992

Assets		Liabilities and Equity	
Cash	$ 1,437,500	Accounts payable	$ 3,139,500
Accounts receivable	3,680,000	Notes payable (8%)	1,437,500
Inventory	5,387,750	Accruals	943,000
Current assets	$10,505,250	Current liabilities	$ 5,520,000
Net fixed assets	14,288,750	Long-term debt (11%)	6,900,000
		Total liabilities	$12,420,000
		Capital stock	$ 4,025,000
		Retained earnings	8,349,000
		Total equity	$12,374,000
		Total liabilities	
Total assets	$24,794,000	and equity	$24,794,000

Table 2

Income Statements for Calendar Year 1992

	First Quarter	Second Quarter	Third Quarter	Fourth Quarter	Total for Year
Sales	$20,083,140	$13,388,760	$15,062,355	$18,409,545	$66,943,800
Cost of goods sold	14,058,198	9,372,132	10,543,649	12,885,992	46,859,971
Gross margin	$ 6,024,942	$ 4,016,628	$ 4,518,706	$ 5,523,553	$20,083,829
Depreciation	357,938	357,938	357,938	357,938	1,431,752
Administrative					
expenses	3,694,666	2,463,110	2,771,000	3,386,778	12,315,554
EBIT	$ 1,972,338	$ 1,195,580	$ 1,389,768	$ 1,778,837	$ 6,336,523
Interest	218,500	218,500	218,500	218,500	874,000
Taxable income	$ 1,753,838	$ 977,080	$ 1,171,268	$ 1,560,337	$ 5,462,523
Taxes (at 40%)	701,535	390,832	468,507	624,135	2,185,009
Net income	$ 1,052,303	$ 586,248	$ 702,761	$ 936,202	$ 3,277,514

Pettingill found that to pay for certain services the bank provides, it requires a compensating balance in the company's demand deposit account, and if the monthly average balance in this account falls below $850,000, the bank will assess a substantial service charge. Over the past two years, Pettingill could not find a single instance when the balance had been less than $1 million, so it appears that this requirement has not posed a problem. When he reported this fact to Brennen, she asked him what the optimal balance would be if there were no compensating balance and pointed out that if it were possible to reduce the cash balance to about $850,000, the company would have a cash turnover ratio more in line with that of previous years.

Two basic models are often used to help determine the optimum cash balance for a corporation: the Baumol model and the Miller-Orr model. Pettingill had studied these models in college, so he and Brennen decided that it would be appropriate for him to look into their use now. Pettingill decided immediately that applying either model to annual data would not be appropriate—there was just too much seasonal variation in the company's operations. However, periods of one quarter could be used, because during each calendar quarter the company has a roughly stable sales rate. Table 3 contains the relevant information from the financial statements reported on a quarterly basis, along with data for the total year. Pettingill also thinks that an opportunity cost of capital of 9 percent per annum is reasonable, as is a fixed transactions cost of $300 for either borrowing or selling securities.

Table 3

Cash Flow Data by Quarters and Total

	First Quarter	Second Quarter	Third Quarter	Fourth Quarter	Total for Year
Average daily net cash flow	$ 60,000	$ 40,000	$ 45,000	$ 55,000	$ 50,000
Standard dev of daily net cash flow	736,900	518,000	582,300	665,300	1,264,610
New net cash needed	5,400,000	3,600,000	4,050,000	4,950,000	18,000,000

After collecting this data, Pettingill met with Brennen, and they began to consider which model, if either, and what cash management policy they should recommend to Zunker. The decision is important for more reasons than just its profitability effects—given Zunker's fetish for "following the best business practices in all areas," if the final decision cannot be justified, then both Pettingill's and Brennen's futures could be in jeopardy. After much discussion, they drew up the following list of questions and agreed that Pettingill would draft answers to them, after which they would discuss the questions before meeting with Zunker. Put yourself in Pettingill's position and answer the questions.

Questions

1. The equation for the Baumol model follows:

$$C = \sqrt{\frac{2FT}{k}} \ .$$

Here C = optimal cash balance; F = fixed costs of financial transactions such as borrowing or selling securities to replenish the cash account; T = total amount of net new cash needed for transactions over the entire period; and k is the opportunity cost of capital (cost of borrowing or rate earned on marketable securities held). Using the Baumol model, calculate the optimal cash balance for each quarter. Remember that the firm must maintain a minimum average balance of $850,000.

2. The equations for the Miller-Orr model follow:

$$Z = \left[\frac{3F\sigma^2}{4k} \right]^{1/3} + L$$

$$H = 3Z - 2L$$

$$\text{Average cash balance} = \frac{4Z - L}{3} \ .$$

Here Z = optimal cash balance; H = upper cash balance limit (point at which cash is used to buy securities or to repay loans); L = lower cash balance limit (point at which securities are sold to raise cash or funds are borrowed to build up the cash account); F = fixed costs of borrowing or selling securities; k = daily opportunity cost of capital; and σ^2 = variance of daily net cash flows about the mean daily net cash flow. What is the optimal cash balance for each quarter using the Miller-Orr model? Again, remember that the $850,000 minimum average balance must be maintained.

3. What are the key assumptions of each model, and which of them do you think would be more appropriate for use in this situation? Explain.

4. Suppose Elite's bank required a *minimum* cash balance of $850,000, instead of an *average* balance of $850,000. How would this affect your answers to Questions 1 and 2? No calculations are required to answer this question, but explain your answer.

5. Using your answers to Questions 1 and 2, calculate the cash turnover ratio that would result from the use of each model. Do these figures fall within the range apparently considered by Elite to be "normal"?

6. What changes in the firm's cash management practices would you recommend? Do not restrict yourself to the two models—consider the full range of potential changes but support your answer.

7. If the firm's arrangements with the bank could be changed so that the required average balance of $850,000 could be reduced to some lower amount, say $500,000, or $250,000, or zero, what would this do to the average balance and the cash turnover ratio as determined by each model? If you are using the *Lotus* model, quantify as well as discuss your answer. Otherwise, just discuss the issue.

8. If the required average balance remained at $850,000, but the opportunity cost of capital increased from 9 percent to some higher number, say 15 percent, or fell to say 6 percent, what would happen to the average cash balance and to the turnover ratios under the Baumol and the Miller-Orr models? Why do these changes occur? Again, if you are using the *Lotus* model, quantify as well as discuss your answer. Otherwise, just discuss the issue.

9. If the required average balance remained at $850,000 and the cost of capital at 9 percent, but the transactions cost could be lowered to $20, or increased to $500, what would happen to the average cash balance and to the turnover ratios under the Baumol and the Miller-Orr models? Why do these changes occur? Again, if you are using the *Lotus* model, quantify as well as discuss your answer. Otherwise, just discuss the issue.

10. Does either model exhibit economies of scale in the use of cash? Explain.

11. The company does not now keep any marketable securities. Do we have enough information to determine if the company should plan to maintain a securities portfolio? If not, what type of data would be required? Would this decision be based primarily on quantitative data, on subjective judgment, or on something else?

12. How could Brennen and Pettingill determine how much it would be worth to Elite to get the bank to relax the required minimum balance? In other words, if the required balance were to compensate the bank for services, then how large a fee could the company pay to get the bank to waive the required balance?

32

Cash Budgeting

Alpine Wear, Inc.

Ann Austin, the recently hired treasurer of Alpine Wear, Inc., was summoned to the office of Billy Joe Durango, the president and chief executive officer. When she got to Billy's office, Ann found him shuffling through a set of worksheets. He told her that because of a recent tightening of credit by the Federal Reserve, hence an impending contraction of bank loans, the firm's bank has asked each of its major loan customers for an estimate of their borrowing requirements for the remainder of 1993 and the first half of 1994.

Billy had a previously scheduled meeting with the firm's bankers the following Monday, so he asked Ann to come up with an estimate of the firm's probable financing requirements for him to submit at that time. Billy was going away on a white-water rafting expedition, a trip that had already been delayed several times, and he would not be back until just before his meeting with the bankers. Therefore, Billy asked Ann to prepare a cash budget while he was away.

Due to the firm's rapid growth over the last few years, no one had taken the time to prepare a cash budget recently; thus Ann was afraid she would have to start from scratch. From information already available, Ann knew that no loans would be needed from the bank before January, so she decided to restrict her budget to the period from January through June 1994. As a first step, she obtained the following sales forecast from the marketing department:

1993	November	$300,000
	December	480,000

1994	January	600,000
	February	720,000
	March	840,000
	April	980,000
	May	780,000
	June	600,000
	July	300,000
	August	240,000

(Note that the sales figures are *before* any discounts; that is, they are *not* net of discounts.)

Alpine Wear's credit policy is 1.5/10, net 30. Hence, a 1.5 percent discount is allowed if payment is made within 10 days of the sale; otherwise, payment in full is due 30 days after the date of sale. On the basis of a previous study, Ann estimates that, generally, 25 percent of the firm's customers take the discount, 65 percent pay within 30 days, and 10 percent pay late, with the late payments averaging about 60 days after the invoice date. For monthly budgeting purposes, discount sales are assumed to be collected in the month of the sale, net sales in the month after the sale, and late sales two months after the sale.

Alpine Wear begins production of goods two months before the anticipated sale date. Variable production costs are made up entirely of purchased materials and labor, which total 60 percent of forecasted sales—20 percent for materials and 40 percent for labor. All materials are purchased just before production begins, or two months before the sale of the finished goods. On average, Alpine Wear pays 50 percent of the materials cost in the month when it receives the materials, and the remaining 50 percent the next month, or one month prior to the sale. Labor expenses follow a similar pattern, but only 30 percent is paid two months prior to the sale, while 70 percent is paid one month before the sale.

Alpine Wear pays fixed general and administrative expenses of approximately $90,000 a month, while lease obligations amount to $36,000 per month. Both expenditures are expected to continue at the same level throughout the forecast period. The firm estimates miscellaneous expenses to be $30,000 monthly, and fixed assets are currently being depreciated by $48,000 per month. Alpine Wear has $1,200,000 (book value) of bonds outstanding. They carry a 10 percent semiannual coupon, and interest is paid on January 15 and July 15. Also, the company is planning to replace an old machine in June with a new one costing $400,000. The old machine has both a zero book and a zero market value. Federal and state income taxes are expected to be $90,000 quarterly, and payments must be made on the 15th of December, March, June, and September. Alpine Wear has a policy of maintaining a minimum cash balance of $300,000, and this amount will be on hand on January 1, 1994.

Assume that you were recently hired as Ann Austin's assistant, and she has turned the job of preparing the cash budget over to you. You must meet with her and Billy Durango on Sunday night to review the budget prior to Billy's meeting with the bankers on Monday. Answer the following questions, which she provided to you for direction, but also think about any other related issues that Ann or Billy, or the bankers, might raise concerning the projections. In particular, be prepared to explain the sources of all the numbers and the effects on the company's funds requirements if any of the basic assumptions turn out to be incorrect. Your predecessor was fired for not really understanding a report he submitted, and you don't want to suffer the same fate!

Questions

1. Construct a monthly cash budget for Alpine Wear for the period January through June 1994. For the purposes of this question, disregard both interest payments on short-term bank loans and interest received from investing surplus funds. Also, assume that all cash flows occur on the 15th of each month. Finally, note that collections from sales in November and December of 1993 will not be completed until January and February of 1994, respectively. (Hint: Use Table 1 as a guide.) If you have access to the *Lotus* model, use it to generate the required numbers. What is the maximum cumulative funds shortfall during the 6-month planning period?

2. Assume that the bank will agree to give Alpine Wear a $400,000 line of credit. Will this be sufficient to cover any expected cash shortfalls? Suppose the bank refused to grant the loan, and thus the company had to obtain short-term financing from other sources. What other sources might be available?

3. The monthly cash budget you have prepared assumes that all cash flows occur on the 15th of each month. Suppose Alpine Wear's outflows tend to cluster at the beginning of the month, while collections tend to be heaviest toward the end of each month. How would this affect the validity of the monthly budget? What could be

done to correct any inaccuracies that might result from the mismatch of inflows and outflows?

4. Now assume that you and Ann decide you need to develop a daily cash budget for the month of January, based on the following assumptions. (Hint: Use Table 2 as a guide.)

   (1) Assume that Alpine Wear normally operates 7 days a week; therefore, use 31 days for your January cash budget.

   (2) Sales are made at a constant rate throughout the month; that is, 1/31st of the January sales are made each day.

   (3) Daily sales follow the 25 percent, 65 percent, 10 percent collection breakdown.

   (4) Discount purchasers take full advantage of the 10-day discount period before paying, and "on time" purchasers wait the full 30 days to pay. Thus, collections during the first 10 days of January will reflect discount sales from the last 10 days of December, plus "regular" sales made in earlier months. Also, on January 31st, Alpine Wear will begin collecting January's net sales and December's late sales.

   (5) The lease payment is made on the first of the month.

   (6) Fifty percent of both labor costs and general and administrative expenses are paid on the 1st and 50 percent are paid on the 15th.

   (7) Materials are delivered on the 1st and paid for on the 5th.

   (8) Miscellaneous expenses are incurred and paid evenly throughout the month; 1/31st each day.

   (9) Required interest payments are made on the 15th.

   (10) The target cash balance is $300,000, and this amount must be in the bank on each day. This minimum balance is required by the firm's bank.

   If you calculated it correctly, the monthly cash budget should have indicated that a bank loan of $184,650 will be required in January. Does the daily cash budget support this conclusion?

5. Think about the mechanics of the bank loan. During a typical month, the funds needed or the cash surplus would be changing daily. Could the company increase or decrease its loan on a daily

basis? If not, would this have any effect on the amount of funds it needs?

6. You are aware that Billy is concerned about the efficient utilization of his firm's cash resources. Specifically, he has questioned whether or not seasonal variations should be incorporated into the firm's target balance. In other words, during months when cash needs are greatest, the target balance would be somewhat higher, while the target would be set at a lower level during slack months. Would you recommend that Alpine Wear follow this strategy? If the firm had any compensating balance requirements, would this affect your answer? How would a variable target balance be incorporated into the monthly cash budget? How would it be incorporated into the daily cash budget?

7. The only receipts shown in Alpine Wear's cash budget are collections. What are some other types of inflows that could occur? Also, the budget ignored short-term interest expense and income. If the company paid interest at 7 percent annually on the short-term bank loan and received interest at 5 percent annually on surplus cash, how could these items be incorporated into the cash budget? Be specific; that is, indicate exactly how the budget would be modified and give an example.

8. Because cash is a nonearning asset, Alpine Wear's cash management policy is to invest any surplus funds in marketable securities. Can you suggest an investment policy that will provide liquidity and safety, yet offer the firm a reasonable return on its marketable securities investment? Specifically, describe the types of securities, the desired maturities, the expected returns, and the risks that would be involved. Would your suggestions be the same for a company whose cash balances were projected to be in the millions of dollars as opposed to Alpine Wear's thousands? Would it matter if the forecasts showed cash surpluses for all future months, going out indefinitely, versus a situation in which surpluses and deficits alternated from month to month due to seasonal factors?

9. The cash budget is a forecast, so many of the cash flows shown are expected values rather than amounts known with certainty. If actual sales, hence collections, were different from the forecasted levels, then the forecasted surpluses and deficits would be incorrect.

You know that Billy and Ann will be interested in knowing how various changes in the key assumptions would affect the cumulative surplus or deficit. For example, if sales fell below the forecasted level, what effect would that have? It would be particularly bad to have a $400,000 line of credit and then find that due to incorrect assumptions the actual cash requirement was $600,000!

With this in mind, answer the following questions. If you are using the *Lotus* model, quantify your answers. Otherwise, just discuss the likely effects of the indicated changes. In either situation, indicate how the company should prepare for the types of events noted. In this discussion, recognize that getting a line of credit is not without cost. Banks typically charge a 1 point, or 1 percent of the maximum amount requested, commitment fee up front. Thus a $400,000 line would require a $4,000 commitment fee, while a $600,000 line would cost $6,000.

a. What would be the impact on the monthly net cash flows from January to June 1994 if actual sales were 20 percent below the forecasted amounts? (In your answer, assume that actual sales for November and December 1993 are 20 percent below the forecasted level. Also, assume that purchases and labor, as well as all other expenses, are set by contract at the start of the 6-month forecast period on the basis of the original expected sales; so the outflows cannot be adjusted downward during the planning period even though sales decline below the forecasted levels.)

b. What if actual sales were only 50 percent of the forecasted level? To answer this question, again assume that all expenses are based on the expected level of sales, not the realized level.

c. Suppose customers changed their payment patterns and began paying as follows: 20 percent in the month of sale, 30 percent in the following month, and 50 percent in the second month versus the old 25-65-10 pattern. Now how large a credit line would the company require?

10. Based on all of your analysis, how large a credit line would you recommend that Billy seek from the firm's bankers? If you find it difficult to identify a defendable number, what other information would you want, and how would you suggest the credit line be established?

Table 1

Monthly Cash Budget Worksheet

I. Collections & Payments

	November	December	January	February	March	April	May	June	July	August
Gross Sales (expected)	$300,000	$300,000	X	X	X	X	$780,000	$600,000	$300,000	$240,000
Gross Sales (realized)	$300,000	$300,000	X	X	X	X	$780,000	$600,000	$300,000	$240,000
Collections:										
Month of Sale	$ 73,875	$118,200	X	X	X	X	$192,075	$147,750		
1 Month after Sale		X	X	X	468,000	546,000	637,000	507,000		
2 Months after Sale			X	X	60,000	72,000	84,000	98,000		
Total Collections		X	$489,750	$615,300	X	X	X	X		
Purchases	$120,000	X	X	X	$156,000	$120,000	$60,000	$48,000		
Payments:										
2 Months before Sale		72,000	84,000	X	X	X	X	X		
1 Month before Sale		60,000	72,000	84,000	X	X	X	X		
Total Payments		X	$156,000	X	X	X	X	$ 54,000		

Table 1
Continued

II. Cash Gain (Loss) for Month

	November	December	January	February	March	April	May	June	July	August
Collections			$489,750	X	X	X	X	X		
Payments:										
Purchases			X	X	X	X	X	$ 54,000		
Labor										
2 Months before Sale			100,800	X	X	X	X	28,800		
1 Month before Sale			201,600	$235,200	$274,400	$218,400	$168,000	84,000		
Administrative Expenses			90,000	X	X	X	X	X		
Lease			36,000	X	X	X	X	X		
Miscellaneous Expenses			30,000	X	X	X	X	X		
Taxes					90,000			90,000		
Interest (on bonds)			60,000							
New Equipment								400,000		
Total Payments			$674,400	X	X	X	X	X		
Net Cash Gain (Loss)			($184,650)	($ 75,500)	X	X	X	X		

Table 1
Continued

	November	December	January	February	March	April	May	June	July	August
III. *Cash Surplus or Loan Requirement*										
Cash at Start (no borrowing)			$300,000	$115,350	X	X	X	X		
Cumulative Cash			$115,350	X	X	X	X	X		
Target Cash Balance			$300,000	X	X	X	X	X		
Surplus Cash or Total Loans Outstanding to Maintain Target Cash Balance			($184,650)	X	X	X	X	X		

Table 2

Daily Cash Budget Worksheet

							Day								
	1	2	***	5	***	10	11	***	14	15	***	28	29	30	31
I. Collections & Payments															
Gross Sales	$ 19,355	X ***		$ 19,355 ***		$19,355	$19,355	***	$19,355	$19,355	***	X		X $19,355	$19,355
Collections:															
Discount Payers	$ 3,813	X ***		X ***		X	$ 4,766	***	X	$ 4,766 ***		X	X	X $ 4,766	$ 4,766
Net Payers	10,065	X ***		X ***		X	10,065	***	X	10,065 ***		X	X	X 10,065	12,581
Late Payers	1,000	X ***		X ***		X	1,000	***	X	1,000 ***		X	X	X 1,000	1,548
Total Collections	$ 14,877	$14,877 ***		$ 14,877 ***		$14,877	$15,831	***	$15,831	$15,831 ***		$15,831	$15,831	$15,831	$18,895
Purchases	$168,000			$156,000 ***											
Payments:															
2 Months before Sale				X											
1 Month before Sale				$ 72,000											
Total Payments	$ 0	$ 0 ***		$156,000 ***		$ 0	$ 0 ***		$ 0	$ 0 ***		$ 0	$ 0	$ 0	$ 0

Table 2

Continued

	Day														
	1	2	***	5	***	10	11	***	14	15	***	28	29	30	31
II. Cash Gain (Loss) for Day															
Collections	$14,877	$14,877	***	$14,877	***	X	X	***	$15,831	$15,831	***	$15,831	$15,831	$15,831	$18,895
Payments:															
Purchases				$156,000											
Labor															
2 Months before Sale	$50,400									$50,400					
1 Month before Sale	100,800									100,800					
Admin. Expenses	45,000									45,000					
Lease	X														
Miscellaneous Exp.	968	968		968		968	968		968	968		968	968	968	968
Taxes															
Interest (on bonds)										60,000					
Total Payments	$233,168	$ 968	***	$156,968	***	$ 968	968	***	$ 968	$257,168	***	968	$ 968	968	$ 968
Net Cash Gain (Loss)	($218,290)	X	***	($142,090)	***	$13,910	$14,863	***	$14,863	($241,337)	***	$14,863	$14,863	$14,863	$17,927

Table 2
Continued

									Day						
	1	2	***	5	***	10	11	***	14	15	***	28	29	30	31
III. Cash Surplus or Loan Requirement															
Cash at start (no borrowing)	$300,000	$ 81,710	***	$123,439	***	$ 36,987	$ 50,897	***	$ 95,485	$110,348	***	$ 47,366	X	$ 77,092	$ 91,955
Cumulative cash	$ 81,710	$ 95,619		($ 18,652)		$ 50,897	$ 65,760			X ($130,989)		X	X	$ 91,955	$109,882
Target cash Balance	300,000	300,000		300,000		300,000	300,000		X	300,000		X	X	300,000	300,000
Surplus cash or total loans outstanding to maintain target cash balance	($218,290)	($204,381)	***	($318,652)	***	($249,103)	($234,240)	***	X	($430,989)	***	($237,771)	($222,908)	($208,045)	($190,118)

33

Credit Policy

Upscale Toddlers, Inc.

Upscale Toddlers, Inc., manufactures children's clothing, including such accessories as socks and belts. The company has been in business since 1955, mainly supplying private label merchandise to large department stores. In 1990, however, the company started producing its own line of children's clothing under the brandname "Yuppiewear." An increasing number of two-income families has been accompanied by an increasing demand for high-status children's clothing, and Toddlers was the first in its field to recognize this trend.

When Toddlers' sales were primarily for private labels, the firm's financial manager did not have to worry much about its overall credit policy. Most of its sales were negotiated directly with department store buyers, and the resulting contracts contained specific credit terms. The new line, however, represents a significant change—it is sold through numerous wholesalers under standard credit terms, so credit policy per se has become important. Elizabeth Hardin, the assistant treasurer, has been assigned the task of reviewing the company's current credit policy and recommending any desirable changes.

Toddlers' current credit terms are 2/10, net 30. Thus, wholesalers buying from Toddlers receive a 2 percent discount off the gross purchase price if they pay within 10 days, while customers who do not take the discount must pay the full amount within 30 days. The company does check the financial strength of potential customers, but its standards for granting credit are not high. Similarly, it does have procedures for collecting past-due accounts, but its collections policy could best be described as passive. Gross sales to wholesalers average about $15 million a year, and 50 percent of the paying wholesalers take the discount and pay, on average, on Day 10. Another 30 percent of the payers generally pay the full amount on Day 30, while 20 percent tend to stretch Toddlers' terms and do not actually pay, on average, until Day 40. Two percent of Toddlers' gross sales to wholesalers end up as bad debt losses.

Nathan Langly, the treasurer and Hardin's boss, is convinced that the firm should tighten up its credit policy. According to Langly, good customers will pay on time regardless of the terms, and the ones who would complain about a tighter policy are probably not good customers. Hardin must make an analysis and then recommend a course of action. For political reasons, she has decided to focus on a tighter policy, under which a 4 percent discount would be offered to customers who pay cash on delivery (COD) and 20 days of credit would be offered to customers who elect not to take the discount. Also, under the new policy stricter credit standards would be applied, and a tougher collection policy would be enforced. This policy has been dubbed 4/COD, net 20.

Langly likes this policy—he believes that increasing the discount would both bring in new customers and also encourage more of Toddlers' existing customers to take the discount. As a result, he believes that sales to wholesalers would increase from $15 million to $16.5 million annually, that 60 percent of the paying customers would take the discount, that 30 percent of the payers would pay on Day 20, that 10 percent would pay late on Day 30, and that bad debt losses would be reduced to 1 percent of gross sales. Langly's is not the only position, though—Arnold Quayle, the sales manager, has argued for an easier credit policy. Quayle thinks that the proposed change would result in a drastic loss of sales and profits.

Toddlers' variable cost-to-sales ratio is 80 percent; its pre-tax cost of carrying receivables is 12 percent; and the company can expand without any problems (or any cost increases) because it can subcontract production that it cannot handle in-house. Further, Langly is convinced that neither the variable cost ratio nor the cost of capital would change as a result of a credit policy change. Arnold Quayle, however, thinks that the variable cost ratio might increase significantly if sales rise so much that the company is forced to use outside suppliers. Also, after discussions with the cost accounting staff, Quayle thinks that the variable cost ratio might rise as high as 90 percent this coming year, even without an increase in sales, due to higher labor costs under a contract now being negotiated. Everyone agrees that there is little chance that costs will decline, regardless of the credit policy decision. Toddlers' federal-plus-state tax rate is 40 percent.

Now Hardin must conduct an analysis to estimate the effect of the proposed credit policy change on Toddlers' profitability. She and Langly are very much concerned about the analysis, both because of its importance to the company and also because of its "political implications"—the sales and production people have been lobbying against any credit tightening because they do not want to take a chance on losing sales and having to cut production, and also because they question the assumptions Langly wants to use. Therefore, Hardin knows that her report will be critically reviewed. Working with Langly, she prepared the following set of questions for use as a guide in drafting her report. Put yourself in her position and answer the following questions. As you answer each question, think about follow-up questions that other people, such as those in sales and production, might ask when the report is being reviewed.

Questions

1. What are the four variables which make up a firm's credit policy? How likely (and how quickly) are competitors to respond to a change in each variable, and is their response likely to be the same for a change toward tightness as one toward looseness?

2. What is Toddlers' current days sales outstanding (DSO) [also called average collection period (ACP)]? What would the expected DSO be if the credit policy change were made?

3. What is the dollar amount of bad debt losses under the current policy? What would be the expected losses under the proposed policy?

4. What is the cost of granting discounts under the current policy? What would be the expected cost under the new policy?

5. What is Toddlers' dollar cost of carrying receivables under the current policy? What would be the expected cost under the new policy? (Use a 360 day year.)

6. What is the expected incremental profit associated with the proposed change in credit terms? Should Toddlers make the change? (Hint: Construct income statements under each policy and focus on the expected change. See Table 1 for a guide.)

7. Does your analysis up to this point consider the risks involved with a credit policy change? If not, how could risk be assessed and incorporated into the analysis?

8. Suppose the firm makes the change to COD/4, net 20, but Toddlers' competitors react by making similar changes in their terms. The net

result is that Toddlers' gross sales remain at the current $15 million level. If the remainder of Hardin's assumptions are correct, what would be the impact on Toddlers' profitability?

9. Hardin expects both the sales and production managers to question her assumptions, so she would like to know which variables are most critical in the sense that profitability is very sensitive to them. Then, she would like to know just how far off her assumption could be before the change to a tighter credit policy would be incorrect. If you are using the *Lotus* model, do some sensitivity analyses, changing one variable at a time while leaving the others at their base case values. Which variables are most important in terms of their effects on profits, and how large an error could there be in the assumptions which you regard as being most critical before the decision should be reversed?

10. Also, if she could, Hardin would like to have a better basis for the assumptions used in her report—as it stands, all she has to rely on is Langly's judgment, which is contrary to that of two other senior executives. What are some actions that Hardin might take to improve the accuracy of her forecasts?

The following question presents an algebraic approach to analyzing changes in credit policy. Answer it only if it is assigned by your instructor.

11. As an alternative to constructing profit statements, an algebraic approach has been developed that focuses directly on the change in profits. To use this approach, it is first necessary to define the following symbols:

S_0 = current gross sales

S_N = new gross sales after the change in credit policy. Note that S_N can be greater than or less than S_0.

V = variable costs as a percentage of gross sales. V includes production costs, inventory carrying costs, the cost of administering the credit department, and all other variable costs except bad debt losses, receivables carrying costs, and the cost of giving discounts.

$1 - V$ = contribution margin, or the proportion of gross sales that goes toward covering fixed costs and increasing profits

k = cost of financing the firm's receivables

DSO_0 = current days sales outstanding

DSO_N = new average days sales outstanding after change in credit policy

B_0 = current bad debt losses as a proportion of current gross sales

B_N = new bad debt losses as a proportion of new gross sales

P_0 = proportion of current-collected gross sales that are discount sales

P_N = proportion of new-collected gross sales that are discount sales

D_0 = current discount offered

D_N = discount offered under new policy

T = tax rate

Calculate values for the incremental change in the firm's investment in receivables, ΔI, and the incremental change in after-tax profits, ΔP, as follows:

$$\Delta I = V[(DSO_N - DSO_0)(S_0/360)] + V[(DSO_N)(S_N - S_0)/360].$$

$$\Delta P = (1 - T)(S_N - S_0)(1 - V) - k\Delta I - (B_N S_N - B_0 S_0)$$

$$- [D_N S_N P_N(1 - B_N) - D_0 S_0 P_0(1 - B_0)].$$

Note that, in the profit equation, the first term $\{(1 - T)(S_N - S_0)(1 - V)\}$ is the incremental after-tax gross profit, the second term $\{k\ \Delta I\}$ is the incremental cost of carrying receivables, the third term $\{B_N S_N - B_0 S_0\}$ is the incremental bad debt losses, and the last term $\{D_N S_N P_N(1 - B_N) - D_0 S_0 P_0(1 - B_0)\}$ is the incremental cost of discounts.[1]

Use the equations presented here to estimate the change in profits associated with the new policy.

---

[1] Note that the analysis presented here is somewhat simplified in that the opportunity cost of the incremental investment in receivables from current customers is not considered. For a complete discussion of the analysis, see Eugene F. Brigham and Louis C. Gapenski, *Intermediate Financial Management*, 4th ed., Chapter 23.

Table 1

Projected Income Statements

	Proposed Policy	Current Policy	Difference
Gross sales	X	$15,000,000	X
Discounts taken	X	147,000	X
Net sales	X	$14,853,000	X
Production costs	X	12,000,000	X
Net earnings before credit costs	X	$ 2,853,000	X
Credit-related costs:			
Receivables carrying cost	X	88,000	X
Bad debt losses	X	300,000	X
Net earnings before tax	X	$ 2,465,000	X
Taxes (40%)	X	986,000	X
After-tax profit	X	$ 1,479,000	X

34

Receivables Management

Texas Rose Company

Desmond Tyler received his masters degree in landscape architecture ten years ago from the University of Arkansas. After graduation, he went to work for a landscaping firm in Little Rock, where he made many contacts throughout the South. He moved to Texas after five years, taking a position on the horticulture staff at the Alamo, in San Antonio. Although both of his jobs were professionally rewarding, Tyler's primary goal has always been to start his own wholesale nursery.

Tyler is currently developing a business plan which he will present at a venture capital seminar to be held in Houston. The main purpose of the seminar is to match entrepreneurs with venture capitalists who are interested in providing capital to fledgling firms. Tyler has spent a lot of time thinking about how his proposed firm's receivables should be managed—he is concerned about this issue because he has seen several firms get into financial difficulty due to poor receivables management that led to large bad debt losses.

The proposed firm, Texas Rose Company, would sell roses primarily to retail nurseries and to landscapers. Tyler has actually been growing seedlings for the past several years and has sufficient inventory on hand to open for business in January. Of course, he cannot produce a full line of roses for several more years, so he has lined up suppliers to furnish those plants which are not available from his own stock. Sales will be highly seasonal; wholesale plant sales are slow during the cold winter months, but they pick up dramatically in the spring, when most planting takes place. Business falls off again in the summer, when it becomes too hot to plant most varieties, and sales continue low until the following spring. Tyler's sales forecasts for the first six months of operations are given in Table 1.

Tyler does not plan to give discounts for early payment—discounts are not widely used in the industry. Approximately 30 percent of the customers (by dollar value) are expected to pay in the month of sale, 55 percent are expected to pay in the month following the sale, and the remaining 15 percent are expected to pay 2 months after the sale. Tyler does not foresee any problems with bad debt losses—he plans to screen his customers very carefully, and he thinks this will eliminate such losses. Still, Tyler is concerned about the level of receivables, and he wants to have a monitoring system in place that will allow him to spot quickly any adverse trends as they develop.

Assume that Tyler has hired you as a consultant to help him in setting up his receivables management system. After extended discussions, you and Tyler developed the following set of questions. Your task now is to answer them and then to help Tyler with his presentation to the venture capitalists. You are well aware that the venture capitalists are extremely knowledgeable, and if Tyler is to be able to raise the needed capital, both of you must be ready for some additional and very probing questions.

Questions

1. Tyler's total sales forecast for the nursery's first full year of operations is 228,000 plants at an average sales price of $5 per plant. As a first approximation, assume that 30 percent of the firm's customers will pay 10 days after the sale, 55 percent will pay on the 30th day, and 15 percent will pay on the 60th day.

   a. What is the firm's projected days sales outstanding (DSO)?

   b. What is the projected average daily sales? (Use a 360-day year.)

   c. What is Texas Rose's projected average receivables level?

   d. If Tyler is estimating a gross profit margin, or contribution margin, of 40 percent, how much of the receivables balance must actually be financed? What would Texas Rose's balance sheet figures for accounts receivable and notes payable be at the end of the year if notes payable are used to finance the investment in receivables?

   e. If short-term bank loans cost 12 percent, what is the projected annual cost of carrying the receivables?

2. In general, what are the primary factors which influence the level of receivables outstanding, and thus which might change and cause a change in the firm's level of receivables? What factors influence the dollar cost of carrying the receivables?

3. Refer to the monthly sales forecasts given in Table 1. Assume that these amounts are realized and that the firm's customers pay exactly as predicted.

   a. What would the receivables level be at the end of March and at the end of June?

   b. What is the firm's forecasted average daily sales for the first three months of operations? For the entire half-year?

   c. What is the implied DSO at the end of March? At the end of June? (Hint: Complete Table 2.) What is the relationship between the DSO and the average collection period?

   d. Does the DSO indicate that the firm's customers have changed their payment behavior from the first to second quarter? Is DSO a good management tool in this situation? If not, why not?

4. Construct aging schedules as of the end of March and the end of June by completing Table 3. What do these schedules indicate about the customers' payment patterns? Explain.

5. Construct the uncollected balances schedule as of the end of March and the end of June by completing Table 4. Do these schedules properly measure customers' payment patterns? If you wanted to monitor one number from Table 4, what would be the best one? Explain your answers.

6. Assume that Texas Rose does receive financing and is now an unqualified success, and that Tyler is developing the firm's pro forma financial statements for the second year of operations. His sales forecast for the first 6 months of the second year is as follows:

Month	Sales
January	$ 80,000
February	140,000
March	200,000
April	280,000
May	220,000
June	140,000

What is the best forecast of the firm's receivables at the end of March and the end of June? Explain.

7. You anticipate that the venture capitalists will ask some questions that can best be answered if you have done some sensitivity analyses of the effects of various inputs on the key outputs. To begin, assume that sales are a constant $160,000 in each month. What would the DSOs, aging schedules, and uncollected balances schedules be at the end of March and June? If you are using the *Lotus* model, quantify your answer. Otherwise, just discuss the general effects of the change in the sales pattern.

8. Return to the original sales estimates. Now suppose customers act as follows: 10 percent pay in the month of sale, 40 percent pay in the month following the sales month, and 50 percent pay two months after the sale. What would be the DSOs, aging schedules, and uncollected balances schedules at the ends of March and June in this situation?

9. How could Tyler use the information developed above to establish a practical method for monitoring receivables and then taking action to ensure that his credit policy and collection practices are under control?

Table 1

Sales Forecasts

Month	Sales
January	$ 40,000
February	100,000
March	160,000
April	240,000
May	180,000
June	120,000

Table 2

Calculation of Days Sales Outstanding

	End of Month	
	March	June
Receivables balance	$127,000.00	X
Average daily sales	$3,333.33	X
DSO	38.1 days	X

Table 3

Aging Schedules

Age of Account in Days	End of March			End of June	
	A/R	%		A/R	%
0–30	$112,000	88		X	X
30–60	15,000	12		X	X
60–90	0	0		X	X
Total	$127,000	100		$111,000	100

Table 4

Uncollected Balances Schedules

End of March:

Month	Sales	Accts Rec from Month	Rec/Sales
January	$ 40,000	$ 0	0%
February	X	X	X
March	160,000	112,000	70
		$127,000	85%

End of June:

Month	Sales	Accts Rec from Month	Rec/Sales
April	$240,000	$ 0	0%
May	X	X	X
June	120,000	84,000	70
		$ X	X%

VIII

Financial Analysis
and Forecasting

35

*Financial Analysis
and Forecasting*

Mark X Company (A)

Mark X Company manufactures farm and specialty trailers of all types. More than 85 percent of the company's sales come from the western part of the United States, particularly California, although a growing market for custom horse transport vans designed and produced by Mark X is developing nationally and even internationally. Also, several major boat companies in California and Washington have had Mark X design and manufacture trailers for their new models, and these boat-trailer "packages" are sold through the boat companies' nationwide dealer networks.

Steve Wing, the president of Mark X, recently received a call from Karen Dennison, senior vice president of Wells Fargo Bank. Karen told Steve that a deficiency report generated by the bank's computerized analysis system had been filed because of Mark X's deteriorating financial position. The bank requires quarterly financial statements from each of its major loan customers. Information from such statements is fed into the computer, which then calculates key ratios for each customer and charts trends in these ratios. The system also compares the statistics for each company with the average ratios of other firms in the same industry and against any protective covenants in the loan agreements. If any ratio is significantly worse than the industry average, reflects a marked adverse trend, or fails to meet contractual requirements, the computer highlights the deficiency.

The latest deficiency report on Mark X revealed a number of significant adverse trends and several potentially serious problems (see Tables 1 through 6 for Mark X's historical financial statements). Particularly disturbing were the 1992 current, quick, and debt ratios, all of which failed to meet the contractual limits of 2.0, 1.0, and 55 percent, respectively. Technically, the bank had a legal right to call all the loans it had extended to Mark X for immediate repayment and, if the loans were not repaid within ten days, to force the company into bankruptcy.

Karen hoped to avoid calling the loans if at all possible, as she knew this would back Mark X into a corner from which it might not be able to emerge. Still, her own bank's examiners had recently become highly sensitive to the issue of problem loans, because the recent spate of bank failures had forced regulators to become more strict in their examination of bank loan portfolios and to demand earlier identification of potential repayment problems.

One measure of the quality of a loan is the Altman Z score, which for Mark X was 2.97 for 1992, just below the 2.99 minimum that is used to differentiate strong firms, with little likelihood of bankruptcy in the next two years, from those deemed likely to go into default. This will put the bank under increased pressure to reclassify Mark X's loans as "problem loans," to set up a reserve to cover potential losses, and to take whatever steps are necessary to reduce the bank's exposure. Setting up the loss reserve would have a negative effect on the bank's profits and reflect badly on Karen's performance.

To keep Mark X's loan from being reclassified as a "problem loan," the Senior Loan Committee will require strong and convincing evidence that the company's present difficulties are only temporary. Therefore, it must be shown that appropriate actions to overcome the problems have been taken and that the chances of reversing the adverse trends are realistically good. Karen now has the task of collecting the necessary information, evaluating its implications, and preparing a recommendation for action.

The recession that plagued the U.S. economy in the early 1990s had caused severe, though hopefully temporary, problems for companies like Mark X. Farm commodity prices have remained low, thus farmers have held their investments in new equipment to the bare minimum. On top of this, the luxury tax imposed in 1991 has had a disastrous effect on top-of-the-line boat/trailer sales. Finally, the Tax Reform Act of 1986 reduced many of the tax benefits associated with horse breeding, leading to a drastic curtailment of demand for new horse transport vans. In light of the softening demand, Mark X had aggressively reduced prices in 1991 and 1992 to stimulate sales. This, the company believed, would allow it to realize greater economies of scale in production and to ride the learning, or experience, curve down to a lower cost position. Mark X's management had full confidence that national economic policies would revive the ailing economy and that the downturn in demand would be only a short-term problem. Consequently, production continued unabated, and inventories increased sharply.

In a further effort to reduce inventory, Mark X relaxed its credit standards in early 1992 and improved its already favorable credit terms. As a result, sales growth did remain high by industry standards through the third quarter of 1992, but not high enough to keep inventories from continuing to rise. Further, the credit policy changes had caused accounts receivable to increase dramatically by late 1992.

To finance its rising inventories and receivables, Mark X turned to the bank for a long-term loan in 1991 and also increased its short-term credit lines in both 1991 and 1992. However, this expanded credit was insufficient to cover the asset expansion, so the company began to delay payments of its accounts payable until the second late notice had been received. Management realized that this was not a particularly wise decision for the long run, but they did not think it would be necessary to follow the policy for very long. They predicted that the national economy would pull out of the weak growth scenario in late 1992. Also, there has been some talk in Congress of killing the luxury tax and even giving some tax benefits back to horse breeders. Thus, the company was optimistic that its stable and profitable markets of the past would soon reappear.

After Karen's telephone call, and the subsequent receipt of a copy of the bank's financial analysis of Mark X, Steve began to realize just how precarious his company's financial position had become. As he started to reflect on what could be done to correct the problems, it suddenly dawned on him that the company was in even more trouble than the bank imagined. Steve had recently signed a firm contract for a plant expansion that would require an additional $6,375,000 of capital during the first quarter of 1993, and he had planned to obtain this money with a short-term loan from the bank to be repaid from profits expected in the last half of 1993 as a result of the expansion. In his view, once the new production facility went on line, the company would be able to increase output in several segments of the trailer market. It might have been possible to cut back on the expansion plans and to retrench, but because of the signed construction contracts and the cancellation charges that would be imposed if the plans were canceled, Steve correctly regards the $6,375,000 of new capital as being essential for Mark X's very survival.

Steve quickly called his senior management team in for a meeting, explained the situation, and asked for their help in formulating a solution. The group concluded that if the company's current business plan were carried out, Mark X's sales would grow by 10 percent from 1992 to 1993 and by another 15 percent from 1993 to 1994. Further, they concluded that Mark X should reverse its recent policy of aggressive pricing and easy credit, returning to pricing that fully covered costs plus normal profit margins and to standard industry credit practices. These changes should enable the company to reduce the cost of goods sold from over 85 percent of sales in 1992 to about 82.5 percent in 1993 and then to 80 percent in 1994. Similarly, the management group felt that the company could reduce administrative and selling expenses from almost 9 percent of sales in 1992 to 8 percent in 1993 and then to 7.5 percent in 1994. Significant cuts should also be possible in miscellaneous expenses, which should fall from 2.92 percent of 1992 sales to approximately 1.75 percent of sales in 1993 and to 1.25 percent in 1994. These cost reductions represented "trimming the fat," so they were not expected to degrade the quality of the firm's products or the effectiveness of its sales efforts. Further, to appease suppliers, future bills would be paid more promptly, and, to convince the bank how serious management is about correcting the company's problems, cash dividends would be eliminated until the firm regains its financial health.

Assume that Steve has hired you as a consultant to first verify the bank's evaluation of the company's current financial situation and then to put together a forecast of Mark X's expected performance for 1993 and 1994. Steve asks you to develop some figures that ignore the possibility of a reduction in the credit lines and that assume the bank will increase the line of credit by the $6,375,000 needed for the expansion and supporting working capital. Also, you and Steve do not expect the level of interest rates to change substantially over the two-year forecast period; however, you both think that the bank will charge 12 percent on both the additional short-term loan, if it is granted, and on the existing short-term loans, if they are extended. The assumed 40 percent combined federal and state tax rate should also hold for two years. Finally, if the bank cooperates, and if Steve is able to turn the company around, the P/E ratio should be 10 in 1993 and should rise to 12 in 1994.

Your first task is to construct a set of pro forma financial statements that Steve and the rest of the Mark X management team can use to assess the company's position and also to convince Karen that her bank's loan is safe, provided the bank will extend the firm's line of credit. Then, you must present your projections, with recommendations for future action, to Mark X's management and to Karen. To prepare for your presentations, answer the following questions, keeping in mind that both the Mark X managers and, particularly, Karen and possibly her bosses, could ask you some tough questions about your analysis and recommendations. Put another way, the following questions are designed to help you focus on the issues, but they are not meant to be a complete and exhaustive list of all the relevant points.

Questions

1. Complete the 1992 columns of Tables 3 through 6, disregarding for now the projected data in the 1993 and 1994 columns. If you are using the *Lotus* model, use it to complete the tables. Be sure you *understand* all the numbers, as it would be most embarrassing (and harmful to your career) if you were asked how you got a particular number and you could not give a meaningful response.

2. Based on the information in the case and on the results of your calculations in Question 1, prepare a list of Mark X's strengths and weaknesses. In essence, you should look at the common size statements and each group of key ratios (for example, the liquidity ratios) and see what those ratios indicate about the company's operations and financial condition. As a part of your answer, use the extended Du Pont equation to highlight the key relationships.

3. Recognizing that you might want to revise your opinion later, does it appear, based on your analysis to this point, that the bank should lend the requested money to Mark X? Explain.

4. Now complete the tables to develop pro forma financial statements for 1993 and 1994. For these calculations, assume that the bank is willing to maintain the present credit lines and to grant an additional $6,375,000 of short-term credit on January 1, 1993. In the analysis, take account of the amounts of inventory and accounts receivable that would be carried if inventory utilization (based on the cost of goods sold) and days sales outstanding were set at industry-average levels. Also, assume in your forecast that all of Mark X's plans and predictions concerning sales and expenses materialize, and that the firm pays no cash dividends during the forecast period. Finally, in your calculations use the cash and marketable securities account as the residual balancing figure.

In responding to Questions 5 through 8, no Lotus model modifications are required. Answers should be based solely on the data contained in the financial statements completed in response to Question 4.

5. Assume Mark X has determined that its optimal cash balance is 5 percent of sales and that funds in excess of this amount will be invested in marketable securities, which on average will earn

7 percent interest. Based on your forecasted financial statements, will Mark X be able to invest in marketable securities in 1993 and 1994? If so, what is the amount of excess funds Mark X should invest in marketable securities? Do your financial forecasts reveal any developing conditions that should be corrected?

6. Based on the forecasts developed earlier, would Mark X be able to retire all of the outstanding short-term loans by December 31, 1993?

7. If the bank decides to withdraw the entire line of credit and to demand immediate repayment of the two existing loans, what alternatives would be available to Mark X?

8. Under what circumstances might the validity of comparative ratio analysis be questionable? Answer this question in general, not just for Mark X, but use Mark X data to illustrate your points.

9. Now revise your pro forma financial statements for 1993 and 1994 assuming the following conditions:

   a. Short-term loans will be repaid when sufficient cash is available to do so without reducing the liquidity of the firm below the minimum requirements set by the bank and when the company is able to maintain at least the minimum cash balance (5 percent).

   b. When the loans are repaid, the repayments will occur at a constant rate throughout the year. Therefore, on average, the amount of short-term loans outstanding will be half of the beginning-of-year amount.

   c. Mark X will reinstate a 25 percent cash dividend in the year that all short-term loans and credit lines have been fully cleaned up (paid in full).

10. It is apparent that Mark X's future (and that of the bank loan) is critically dependent on the company's performance in 1993 and 1994. Therefore, it would be useful if you could, as part of your consulting report, inform management—and the bank—as to how sensitive the results are to such things as the sales growth rate, the cost of goods sold percentage, and the administrative expense ratio. If the results would still look fairly good even if those factors were not as favorable as initially forecasted, the bank would have greater confidence in extending the requested credit. On the other hand, if even tiny changes in these variables would

lead to a continuation of the past downward trend, then the bank should be leery. If you are using the *Lotus* model, do some sensitivity analyses (using data tables) to shed light on this issue. (Hint: See the bottom part of the model labeled "SENSITIVITY ANALYSES" for some ideas.) If you do not have access to the model, describe how one would go about a sensitivity (or scenario) analysis, but do not quantify your answer.

11. On the basis of your analyses, do you think Karen should recommend that the bank extend the existing short- and long-term loans and grant the additional $6,375,000 loan or that the bank demand immediate repayment of all existing loans? If she does recommend continuing to support the company, what conditions (for example, collateral, guarantees, or other safeguards) might the bank impose to help protect against losses should Mark X's plans go awry?

Table 1

Historical and Pro Forma Balance Sheets
for Years Ended December 31
(in Thousands of Dollars)

	1990	1991	1992	Proforma 1993	Proforma 1994
Assets:					
Cash and marketable					
securities	$ 5,149	$ 4,004	$ 3,906	X	X
Accounts receivable	17,098	18,462	29,357	X	X
Inventory	18,934	33,029	46,659	X	X
Current assets	$ 41,181	$ 55,495	$ 79,922	X	X
Land, buildings, plant, and					
equipment	$ 17,761	$ 20,100	$ 22,874	$ 29,249	$ 30,126
Accumulated depreciation	(2,996)	(4,654)	(6,694)	(9,117)	(10,940)
Net fixed assets	$ 14,765	$ 15,446	$ 16,180	$ 20,132	$ 19,186
Total assets	$ 55,946	$ 70,941	$ 96,102	X	X
Liabilities and Equity:					
Short-term bank loans	$ 3,188	$ 5,100	$ 18,233	X	X
Accounts payable	6,764	10,506	19,998	15,995	16,795
Accruals	3,443	5,100	7,331	9,301	11,626
Current liabilities	$ 13,395	$ 20,706	$ 45,562	X	X
Long-term bank loans	$ 6,375	$ 9,563	$ 9,563	$ 9,563	$ 9,563
Mortgage	2,869	2,601	2,340	2,104	1,894
Long-term debt	$ 9,244	$ 12,164	$ 11,903	$ 11,667	$ 11,457
Total liabilities	$ 22,639	$ 32,870	$ 57,465	X	X
Common stock	$ 23,269	$ 23,269	$ 23,269	$ 23,269	$ 23,269
Retained earnings	10,038	14,802	15,368	X	X
Total equity	$ 33,307	$ 38,071	$ 38,637	X	X
Total liabilities and equity	$ 55,946	$ 70,941	$ 96,102	X	X

Notes:
a. 3,500,000 shares of common stock were outstanding throughout the period 1990 through 1992.
b. Market price of shares: 1990—$17.78; 1991—$9.71; 1992—$3.67.
c. Price/earnings (P/E) ratios: 1990—6.61; 1991—5.35; 1992—17.0. The 1992 P/E ratio is high because of the depressed earnings that year.
d. Assume that all changes in interest-bearing loans and gross fixed assets occur at the start of the relevant years.
e. The mortgage loan is secured by a first-mortgage bond on land and buildings.

Table 2

Historical and Pro Forma Income Statements
for Years Ended December 31
(Thousands of Dollars)

	1990	1991	1992	Pro Forma 1993	1994
Net sales	$170,998	$184,658	$195,732	X	X
Cost of goods sold	187,684	151,761	166,837	X	X
Gross profit	$ 33,314	$ 32,897	$ 28,895	$37,678	$49,520
Administration and selling expenses	$ 12,790	$ 15,345	$ 16,881	$17,224	X
Depreciation	1,594	1,658	2,040	2,423	1,823
Miscellaneous expenses	2,027	3,557	5,725	3,768	X
Total operating expenses	$ 16,411	$ 20,560	$ 24,646	X	X
EBIT	$ 16,903	$ 12,337	$ 4,249	$14,263	X
Interest on short-term loans	$ 319	$ 561	$ 1,823	$ 2,953	$ 2,953
Interest on long-term loans	638	956	956	X	956
Interest on mortgage	258	234	211	X	170
Total interest	$ 1,215	$ 1,751	$ 2,990	$ 4,098	$ 4,079
Before-tax earnings	$ 15,688	$ 10,586	$ 1,259	X	$21,953
Taxes	6,275	4,234	504	4,066	8,781
Net income	$ 9,413	$ 6,352	$ 755	X	X
Dividends on stock	2,353	1,588	189	$ 0	X
Additions to retained earnings	$ 7,060	$ 4,764	$ 567	X	X

Notes:
  a. Earnings per share (EPS): 1990—$2.69; 1991—$1.81; 1992—$0.22.
  b. Interest rates on borrowed funds:
       Short-term loan: 1990—10%; 1991—11%; 1992—10%.
       Long-term loan: 10% for each year.
       Mortgage: 9% for each year.
  c. For purposes of this case, assume that expenses other than depreciation and interest are
       totally variable with sales.

Table 3

Common Size Balance Sheets
for Years Ended December 31

	1990	1991	1992
Assets:			
Cash and marketable securities	9.20%	5.64%	4.06%
Accounts receivable	30.56	26.02	X
Inventory	33.84	46.56	48.55%
Current assets	73.61%	78.23%	X
Land, buildings, plant, and equipment	31.75%	28.33%	X
Accumulated depreciation	(5.36)	(6.56)	(6.97)
Net fixed assets	26.39%	21.77%	16.84%
Total assets	100.00%	100.00%	100.00%
Liabilities and Equities:			
Short-term bank loans	5.70%	7.19%	18.97%
Accounts payable	12.09	14.81	20.81
Accruals	6.15	7.19	7.63
Current liabilities	23.94%	29.19%	47.41%
Long-term bank loans	11.39%	13.48%	X
Mortgage	5.13	3.67	2.43
Long-term debt	16.52%	17.15%	X
Total liabilities	40.47%	46.33%	59.80%
Common stock	41.59%	32.80%	24.21%
Retained earnings	17.94	20.86	X
Total equity	59.53%	53.67%	X
Total liabilities and equity	100.00%	100.00%	100.00%

Note: Rounding differences occur in this table.

Table 4

Common-Size Income Statements
for Years Ended December 31

	1990	1991	1992
Net sales	100.00%	100.00%	100.00%
Cost of goods sold	80.52	82.18	X
Gross profit	19.48%	17.82%	X
Administrative and selling expenses	7.48%	8.31%	8.62%
Depreciation	0.93	0.90	X
Miscellaneous expenses	1.19	1.93	2.92
Total operating expenses	9.60%	11.13%	X%
EBIT	9.88%	6.68%	2.17%
Interest on short-term loans	0.19%	0.30%	X
Interest on long-term loans	0.37	0.52	X
Interest on mortgage	0.15	0.13	0.11
Total interest	0.71%	0.95%	1.53%
Before-tax earnings	9.17%	5.73%	0.64%
Taxes	3.67	2.29	X
Net income	5.50%	3.44%	0.39%
Dividends on stock	1.38%	0.86%	0.10%
Additions to retained earnings	4.13%	2.58%	0.29%

Table 5

Statement of Cash Flows
for Years Ended December 31
(in Thousands of Dollars)

	1991	1992
Cash Flow from Operations:		
Sales	$184,658	$195,732
Increase in receivables	(1,364)	X
Cash sales	$183,294	X
Cost of goods sold	(151,761)	(166,837)
Increase in inventories	(14,095)	(13,630)
Increase in accounts payable	3,742	9,492
Increase in accruals	1,657	X
Cash cost of goods	($160,457)	X
Cash margin	$ 22,837	X
Administrative and selling expenses	(15,345)	($ 16,881)
Miscellaneous expenses	(3,557)	(5,725)
Taxes	(4,234)	(504)
Net cash flow from operations	($ 299)	X
Cash Flow from Fixed Asset Investment:		
Investment in fixed assets	($ 2,339)	($ 2,774)
Cash Flow from Financing Activities:		
Increase in short-term debt	$ 1,912	$ 13,133
Increase in long-term debt	3,188	X
Repayment of mortgage	(268)	(261)
Interest expense	(1,751)	(2,990)
Common dividends	(1,588)	(189)
Net cash flow from financing activities	$ 1,493	$ 9,693
Increase (decrease) in cash and marketable securities	($ 1,145)	X

Table 6

Historical and Pro Forma Ratio Analysis
for Years Ended December 31

	1990	1991	1992	Pro Forma 1993	Pro Forma 1994	Industry Average
Liquidity Ratios:						
Current ratio	3.07	2.68	X	X	X	2.50
Quick ratio	1.66	1.08	0.73	1.10	X	1.00
Debt Management Ratios:						
Debt ratio	40.47%	46.33%	X	X	52.69%	50.00%
TIE coverage	13.91	7.05	1.42	X	6.38	7.70
Asset Management Ratios:						
Inventory turnover (cost)[a]	7.27	4.59	3.58	5.70	5.70	5.70
Inventory turnover (sales)[b]	9.03	5.59	4.19	X	X	7.00
Fixed asset turnover	11.58	11.96	12.10	10.69	12.91	12.00
Total asset turnover	3.06	2.60	X	2.03	X	3.00
Days sales outstanding (ACP)[c]	36.00	35.99	53.99	X	32.00	32.00
Profitability Ratios:						
Profit margin	5.50%	3.44%	0.39%	X	X	2.90%
Gross profit margin	19.48%	17.82%	14.76%	17.50%	20.00%	18.00%
Return on total assets	16.82%	8.95%	X	5.74%	10.76%	8.80%
ROE	28.26%	16.68%	1.96%	X	X	17.50%
Other Ratios:						
Altman Z score[d]	6.55	4.68	X	X	5.08	4.65
Payout ratio	25.00%	25.00%	25.00%	0.00%	X	20.00%

Notes:
a. Uses cost of goods sold as the numerator.
b. Uses net sales as the numerator.
c. Assume a 360-day year.
d. Altman's function is calculated as

$$Z = 0.012X_1 + 0.014X_2 + 0.033X_3 + 0.006X_4 + 0.999X_5$$

Here,
X_1 = net working capital/total assets
X_2 = retained earnings/total assets
X_3 = EBIT/total assets
X_4 = market value of common and preferred stock/book value of all debt
X_5 = sales/total assets.

The "Altman Z score" range of 1.81–2.99 represents the so-called "zone of ignorance." Note that the first four variables are expressed as percentages. Refer to Chapter 26 of Eugene F. Brigham and Louis C. Gapenski, *Intermediate Financial Management,* Fourth Edition (Fort Worth: Dryden Press, 1993), for details.

e. Year-end balance-sheet values were used throughout in the computation of ratios embodying balance-sheet items.
f. Assume constant industry-average ratios throughout the period 1990 through 1994.

36

*Financial Analysis
and Forecasting*

Garden State Container Corporation

Garden State Container Corporation manufactures boxes and other containers primarily for farm products.   More than 85 percent of the company's sales come from the northeastern part of the United States, especially Pennsylvania, New Jersey, New York, and Maryland, although the company's patented egg cartons are distributed throughout the United States. Jim Jackson, the founder and president, recently received a call from Martha Menendez, vice president of Atlantic First National Bank. Menendez told him that a negative report had been generated by the bank's computerized analysis system; the report showed that Garden State's financial position was bad and getting worse.

The bank requires quarterly financial statements from each of its major loan customers. Information from these statements is fed into the computer, which then calculates key ratios for each customer and charts trends in these ratios. The system also compares the statistics for each company with the average ratios of other firms in the same industry and against any protective covenants in the loan agreements. If any ratio is significantly worse than the industry average, reflects a marked adverse trend, or fails to meet contractual requirements, the computer highlights the deficiency.

The latest report on Garden State revealed a number of adverse trends and several potentially serious problems (see Tables 1 through 6 for Garden State's historical financial statements).   Particularly disturbing were the 1992 current, quick, and debt ratios, all of which failed to meet the contractual limits of 2.0, 1.0, and 55 percent, respectively. Technically, the bank had a legal right to call all the loans it had extended to Garden State for immediate repayment and, if the loans were not repaid within ten days, to force the company into bankruptcy.

Martha hoped to avoid calling the loans if at all possible, as she knew this would back Garden State into a corner from which it might not be able to emerge. Still, her own bank's examiners had recently become highly sensitive to the issue of problem loans, because the recent spate of bank failures had forced regulators to become more strict in their examination of bank loan portfolios and to demand earlier identification of potential repayment problems.

One measure of the quality of a loan is the Altman Z score, which for Garden State was 3.04 for 1992, slightly below the 3.20 minimum that Martha's bank uses to differentiate strong firms with little likelihood of bankruptcy in the next two years from those deemed likely to go into default. This will put the bank under increased pressure to reclassify Garden State's loans as "problem loans," to set up a reserve to cover potential losses, and to take whatever steps are necessary to reduce the bank's exposure. Setting up the loss reserve would have a negative effect on the bank's profits and reflect badly on Martha's performance.

To keep Garden State's loan from being reclassified as a "problem loan," the Senior Loan Committee will require strong and convincing evidence that the company's present difficulties are only temporary. Therefore, it must be shown that appropriate actions to overcome the problems have been taken and that the chances of reversing the adverse trends are realistically good. Martha now has the task of collecting the necessary information, evaluating its implications, and preparing a recommendation for action.

The recession that plagued the U.S. economy in the early 1990s caused severe, though hopefully temporary, problems for companies like Garden State. On top of this, disastrous droughts for two straight summers had devastated vegetable crops in the area, leading to a drastic curtailment of demand for produce shipping containers. In light of the softening demand, Garden State had aggressively reduced prices in 1991 and 1992 to stimulate sales. Higher sales, the company believed, would allow it to realize greater economies of scale in production and to ride the learning, or experience, curve down to a lower cost position. Garden State's management had full confidence that normal weather and national economic policies would revive the ailing economy and that the downturn in demand would be only a short-term problem. Consequently, production continued unabated, and inventories increased sharply.

In a further effort to reduce inventory, Garden State relaxed its credit standards in early 1992 and improved its already favorable credit terms. As a result, sales growth did remain high by industry standards through the third quarter of 1992, but not high enough to keep inventories from continuing to rise. Further, the credit policy changes had caused accounts receivable to increase dramatically by late 1992.

To finance its rising inventories and receivables, Garden State turned to the bank for a long-term loan in 1991 and also increased its short-term credit lines in both 1991 and 1992. However, this expanded credit was insufficient to cover the asset expansion, so the company began to delay payments of its accounts payable until the second late notice had been received. Management realized that this was not a particularly wise decision for the long run, but they did not think it would be necessary to follow the policy for very long—the 1992 summer vegetable crop looked like a record breaker, and it was unlikely that a severe drought would again hurt the crop. They also predicted that the national economy would pull out of the weak growth scenario in late 1992. Thus, the company was optimistic that its stable and profitable markets of the past would soon reappear.

After Martha's telephone call, and the subsequent receipt of a copy of the bank's financial analysis of Garden State, Jim began to realize just how precarious his company's financial position had become. As he started to reflect on what could be done to correct the problems, it suddenly dawned on him that the company was in even more trouble than the bank imagined. Jim had recently signed a firm contract for a plant expansion that would require an additional $12,750,000 of capital during the first quarter of 1993, and he had planned to obtain this money with a short-term loan from the bank to be repaid from profits expected in the last half of 1993 as a result of the expansion. In his view, once the new production facility went on line, the company would be able to increase output in several segments of the shipping container market. It might have been possible to cut back on the expansion plans and to retrench, but because of the signed construction contracts and the cancellation charges that would be imposed if the plans were canceled, Jim correctly regards the $12,750,000 of new capital as being essential for Garden State's very survival.

Jim quickly called his senior management team in for a meeting, explained the situation, and asked for their help in formulating a solution. The group concluded that if the company's current business plan were carried out, Garden State's sales would grow by 10 percent from 1992 to 1993 and by another 15 percent from 1993 to 1994.   Further, they concluded that Garden State should reverse its recent policy of aggressive pricing and easy credit, returning to pricing that fully covered costs plus normal profit margins and to standard industry credit practices. These changes should enable the company to reduce the cost of goods sold from over 85 percent of sales in 1992 to about 82.5 percent in 1993 and then to 80 percent in 1994. Similarly, the management group felt that the company could reduce administrative and selling expenses from almost 9 percent of sales in 1992 to 8 percent in 1993 and then to 7.5 percent in 1994. Significant cuts should also be possible in miscellaneous expenses, which should fall from 2.92 percent of 1992 sales to approximately 1.75 percent of sales in 1993 and to 1.25 percent in 1994. These cost reductions represented "trimming the fat," so they were not expected to degrade the quality of the firm's products or the effectiveness of its sales efforts. Further, to appease suppliers, future bills would be paid more promptly, and to convince the bank how serious management is about correcting the company's problems, cash dividends would be eliminated until the firm regains its financial health.

Assume that Jim has hired you as a consultant to first verify the bank's evaluation of the company's current financial situation and then to put together a forecast of Garden State's expected performance for 1993 and 1994. Jim asks you to develop some figures that ignore the possibility of a reduction in the credit lines and that assume the bank will increase the line of credit by the $12,750,000 needed for the expansion and supporting working capital. Also, you and Jim do not expect the level of interest rates to change substantially over the two-year forecast period; however, you both think that the bank will charge 12 percent on both the additional short-term loan, if it is granted, and on the existing short-term loans, if they are extended. The assumed 40 percent combined federal and state tax rate should also hold for two years. Finally, if the bank cooperates, and if Jim is able to turn the company around, the P/E ratio should be 12 in 1993 and should rise to 14 in 1994.

Your first task is to construct a set of pro forma financial statements that Jim and the rest of the Garden State management team can use to assess the company's position and also to convince Martha that her bank's loan is safe, provided the bank will extend the firm's line of credit. Then, you must present your projections, with recommendations for future action, to Garden State's management and to Martha. To prepare for your presentations, answer the following questions, keeping in mind that the Garden State managers and, particularly, Martha and her bosses, could ask you some tough questions about your analysis and recommendations. Put another way, the following questions are designed to help you focus on the issues, but they are not meant to be a complete and exhaustive list of all the relevant points.

Questions

1. Complete the 1992 columns of Tables 3 through 6, disregarding for now the projected data in the 1993 and 1994 columns. If you are using the *Lotus* model, use it to complete the tables. Be sure you *understand* all the numbers, as it would be most embarrassing (and harmful to your career) if you were asked how you got a particular number, and you could not give a meaningful response.

2. Based on the information in the case and on the results of your calculations in Question 1, prepare a list of Garden State's strengths and weaknesses. In essence, you should look at the common-size statements and each group of key ratios (for example, the liquidity ratios) and see what those ratios indicate about the company's operations and financial condition. As a part of your answer, use the extended Du Pont equation to highlight the key relationships.

3. Recognizing that you might want to revise your opinion later, does it appear, based on your analysis to this point, that the bank should lend the requested money to Garden State? Explain.

4. Now complete the tables to develop pro forma financial statements for 1993 and 1994. For these calculations, assume that the bank is willing to maintain the present credit lines and to grant an additional $12,750,000 of short-term credit on January 1, 1993. In the analysis, take account of the amounts of inventory and accounts receivable that would be carried if inventory utilization (based on the cost of goods sold) and days sales outstanding were set at industry-average levels. Also, assume in your forecast that all of Garden State's plans and predictions concerning sales and expenses materialize and that the firm pays no cash dividends during the forecast period. Finally, in your calculations use the cash and marketable securities account as the residual balancing figure.

In responding to Questions 5 through 8, no Lotus model modifications are required. Answers should be based solely on the data contained in the financial statements developed in response to Question 4.

5. Assume Garden State has determined that its optimal cash balance is 5 percent of sales and that funds in excess of this amount will be invested in marketable securities which, on average, will earn 7 percent interest. Based on your forecasted financial statements, will Garden State be able to invest in marketable securities in 1993 and 1994? If so, what is the amount of excess funds Garden State should

invest in marketable securities? Do your financial forecasts reveal any developing conditions that should be corrected?

6. Based on the forecasts developed earlier, would Garden State be able to retire all of the outstanding short-term loans by December 31, 1993?

7. If the bank decides to withdraw the entire line of credit and to demand immediate repayment of the two existing loans (the short-term and long-term loans) extended to Garden State, what alternatives would be available to Garden State?

8. Under what circumstances might the validity of comparative ratio analysis be questionable? Answer this question in general, not just for Garden State, but use Garden State data to illustrate your points.

9. Now revise your pro forma financial statements for 1993 and 1994 assuming the following conditions:

    a. Short-term loans will be repaid when sufficient cash is available to do so without reducing the liquidity of the firm below the minimum requirements set by the bank, and when the company is able to maintain at least the minimum cash balance (5 percent).

    b. When loans are repaid, the repayments will occur at a constant rate throughout the year. Therefore, on average, the amount of short-term loans outstanding will be half of the beginning-of-year amount.

    c. Garden State will reinstate a 25 percent cash dividend in the year that all short-term loans and credit lines have been fully cleaned up (paid in full).

10. It is apparent that Garden State's future (and that of the bank loan) is critically dependent upon the company's performance in 1993 and 1994. Therefore, it would be useful if you could, as part of your consulting report, inform management—and the bank—as to how sensitive the results are to such things as the sales growth rate, the cost of goods sold percentage, and the administrative expense ratio. If the results would still look fairly good even if those factors were not as favorable as initially forecasted, the bank would have greater confidence in extending the requested credit. On the other hand, if even tiny changes in these variables would lead to a continuation of the past downward trend, then the bank should be leery. If you are using the *Lotus* model, do some sensitivity analyses (using data

tables) to shed light on this issue. (Hint: See the bottom part of the model labeled "SENSITIVITY ANALYSES" for some ideas.) If you do not have access to the model, describe how one would go about a sensitivity (or scenario) analysis, but do not quantify your answer.

11. On the basis of your analyses, do you think Martha should recommend that the bank extend the existing short- and long-term loans and grant the additional $12,750,000 loan or that the bank demand immediate repayment of all existing loans? If she does recommend continuing to support the company, what conditions (for example, collateral, guarantees, or other safeguards) might the bank impose to help protect against losses should Garden State's plans go awry?

Table 1

Historical and Pro Forma Balance Sheets
for Years Ended December 31
(in Thousands of Dollars)

	1990	1991	1992	Pro Forma 1993	Pro Forma 1994
Assets:					
Cash and marketable securities	$ 9,930	$ 7,363	$ 6,550	X	X
Accounts receivable	34,196	36,924	58,714	X	X
Inventory	39,791	69,361	97,984	X	X
Current assets	$ 83,888	$ 113,647	$ 163,249	X	X
Land, buildings, plant, and equipment	$ 34,634	$ 39,195	$ 44,604	$ 57,036	$ 58,746
Accumulated depreciation	(5,992)	(9,308)	(13,388)	(18,234)	(21,880)
Net fixed assets	$ 28,642	$ 29,887	$ 31,216	$ 38,802	$ 36,866
Total assets	$ 112,530	$ 143,534	$ 194,465	$ 215,375	X
Liabilities and Equity:					
Short-term bank loans	$ 6,376	$ 10,200	$ 36,466	X	X
Accounts payable	13,528	21,012	39,996	31,990	$ 33,590
Accruals	6,886	10,200	14,662	18,602	23,252
Current liabilities	$ 26,790	$ 41,412	$ 91,124	X	X
Long-term bank loans	$ 13,388	$ 20,082	$ 20,082	$ 20,082	$ 20,082
Mortgage	5,738	5,202	4,680	4,208	3,788
Long-term debt	$ 19,126	$ 25,284	$ 24,762	$ 24,290	$ 23,870
Total liabilities	$ 45,916	$ 66,696	$ 115,886	X	X
Common stock	$ 46,538	$ 46,538	$ 46,538	$ 46,538	$ 46,538
Retained earnings	20,076	30,300	32,041	X	X
Total equity	$ 66,614	$ 76,838	$ 78,579	X	X
Total liabilities and equity	$ 112,530	$ 143,534	$ 194,465	X	X

Notes:
a. 7,000,000 shares of common stock were outstanding throughout the period 1990 through 1992.
b. Market price of shares: 1990—$17.78; 1991—$9.70; 1992—$3.74.
c. Price/earnings (P/E) ratios: 1990—6.29; 1991—4.98; 1992—11.28. The 1992 P/E ratio is high because of the depressed earnings that year.
d. Assume that all changes in interest-bearing loans and gross fixed assets occur at the start of the relevant years.
e. The mortgage loan is secured by a first-mortgage bond on land and buildings.

Table 2

Historical and Pro Forma Income Statements
for Years Ended December 31
(Thousands of Dollars)

	1990	1991	1992	Pro Forma 1993	Pro Forma 1994
Net sales	$350,546	$378,549	$401,251	$ 441,376	$ 507,583
Cost of goods sold	282,252	311,110	342,016	364,135	X
Gross profit	$ 68,294	$ 67,439	$ 59,235	$ 77,241	$ 101,517
Administration and selling expenses	$ 25,580	$ 30,690	$ 33,762	X	X
Depreciation	3,188	3,316	4,080	4,846	3,646
Miscellaneous expenses	4,054	7,114	11,450	X	6,345
Total operating expenses	$ 32,822	$ 41,120	$ 49,292	X	X
EBIT	$ 35,472	$ 26,319	$ 9,943	$ 29,361	X
Interest on short-term loans	$ 638	$ 1,122	$ 3,647	$ 5,906	$ 5,906
Interest on long-term loans	1,339	2,008	2,008	1,912	1,912
Interest on mortgage	516	468	421	379	341
Total interest	$ 2,493	$ 3,598	$ 6,076	$ 8,197	$ 8,159
Before-tax earnings	$ 32,979	$ 22,721	$ 3,867	X	$ 45,298
Taxes	13,192	9,088	1,547	X	18,119
Net income	$ 19,787	$ 13,632	$ 2,320	X	X
Dividends on stock	4,947	3,408	580	0	X
Additions to retained earnings	$ 14,841	$ 10,224	$ 1,740	X	X

Notes:
a. Earnings per share (EPS): 1990—$2.69; 1991—$1.81; 1992—$0.22.
b. Interest rates on borrowed funds:
   Short-term loan: 1990—10%; 1991—11%; 1992—10%.
   Long-term loan: 10% for each year.
   Mortgage: 9% for each year.
c. For purposes of this case, assume that expenses other than depreciation and interest are totally variable with sales.

Table 3

Common-Size Balance Sheets
for Years Ended December 31

	1990	1991	1992
Assets:			
Cash and marketable securities	8.82%	5.13%	3.37%
Accounts receivable	30.39	25.72	X
Inventory	35.36	48.32	50.39
Current assets	74.55%	79.18%	X
Land, buildings, plant, and equipment	30.78%	27.31%	X%
Accumulated depreciation	(5.32)	(6.48)	(6.88)
Net fixed assets	25.45%	20.82%	16.05%
Total assets	100.00%	100.00%	100.00%
Liabilities and Equities:			
Short-term bank loans	5.67%	7.11%	18.75%
Accounts payable	12.02	14.64	20.57
Accruals	6.12	7.11	7.54
Current liabilities	23.81%	28.85%	46.86%
Long-term bank loans	11.90%	13.99%	X
Mortgage	5.10	3.62	2.41
Long-term debt	17.00%	17.62%	X
Total liabilities	40.80%	46.47%	59.59%
Common stock	41.36%	32.42%	23.93%
Retained earnings	17.84	21.11	X
Total equity	59.20%	53.53%	40.41%
Total liabilities and equity	100.00%	100.00%	100.00%

Note: Rounding differences occur in this table.

Table 4

Common-Size Income Statements
for Years Ended December 31

	1990	1991	1992
Net sales	100.00%	100.00%	100.00%
Cost of goods sold	80.52	82.18	X
Gross profit	19.48%	17.82%	14.76%
Administrative and selling expenses	7.30%	8.11%	8.41%
Depreciation	0.91	0.88	X
Miscellaneous expenses	1.16	1.88	2.85
Total operating expenses	9.36%	10.86%	2.28%
EBIT	10.12%	6.95%	2.48%
Interest on short-term loans	0.18%	0.30%	X
Interest on long-term loans	0.38	0.53	X
Interest on mortgage	0.15	0.12	0.10
Total interest	0.71%	0.95%	1.51%
Before-tax earnings	9.41%	6.00%	0.96%
Taxes	3.76	2.40	X
Net income	5.64%	3.60%	0.58%
Dividends on stock	1.41%	0.90%	0.14%
Additions to retained earnings	4.23%	2.70%	0.43%

309

Table 5

Statement of Cash Flows
for Years Ended December 31
(in Thousands of Dollars)

	1991	1992
Cash Flow from Operations:		
Sales	$ 378,549	$ 401,251
Increase in receivables	(2,728)	X
Cash sales	$ 375,821	$ 379,461
Cost of goods sold	(311,110)	(342,016)
Increase in inventories	(29,570)	(28,623)
Increase in accts payable	7,484	18,984
Increase in accruals	3,314	X
Cash cost of goods	($ 329,882)	X
Cash margin	$ 45,939	X
Administrative and selling expenses	(30,690)	($ 33,762)
Miscellaneous expenses	(7,114)	(11,450)
Taxes	(9,088)	(1,547)
Net Cash Flow from operations	($ 953)	X
Cash Flow from Fixed Asset Investment:		
Investment in fixed assets	($ 4,561)	($ 5,409)
Cash Flow from Financing Activities:		
Increase in short-term debt	$ 3,824	$ 26,266
Increase in long-term debt	6,694	X
Repayment of mortgage	(536)	(522)
Interest expense	(3,598)	(6,076)
Common dividends	(3,408)	(580)
Net Cash Flow from financing activities	$ 2,976	$ 19,088
Increase (decrease) in cash		
and marketable securities	($ 2,539)	X

Table 6

Historical and Pro Forma Ratio Analysis
for Years Ended December 31

	1990	1991	1992	Pro Forma 1993	Pro Forma 1994	Industry Average
Liquidity Ratios:						
Current ratio	3.13	2.74	X	X	X	2.50
Quick ratio	1.65	1.07	0.72	1.13	X	1.00
Leverage Ratios:						
Debt ratio	40.80%	46.47%	X	X	52.31%	50.00%
TIE coverage	14.23	7.31	1.64	X	6.55	7.70
Asset Managment Ratios:						
Inventory turnover (cost)a	7.09	4.49	3.49	5.70	5.70	5.70
Inventory turnover (sale)b	8.81	5.46	4.10	X	X	7.00
Fixed asset turnover	12.24	12.67	12.85	11.38	13.77	12.00
Total asset turnover	3.12	2.64	X	2.05	X	3.00
Days sale outstanding (ACP)c	35.12	35.11	52.68	X	32.00	32.00
Profitability Ratios:						
Profit margin	5.64%	3.60%	0.58%	X	X	2.90%
Gross profit margin	19.48%	17.82%	14.76%	17.50%	20.00%	18.00%
Return on total assets	17.58%	9.50%	X	5.90%	10.94%	8.80%
ROE	29.70%	17.74%	2.95%	X	X	17.50%
Other Ratios						
Altman Z scored	6.64	4.75	X	3.95	5.42	4.65
Payout ratio	25.00%	25.00%	25.00%	0.00%	X	20.00%

Notes:
a. Uses cost of goods sold as the numerator.
b. Uses net sales as the numerator.
c. Assume a 360-day year.
d. Altman's function is calculated as

$$Z = 0.012X_1 + 0.014X_2 + 0.033X_3 + 0.006X_4 + 0.999X_5$$

Here,
X_1 = net working capital/total assets.
X_2 = retained earnings/total assets
X_3 = EBIT/total assets
X_4 = market value of common and preferred stock/book value of all debt
X_5 = sales/total assets
The "Altman Z score" range of 1.81–2.99 typically represents the so-called "zone of ignorance." Note that the first four variables are expressed as percentages. Refer to Chapter 26 of Eugene F. Brigham and Louis C. Gapenski, *Intermediate Financial Management*, Fourth Edition (Fort Worth: Dryden Press, 1993), for details.
e. Year-end balance-sheet values were used throughout in the computation of ratios embodying balance-sheet items.
f. Assume constant industry-average ratios throughout the period 1990 through 1994.

37

Financial Forecasting

Space-Age Materials, Inc.

Most people think of pottery and figurines when they think of ceramics. However, ceramic material is particularly well suited for use under high temperatures and intense pressure, especially if light weight is desirable. Because of these properties, ceramics are ideal for use in high-performance engines used in turbocharged automobiles, jet aircraft, and heavy trucks. Unfortunately, though, ceramics are also very brittle, and this characteristic has long prevented their widespread use in such engines.

In 1986, however, Daniel Alexander, a materials engineer, and Roger Avalon, a chemical engineer, succeeded in combining silicon carbide fibers with ceramic materials in a manner that preserved the desirable properties of ceramics but eliminated most of the brittleness. They then formed Space-Age Materials, Inc., and used their own limited capital to build 50 prototype turbine blades with the new ceramic material. On the basis of extensive testing by a number of large aerospace companies, the new firm began receiving production-quantity orders for the new blades.

The new business was an immediate success. Production began in the summer of 1987. Operating losses were incurred during the first short year, but the company has earned a profit in each subsequent year. During 1991 and 1992 the number of new orders exceeded Alexander and Avalon's projections. By the end of 1992, it was obvious to all—including Alexander and Avalon—that additional expansion would be required if the firm was to attain its full growth potential or even to keep competitors from eroding its position.

Ironically, Alexander and Avalon's technological successes were making their financial forecasts incorrect. Consequently, they hired Sue

Li, an MBA, as the company's financial manager to develop a detailed financial plan. Li knew that the company had been lucky and that some large chemical companies, including Monsanto and DuPont, were thinking about entering the market. Space-Age, however, had not been sitting idle. In 1991, the company's research-and-development people produced some exciting breakthroughs, while at the same time there was an increasing trend toward using ceramics in jet engines. As a result, it became apparent that additional funds were probably needed if the company were to maintain, let alone increase, its market share. Therefore, a good financial plan accurately forecasting the future needs of the company is critical to the future success, and probably to the continued existence, of the company.

Li organized Space-Age's financial planning process into five steps:

(1)   A study is made of basic trends in the materials industry and also in the aerospace and other markets where Space-Age expects to operate. How will our customers' needs change over the next five years, and what can we do to meet any existing or developing needs?

(2)   A set of pro forma financial statements is developed and used to analyze the effects of alternative operating plans on projected profits and financial ratios. The plan encompasses five years, with the projections being relatively detailed for the coming year and much less detailed for the following four years. The entire plan is updated every year in November.

(3)   The specific financial requirements needed to support the company's base-case operating plan are determined. This information is obtained from the pro forma statements.

(4)   The specific sources of capital that will be used to meet the financial requirements are identified.

(5)   The initially projected financial statements are then modified to include the addition of the capital needed to finance the projected assets. This involves adjusting the pro forma income statement to include the interest charges associated with any additional debt and an adjustment to dividends paid if new stock must be issued. These modifications change the initially projected retained earnings, and thus change the "external funds needed" to finance the asset expansion. These feedback effects require the use of an iterative process to produce a consistent final set of financial statements. In the past, all this has been done manually—which takes a good bit of time—but Li has been working to develop a computerized model to speed up the process.

Space-Age's 1988 through 1992 historical financial statements, along with three key ratios and industry averages, are given in Tables 1 and 2. The company was operating its fixed assets at full capacity in 1992, so its $88.73 million of sales represented full-capacity sales. Since the firm's marketing department is forecasting a 20 percent increase in sales for 1993, new assets will have to be added. For planning purposes, Li assumes (1) that accounts payable and accruals will spontaneously increase in accordance with standard industry practices, (2) that new long-term capital will be raised in accordance with the firm's target capitalization ratios, which call for 20 percent long-term debt and 80 percent common equity (measured at market value), and (3) that short-term bank loans, reported as notes payable, will be assumed to grow along with sales, since they are used to finance the firm's working capital needs. (Note that new common equity includes both new retained earnings and new common stock sales.)

Space-Age currently has 4 million shares of common stock outstanding, and the market price is $9. The dividend in 1992 was $0.375 per share, and management does not intend to increase the dividend in 1993. New long-term debt would carry a 12.0 percent coupon, and it would be issued at par. New short-term debt will cost 10.0 percent. The combined federal and state tax rate is 40 percent.

Space-Age's senior managers go off on a one week retreat each November to work on the five-year plan and the budget for the coming year. Prior to the retreat, the various division managers must prepare reports which the top executives will review beforehand and then discuss at the retreat. As financial manager, Li normally prepares some first approximation financial forecasts which are then modified during the retreat as a result of strategic decisions made at that time. The modified statements are used to show the financial implications of different operating plans. However, Li recently underwent a difficult ulcer operation and, because of a slow recovery, she will neither be able to attend the retreat, nor to prepare the background report for it. Therefore, as her assistant, ready or not, you must assume her duties.

Even though she could not get out of bed, Li called you to the hospital to discuss what needed to be done. First, Li told you she had almost finished a computerized model that would aid in the process. Li also indicated that the model needed to be debugged, or at least checked out, by first making "by-hand" projections and then seeing if the model generated the same set of data. If a discrepancy is discovered, it will be necessary to find out where the error lies. Li also cautioned you that it will be necessary to explain to the executives how any changes in operating conditions would affect the funds requirements and also how any changes in the financing mix would affect other financial variables, including external funding requirements, earnings per share, and the stock price. In particular, Li warned you not to try to defend the inputs to the forecasting process; rather, the critical thing is to be able to make adjustments in the likely event the senior executives don't like all the assumptions used in the forecast. As Li pointed out, "It's the top managers' job to understand the business and to make the final assumptions used in the forecast and the budget. It's our job to tell them how those assumptions interact, and what the final outcome will be if their assumptions hold true. We ought to use reasonable inputs for our report and basic forecasts, but our real job in the planning process is to show top management what will happen under different operating conditions."

Finally, you will also have to make a presentation to the company's management. In preparation for the presentation, answer the following questions.

Questions

1. To begin, consider the percentage of sales formula used to determine external funds needed:

External funds needed	=	Required increase in assets	–	Spontaneous increase in liabilities	–	Increase in retained earnings

$$EFN = (A/S)\Delta S - (L/S)\Delta S - MS_1(1 - d).$$

Here,

A/S = Assets/Sales = required dollar increase in assets per $1 increase in sales.

L/S = Spontaneous liabilities/Sales = spontaneously generated financing per $1 increase in sales.

S_1 = total sales projected for next year (S_0 = last year's sales).

ΔS = change in sales = $S_1 - S_0$.

M = profit margin.

d = dividend payout ratio.

Use this equation to calculate Space-Age's EFN for 1993.

2. Now, use the proportional growth (percentage of sales) method to forecast the firm's financial statements and EFN for 1993. (Hint: Table 3 has been provided to speed up your work.) Compare the EFN obtained here with that obtained from the percentage of sales formula given in Question 1. Why are the results different?

3. The major assumption inherent in the proportional growth (percentage of sales) method is that all assets increase proportionally with sales. In effect, this means that the regression of each asset account against sales would result in a straight line that passes through the origin. To check on this assumption, used both in the formula and in Table 3, you could run a regression of each asset against sales, using data from Table 1. As a quick check, run a regression of total assets on sales to test the assumption. (Hint: You can use a financial calculator or the *Lotus 1-2-3* model, or you can get an approximation from a graph.)

   a. Does it appear that the proportionality assumption holds true? Explain.

   b. Repeat the Part a. regression analyses assuming the following data:

Year	Sales	Total Assets
1988	$30.00	$29.40
1989	42.00	31.88
1990	54.59	37.73
1991	68.25	43.08
1992	88.73	44.34

      Under these conditions, does it appear that the proportionality assumption holds true? Explain.

   c. Which of the situations above is likely to hold for most firms? What implications does your answer here have for the percentage of sales method?

4. Assume that you are now at the retreat, discussing the forecast with Space-Age's senior executives. The vice president for manufacturing informs you that fixed assets were actually being operated at only 80 percent of capacity in 1992. What effect would this have on your projected external capital requirement for 1993? In answering this question, disregard any financing feedback effects and answer the question by modifying the 1st pass columns of Table 3, but explain how you could go on to reach a balanced solution. Also, in answering

this and the next question, assume that depreciation expenses remain constant as a percentage of sales.

5. In the 80 percent of capacity utilization scenario, excess funds will be generated. Suppose one of the senior executives asked you, as the finance representative, what you would recommend doing with the money. How would you answer? If you are using the *Lotus* model, how could it be modified to handle EFN surpluses?

6. a. Re-do Question 4 under the assumption that Space-Age was operating at 90 percent of capacity in 1992.

   b. Discuss the general relationship between capacity utilization and projected capital requirements in situations (a) where assets are "lumpy" and (b) where they are not lumpy.

   c. If you are using the *Lotus* model, set up a data table and then graph the relationship between EFN and 1992 capacity utilization.

7. In general, what impacts do a firm's dividend policy, profitability, and capital intensity have on its financing requirements? (Again, if you are using the *Lotus* model, you could do a sensitivity analysis wherein you change certain input data and then observe the effect on EFN. It would be relatively easy to change the input data section to use a payout ratio rather than dividends per share in the event that management wanted to see the relationship between the payout and EFN. To change the profit margin, it would be necessary to change some of the income statement data. This would, of course, depart from the assumption that the 1993 ratios will be the same as 1992 ratios.)

8. The percentage of sales method has been used to forecast the firm's financial statements. Suppose one of the senior executives asked you what assumptions are implied when one uses the percentage of sales method. That is, under what circumstances would the percentage of sales method produce a valid, as opposed to an incorrect, forecast? How would you answer?

9. What are some other methods that could be used to forecast the asset-and-liability balances and, thus, the forecasted financial requirements? If the senior executives asked you to incorporate these procedures into your analysis, how would you do it, how long would it take, and what additional data would you require?

10. The case states that Space-Age's optimal capital structure calls for 20 percent long-term debt and 80 percent common equity. However, according to the 1992 balance sheet, the firm's capitalization ratio is Long-term debt/Total permanent capital = $12,570,000/($12,570,000 + $17,490,000 + 11,310,000) = 0.304 = 30.4 percent, and its total-debt-to-total-assets ratio is $15,540,000/$44,340,000 = 35.1 percent. Do these figures indicate that the capital structure is seriously out of balance, that the company is using far too much debt, and that you should modify the mix of debt and equity used in the forecasts? (Hint: Think about whether the optimal capital structure should be stated in book value or market value terms.)

11. Regardless of whether or not you think the capital structure *should* be changed, if it were changed, how would a change affect the other elements in the forecast, including the interest rate, the stock price, and the projected earnings per share? If you are using the *Lotus* model, conduct a sensitivity analysis.

12. Calculate the following values based on the 1992 financial statements: (a) current ratio, (b) profit margin, (c) ROE, and (d) EPS. Then calculate those projected values for 1993 and discuss how the projected ratios would change as such things as the sales growth rate, the payout ratio, the capital structure, and the profit margin change. Do you think the senior executives at the retreat would be interested in this type of data? If so, could you provide them with it on a "real time" basis? Explain.

Table 1

Historical Financial Statements
(in Millions of Dollars)

	1988	1989	1990	1991	1992
Balance Sheets:					
Cash and securities	$ 0.75	$ 1.05	$ 1.36	$ 1.71	$ 2.18
Accounts receivable	2.40	3.36	4.37	5.46	7.10
Inventories	2.85	3.99	5.19	6.48	8.43
Current assets	$ 6.00	$ 8.40	$ 10.92	$ 13.65	$ 17.71
Net fixed assets	9.00	12.60	16.38	20.48	26.63
Total assets	$ 15.00	$ 21.00	$ 27.30	$ 34.13	$ 44.34
Accounts payable	$ 0.29	$ 0.40	$ 0.53	$ 0.65	$ 0.84
Notes payable	1.81	2.18	0.75	0.94	1.23
Accrued wages & taxes	0.30	0.42	0.54	0.69	0.90
Current liabilities	$ 2.40	$ 3.00	$ 1.82	$ 2.27	$ 2.97
Long-term debt	2.11	3.91	7.74	9.67	12.57
Total liabilities	$ 4.51	$ 6.91	$ 9.56	$ 11.94	$ 15.54
Common stock	$ 10.55	$ 11.93	$ 12.86	$ 13.89	$ 17.49
Retained earnings	(0.06)	2.16	4.88	8.30	11.31
Total common equity	$ 10.49	$ 14.09	$ 17.74	$ 22.19	$ 28.80
Total liabilities & equity	$ 15.00	$ 21.00	$ 27.30	$ 34.13	$ 44.34

	1988	1989	1990	1991	1992
Income Statements:					
Sales	$ 30.00	$ 42.00	$ 54.59	$ 68.25	$ 88.73
Cost of goods sold	25.37	35.08	45.76	57.21	74.25
Depreciation	1.80	2.52	3.28	4.10	5.33
Gross profit	$ 2.83	$ 4.40	$ 5.55	$ 6.94	$ 9.15
Interest expense	0.44	0.69	1.01	1.26	1.64
Taxable income	$ 2.40	$ 3.71	$ 4.54	$ 5.68	$ 7.51
Taxes	0.96	1.49	1.82	2.28	3.00
Net income	$ 1.44	$ 2.22	$ 2.72	$ 3.42	$ 4.51
Dividends	0.00	0.00	0.00	0.00	1.50
Additions to R.E.	$ 1.44	$ 2.22	$ 2.72	$ 3.42	$ 3.01

Note: The figures in the tables were generated using a *Lotus* model; therefore some numbers may not add up properly because of rounding differences.

Table 2

Historical and Industry-Average Ratios

	1988	1989	1990	1991	1992	Industry Average
Current	2.5	2.8	6.0	6.0	6.0	3.3
Debt/assets	30.1%	32.9%	35.0%	35.0%	35.1%	40.0%
ROE	13.7%	15.8%	15.3%	15.4%	15.7%	16.4%

Table 3

Historical 1992 and Projected Financial Statements
(in Millions of Dollars)

	1992	Percentage of Sales	Projected 1993	2nd Pass	3rd Pass	4th Pass
Balance Sheets:						
Cash and securities	$ 2.18	2.46%	$ 2.62	$ 2.62	$ 2.62	X
Accounts receivable	7.10	8.00	X	X	X	X
Inventories	8.43	9.50	10.12	10.12	10.12	X
Current assets	$17.71	N.A.	X	X	X	X
Net fixed assets	26.63	30.01	31.96	31.96	31.96	X
Total assets	$44.34	N.A.	$53.21	$53.21	$53.21	X
Accounts payable	$ 0.84	0.95%	X	X	$ 1.01	X
Notes payable	1.23	1.39	X	X	1.48	X
Accrued wages & taxes	0.90	1.01	1.08	1.08	1.08	X
Current liabilities	$ 2.97	N.A.	X	X	$ 3.56	X
Long-term debt	12.57	N.A.	12.57	13.40	13.45	X
Total liabilities	$15.54	N.A.	$16.13	$16.97	$17.01	X
Common stock	$17.49	N.A.	$17.49	$20.83	$21.00	X
Retained earnings	11.31	N.A.	15.41	15.20	15.19	X
Total common equity	$28.80	N.A.	$32.90	$36.03	$36.19	X
Total liabs. & equity	$44.34	N.A.	$49.04	$52.99	$53.20	X
External funds needed (EFN)			$ 4.17	$ 0.21	$ 0.01	X

Table 3
Continued

	1992	Percentage of Sales	1993	Projected 2nd Pass	3rd Pass	4th Pass
Income Statements:						
Sales	$88.73	100.00%	$106.48	$106.48	$106.48	X
Cost of goods sold	79.58	89.69	95.50	95.50	95.50	X
EBIT	$ 9.15	10.31%	$ 10.98	$ 10.98	$ 10.98	X
Interest expense	1.64	N.A.	X	X	X	X
Taxable income	$ 7.51	N.A.	$ 9.34	$ 9.22	$ 9.21	X
Taxes	3.00	N.A.	3.74	3.69	3.68	X
Net income	$ 4.51	N.A.	$ 5.60	$ 5.53	$ 5.53	X
Dividends	1.50	N.A.	1.50	1.64	1.65	X
Additions to R.E.	$ 3.01	N.A.	$ 4.10	$ 3.89	$ 3.88	X

	1992	1993	Projected 2nd Pass	3rd Pass	4th Pass
External funds needed (EFN)		$4.17	$0.21	$0.01	X
Assumed additional long-term debt		$0.83	$0.04	$0.00	X
Assumed additional stock		$3.34	$0.17	$0.01	X
Additional interest (ST and LT)		$0.12	$0.01	$0.00	X
Additional dividends		$0.14	$0.01	$0.00	X
Selected Ratios (Adjusted for Assumed Financing)					
Current	5.96	5.96	5.96	5.96	X
Profit margin	5.1%	5.3%	5.2%	5.2%	X
ROE	15.7%	15.3%	15.3%	15.3%	X
EPS	$1.13	$1.28	$1.26	$1.26	X

38

Financial Forecasting

Automated Banking Management, Inc.

Automated Banking Management, Inc. (ABM), was founded by two professors from Ohio State University—one in management information systems and one in computer science—to develop expert systems for the banking industry. Expert systems, which are a type of computer program, help managers solve problems. In essence, knowledge concerning a particular subject is placed into the system, and the system draws on that knowledge when trying to answer questions or solve problems related to that subject. The plan was to develop expert systems for banking applications that would be built into a customized computer chip and then be permanently installed in an IBM PC clone. For example, an expert system would be designed to make lending decisions based on the information contained in the customer's loan application and the bank's credit standards. Such a system would provide a bank with greater consistency in its lending decisions throughout the organization and also reduce bank expenses by reducing the number of lending officers needed within the bank. Furthermore, they planned to keep up with developments in the banking industry and to offer periodic updates that would enable their customers to deal efficiently with tax and regulatory changes.

ABM, founded in 1985, was successful from the start. By 1992, it was an industry leader—profitable and growing rapidly. Brent Joseph, an MBA who had been brought in as financial manager, had developed a good initial financial plan, and everything had gone smoothly. Brent knew, though, that the company had been lucky and that some large computer companies, including Microsoft and Apple, were thinking about marketing a competitive system. ABM had not been sitting idle. The company now markets a PC-based personal tax preparation package that sells well, and other products are also in the pipeline. Further, ABM's bank customers are quite satisfied, and word-of-mouth promotion has become one of the company's most important assets. Finally, it would be costly for its bank customers to change systems, so they will probably keep buying ABM's add-ons and modified systems unless some competitor develops a truly outstanding new product.

ABM's financial planning process is broken down into five steps:

(1) A study is made of basic trends in the computer industry as well as in the banking industry and other markets where ABM expects to operate. How will our customers' needs change over the next five years, and what can we do to meet any existing or developing needs?

(2) A set of pro forma financial statements is developed and used to analyze the effects of alternative operating plans on projected profits and financial ratios. The plan encompasses five years, with the projections being relatively detailed for the coming year and much less detailed for the following four years. The entire plan is updated every year in November.

(3) The specific financial requirements needed to support the company's base-case operating plan are determined. This information is obtained from the pro forma statements.

(4) The specific sources of capital that will be used to meet the financial requirements are identified.

(5) The initially projected financial statements are then modified to include the addition of the capital needed to finance the projected assets. This involves adjusting the pro forma income statement to include the interest charges associated with any additional debt and an adjustment to dividends paid if new stock must be issued. These modifications change the initially projected retained earnings and thus change the "external funds needed" to finance the asset expansion. These feedback effects require the use of an iterative process to produce a consistent final set of financial statements. In the past, all this has been done manually—which takes a good bit of time—but Brent has been working to develop a computerized model to speed up the process.

ABM's 1988 through 1992 historical financial statements, along with three key ratios and industry averages, are given in Tables 1 and 2. The company was operating its fixed assets at full capacity in 1992, so its $59.15 million in sales represented full-capacity sales. Since the firm's marketing department is forecasting a 20 percent increase in sales for 1993, new assets will have to be added. For planning purposes, Brent assumes (1) that accounts payable and accruals will spontaneously increase in accordance with standard industry practices, (2) that new long-term capital will be raised in accordance with the firm's target capitalization ratios which call for 20 percent long-term debt and 80 percent common equity (measured at market value), and (3) that short-term bank loans, reported as notes payable, will be assumed to grow along with sales, since they are used to finance the firm's working capital needs. (Note that new common equity includes new retained earnings and new common stock sales.)

ABM currently has 4 million shares of common stock outstanding, and the market price is $6. The dividend in 1992 was $0.25 per share, and management does not intend to increase the dividend in 1993. New long-term debt would carry a 12.0 percent coupon, and it would be issued at par. New short-term debt will cost 10.0 percent. The combined federal and state tax rate is 40 percent.

ABM's senior managers go off on a one week retreat each November to work on the five-year plan and the budget for the coming year. Prior to the retreat, the various division managers must prepare reports which the top executives will review beforehand and then discuss at the retreat. As financial manager, Brent normally prepares some first approximation financial forecasts which are then modified during the retreat as a result of strategic decisions made at that time. The modified statements are used to show the financial implications of different operating plans. However, Brent recently underwent a difficult ulcer operation and, because of a slow recovery, he will neither be able to attend the retreat, nor to prepare the background report for it. Therefore, his assistant, ready or not, must assume his duties.

Even though he could not get out of bed, Brent called his assistant to the hospital, and they discussed what needed to be done. First, Brent told his assistant he had almost finished a computerized model that would aid in the process. Brent also indicated that the model needed to be debugged, or at least checked out, by first making "by-hand" projections and then seeing if the model generated the same set of data. If a discrepancy is discovered, it will be necessary to find out where the error lies. Brent also cautioned his assistant that it should be necessary to explain to the executives how any changes in operating conditions would affect the funds requirements, as well as how any changes in the financing mix would affect *everything*, including external funding requirements, earnings per share, and the stock price. In particular, Brent warned the assistant not to try to defend the inputs to the forecasting process; rather, the critical thing is to be able to make adjustments in the likely event that the senior executives don't like all the assumptions used in the forecast. As Brent pointed out, "It's the top managers' job to understand the business and to make the final assumptions used in the forecast and the budget. It's our job to tell them how those assumptions interact and what the final outcome will be if their assumptions hold true. We ought to use reasonable inputs for our report and basic forecasts, but our real job in the planning process is to show top management what will happen under different operating conditions."

Assume that you are Brent's assistant and that you must take his place at the retreat. Prepare for the event by answering the following questions. Also, think about the types of additional questions that might be asked at the retreat.

Questions

1. To begin, consider the percentage of sales formula used to determine external funds needed:

External funds needed	=	Required increase in assets	–	Spontaneous increase in liabilities	–	Increase in retained earnings
EFN	=	$(A/S)\Delta S$	–	$(L/S)\Delta S$	–	$MS_1(1-d)$.

Here,

A/S = Assets/Sales = required dollar increase in assets per \$1 increase in sales

L/S = Spontaneous liabilities/Sales = spontaneously generated financing per \$1 increase in sales

S_1 = total sales projected for next year (S_0 = last year's sales)

ΔS = change in sales = $S_1 - S_0$

M = profit margin

d = dividend payout ratio.

Use this equation to calculate ABM's EFN for 1993.

2. Now, use the proportional growth (percentage of sales) method to forecast the firm's financial statements and EFN for 1993. (Hint: Table 3 has been provided to speed up your work.) Compare the EFN obtained here with that obtained from the percentage of sales formula given in Question 1. Why are the results different?

3. The major assumption inherent in the proportional growth (percentage of sales) method is that all assets increase proportionally with sales. In effect, this means that the regression of each asset account against sales would result in a straight line that passes through the origin. To check on this assumption, used both in the formula and in Table 3, you could run a regression of each asset against sales, using data from Table 1. As a quick check, run a regression of total assets on sales to test the assumption. (Hint: You can use a financial calculator or the *Lotus 1-2-3* model, or you can get an approximation from a graph.)

   a. Does it appear that the proportionality assumption holds true? Explain.

   b. Repeat the Part a. regression analyses assuming the following data.

Year	Sales	Total Assets
1988	$20.00	$19.60
1989	28.00	21.25
1990	36.40	25.15
1991	45.50	28.72
1992	59.15	29.55

   Under these conditions, does it appear that the proportionality assumption holds true? Explain.

   c. Which of the situations above is likely to hold for most firms? What implications does your answer here have for the percentage of sales method?

4. Assume that you are now at the retreat, discussing the forecast with ABM's senior executives. The vice president for manufacturing informs you that fixed assets were actually being operated at only 80 percent of capacity in 1992. What effect would this have on your projected external capital requirement for 1993? In answering this question, disregard any financing feedback effects and answer the question by modifying the 1st pass columns

of Table 3, but explain how you could go on to reach a balanced solution. Also, in answering this and the next question, assume that depreciation expenses remain constant as a percentage of sales.

5. In the 80 percent of capacity utilization scenario, excess funds will be generated. Suppose one of the senior executives asked you, as the finance representative, what you would recommend doing with the money. How would you answer? If you are using the *Lotus* model, how could it be modified to handle EFN surpluses?

6. a. Re-do Question 4 under the assumption that ABM was operating at 90 percent of capacity in 1992.

   b. Discuss the general relationship between capacity utilization and projected capital requirements in situations (a) where assets are "lumpy" and (b) where they are not lumpy.

   c. If you are using the *Lotus* model, set up a data table and then graph the relationship between EFN and 1992 capacity utilization.

7. In general, what impacts do a firm's dividend policy, profitability, and capital intensity have on its financing requirements? (Again, if you are using the *Lotus* model, you could do a sensitivity analysis wherein you change certain input data and then observe the effect on EFN. It would be relatively easy to change the input data section to use a payout ratio rather than dividends per share in the event that management wanted to see the relationship between the payout and EFN. To change the profit margin, it would be necessary to change some of the income statement data. This would, of course, depart from the assumption that the 1993 ratios will be the same as 1992 ratios.)

8. The percentage of sales method has been used to forecast the firm's financial statements. Suppose one of the senior executives asked you what assumptions are implied when one uses the percentage of sales method. That is, under what circumstances would the percentage of sales method produce a valid, as opposed to an incorrect, forecast? How would you answer?

9. What are some other methods that could be used to forecast the asset and liability balances and, thus, the forecasted financial requirements? If the senior executives asked you to incorporate

these procedures into your analysis, how would you do it, how long would it take, and what additional data would you require?

10. The case states that ABM's optimal capital structure calls for 20 percent long-term debt and 80 percent common equity. However, according to the 1992 balance sheet, the firm's capitalization ratio is Long-term debt/Total permanent capital = $8,380,000/($8,380,000 + $10,680,000 + 8,520,000) = 0.304 = 30.4 percent, and its total-debt-to-total-assets ratio is $10,350,000/$29,585,000 = 35.0 percent. Do these figures indicate that the capital structure is seriously out of balance, that the company is using far too much debt, and that you should modify the mix of debt and equity used in the forecasts? (Hint: Think about whether the optimal capital structure should be stated in book value or market value terms.)

11. Regardless of whether or not you think the capital structure *should* be changed, if it were changed, how would a change affect the other elements in the forecast, including the interest rate, the stock price, and the projected earnings per share? If you are using the *Lotus* model, conduct a sensitivity analysis.

12. Calculate the following values based on the 1992 financial statements: (a) current ratio, (b) profit margin, (c) ROE, and (d) EPS. Then calculate those projected values for 1993 and discuss how the projected ratios would change as such things as the sales growth rate, the payout ratio, the capital structure, and the profit margin change. Do you think the senior executives at the retreat would be interested in this type of data? If so, could you provide them with it on a "real time" basis? Explain.

Table 1

Historical Financial Statements
(in Millions of Dollars)

	1988	1989	1990	1991	1992
Balance Sheets:					
Cash and securities	$ 0.50	$ 0.70	$ 0.91	$ 1.14	$ 1.45
Accounts receivable	1.60	2.24	2.91	3.64	4.73
Inventories	1.90	2.66	3.46	4.32	5.62
Current assets	$ 4.00	$ 5.60	$ 7.28	$ 9.10	$ 11.80
Net fixed assets	6.00	8.40	10.92	13.65	17.75
Total assets	$ 10.00	$ 14.00	$ 18.20	$ 22.75	$ 29.55
Accounts payable	$ 0.19	$ 0.27	$ 0.35	$ 0.43	$ 0.56
Notes payable	1.21	1.45	0.50	0.63	0.82
Accrued wages & taxes	0.20	0.28	0.36	0.46	0.59
Current liabilities	$ 1.60	$ 2.00	$ 1.21	$ 1.52	$ 1.97
Long-term debt	1.41	2.61	5.16	6.45	8.38
Total liabilities	$ 3.01	$ 4.61	$ 6.37	$ 7.96	$ 10.35
Common stock	$ 7.05	$ 7.97	$ 8.59	$ 9.27	$ 10.68
Retained earnings	(0.04)	1.42	3.24	5.52	8.52
Total common equity	$ 6.99	$ 9.39	$ 11.83	$ 14.79	$ 19.20
Total liabilities & equity	$ 10.00	$ 14.00	$ 18.20	$ 22.75	$ 29.55

	1988	1989	1990	1991	1992
Income Statements:					
Sales	$ 20.00	$ 28.00	$ 36.40	$ 45.50	$ 59.15
Cost of goods sold	16.91	23.39	30.51	38.14	49.50
Depreciation	1.20	1.68	2.18	2.73	3.55
Gross profit	$ 1.89	$ 2.93	$ 3.70	$ 4.63	$ 6.10
Interest expense	0.29	0.46	0.67	0.84	1.09
Taxable income	$ 1.60	$ 2.47	$ 3.03	$ 3.79	$ 5.01
Taxes	0.64	0.99	1.21	1.52	2.01
Net income	$ 0.96	$ 1.48	$ 1.82	$ 2.28	$ 3.00
Dividends	0.00	0.00	0.00	0.00	1.00
Additions to R.E.	$ 0.96	$ 1.48	$ 1.82	$ 2.28	$ 2.00

Note: The figures in the tables were generated using a *Lotus* model; therefore some numbers may
not add up properly because of rounding differences.

Table 2

Historical and Industry-Average Ratios

	1988	1989	1990	1991	1992	Industry Average
Current	2.5	2.8	6.0	6.0	6.0	3.3
Debt/assets	30.1%	32.9%	35.0%	35.0%	35.0%	40.0%
ROE	13.7%	15.8%	15.4%	15.4%	15.7%	16.4%

Table 3

Historical 1992 and Projected Financial Statements
(in Millions of Dollars)

	1992	Percentage of Sales	Projected 1993	2nd Pass	3rd Pass	4th Pass
Balance Sheets:						
Cash and securities	$ 1.45	2.45%	$ 1.74	$ 1.74	$ 1.74	X
Accounts receivable	4.73	8.00%	X	X	X	X
Inventories	5.62	9.50%	6.74	6.74	6.74	X
Current assets	$ 11.80	N.A.	X	X	X	X
Net fixed assets	17.75	30.00%	21.29	21.29	21.29	X
Total assets	$ 29.55	N.A.	$ 35.45	$ 35.45	$ 35.45	X
Accounts payable	$ 0.56	0.95%	X	X	$ 0.67	X
Notes payable	0.82	1.39%	X	X	0.98	X
Accrued wages & taxes	0.59	1.00%	0.71	0.71	0.71	X
Current liabilities	$ 1.97	N.A.	X	X	$ 2.36	X
Long-term debt	8.38	N.A.	8.38	8.93	8.96	X
Total liabilities	$ 10.35	N.A.	$ 10.74	$ 11.30	$ 11.33	X
Common stock	$ 10.68	N.A.	$ 10.68	$ 12.90	$ 13.01	X
Retained earnings	8.52	N.A.	11.26	11.12	11.11	X
Total common equity	$ 19.20	N.A.	$ 21.94	$ 24.01	$ 24.12	X
Total liabs. & equity	$ 29.55	N.A.	$ 32.68	$ 35.31	$ 35.45	X
External funds needed (EFN)			$ 2.77	$ 0.14	$ 0.01	X

	1992	Percentage of Sales	1993	Projected 2nd Pass	3rd Pass	4th Pass
Income Statements:						
Sales	$ 59.15	100.00%	$ 70.98	$ 70.98	$ 70.98	X
Cost of goods sold	53.05	89.69	63.66	63.66	63.66	X
EBIT	$ 6.10	10.31%	$ 7.32	$ 7.32	$ 7.32	X
Interest expense	1.09	N.A.	X	X	X	X
Taxable income	$ 5.01	N.A.	$ 6.23	$ 6.15	$ 6.14	X
Taxes	2.01	N.A.	2.49	2.46	2.46	X
Net income	$ 3.00	N.A.	$ 3.74	$ 3.69	$ 3.69	X
Dividends	1.00	N.A.	1.00	1.09	1.10	X
Additions to R.E.	$ 2.00	N.A.	$ 2.74	$ 2.60	$ 2.59	X

	1992	1993	Projected 2nd Pass	3rd Pass	4th Pass
External funds needed (EFN)		$2.77	$0.14	$0.01	X
Assumed additional long-term debt		$0.55	$0.03	$0.00	X
Assumed additional stock		$2.22	$0.11	$0.01	X
Additional interest (ST and LT)		$0.08	$0.00	$0.00	X
Additional dividends		$0.09	$0.00	$0.00	X
Selected Ratios (Adjusted for Assumed Financing)					
Current	5.99	5.99	5.99	5.99	X
Profit margin	5.1%	5.3%	5.2%	5.2%	X
ROE	15.7%	15.3%	15.3%	15.3%	X
EPS	$0.75	$0.86	$0.84	$0.84	X

331

IX

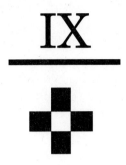

Other Topics

39

Bankruptcy and
Reorganization

Mark X Company (B)

Mark X Company is in a precarious financial position—it is overextended, and unless the company can persuade its bank to continue present loans and also grant substantial additional credit, Mark X may well go under. The company's 1992 year end balance sheet is contained in Table 1.

Before the bank will reach a decision on whether to continue supporting Mark X, Carolyn Mayo, the banker handling the Mark X account, must prepare a report for the bank's Senior Loan Committee. The report must contain a complete bankruptcy analysis which sets forth the bank's exposure in the event of liquidation. To begin her analysis, Mayo estimated what values the assets would have if Mark X were liquidated. Working with the bank's appraisers and liquidation experts, she concluded that the land and buildings could be sold for $5 million, while the equipment would bring in another $3 million. The receivables could be sold for $0.75 on the dollar, but the inventory would bring only $0.50 on the dollar.

Next, Mayo had to make sure that she understood the nature of the claims against Mark X. The accruals currently (that is, at the end of 1992) consist of $5 million of accrued taxes and $2,331,000 of accrued wages. The wages were all earned within the past two weeks, and no single employee is due more than $2,000. Long-term bank loans actually consist of two different loans: $5 million in straight unsecured debt, plus another $4,563,000 in loans that are subordinate to the $5 million loan. Mayo's bank, Wells Fargo, extended both the short-term loan and the senior long-term loan, while a competitor bank holds the subordinated note for $4,563,000. Mayo estimates that the administrative expenses for the trustee in bankruptcy would total $600,000—this amount would be "taken off the top" in any liquidation or reorganization procedure. Finally, Mark X has $6 million in unfunded pension liabilities which would have to be dealt with in any bankruptcy proceedings.

Now assume that you are Carolyn Mayo's assistant, and she has asked you to determine what would happen if the bank called its loans and forced Mark X into bankruptcy. Obviously, Mark X would file for protection under Chapter 11 of the Bankruptcy Act, and it would then either be reorganized or liquidated. Your job is to ascertain how the bank would fare in this event. You will have to make a report to Mayo and, perhaps, also to the Senior Loan Committee, so you should be able to answer any question likely to be thrown at you. To get you started, you and Mayo drew up a list of issues and set them forth in the following questions.

Questions

1. What are the differences between an informal and a formal bankruptcy proceeding, and between a reorganization and a liquidation? Also, explain the meaning of the terms "composition" and "extension" as they are used in bankruptcy proceedings. Could an agreement include both a composition and an extension?

2. What are the standards of "fairness" and "feasibility" as the terms are used in formal bankruptcy reorganizations?

3. What total dollar amount of funds could be expected, before any payments were made, if Mark X were liquidated?

4. Develop a table which shows the distribution of the expected proceeds to the "priority claimants"; that is, those claimants who have precedence over the general creditors. What dollar amount of proceeds would remain after the priority claimants had been paid? (Hint: Complete the top part of Table 2.)

5. Now create a table which shows the distribution to general creditors both before and after the adjustment for subordination. (Hint: Complete the remainder of Table 2.) What is the percentage of each claim (for both senior creditors and general creditors) that would be paid in the final distribution? What would the stockholders get?

6. How would Wells Fargo Bank and its competitor bank fare if Mark X were liquidated, and what, in general terms, is the value to Wells Fargo of the subordination clause in the $4,563,000 long-term loan?

What would be the impact on Wells Fargo if there were no subordination clause?

7. Now consider how the different creditors (and the stockholders) would fare under different assumptions about the amount of the liquidation proceeds. For example, what would the distribution to creditors be if the land and buildings brought only $2 million or if they brought $8 million? Similarly, how would the value received from the equipment, or the inventory, affect the distributions? If you are using the *Lotus* model, quantify your answer; otherwise, just discuss what would happen.

8. *(If you were not assigned Case 35, just discuss what is involved in this question. If you are familiar with Case 35, answer the question more specifically.)* If the assumptions that were used in Part A of the case were used here, in Part B, all of the creditors could be paid off, and the company would earn substantial profits which would give value to the common stock. How should this situation affect the bank's decision as to whether or not to demand repayment of the loan? If the bank did demand repayment, and thus forced Mark X to file for protection under Chapter 11, how would the fact that the distributions depend so heavily on the assumptions used in the forecasts affect the Bankruptcy Court's decision to have the company reorganize versus liquidate? Put another way, do you suppose the court would want to see operating projections based on different sets of assumptions and some evidence as to which of the different sets of assumptions was most likely to be correct? Could probability distributions be used in this regard? Would a financial analyst working for the secured creditors or for the common stockholders be more likely to use a relatively optimistic set of assumptions? Why or why not?

9. *(If you were not assigned Case 35, just discuss what is involved in this question. If you are familiar with Case 35, answer the question more specifically.)* If the company were forced to file for Chapter 11, would you recommend that the Bankruptcy Court order a liquidation or a reorganization under each of the following scenarios: (1) You feel that the projections in Part A, where the projected profits are over $5 million per year, represent the most likely situation and that there is almost no chance that the assets' liquidating value will decline. (2) You regard a second scenario, where annual profits are about $100,000, as most likely, but you also think there is a fairly high probability of either very good or vary bad results. In the event

of a bad outcome, the liquidating value of the assets will fall quickly and sharply from the current level. (3) You regard a third scenario, where annual profits are about – $1.5 million, as being most likely, but you also think there is about a 25 percent probability that the company's optimistic forecast would prove correct. Justify your choices.

10. Based on all the information at hand, should Carolyn Mayo recommend that the bank force Mark X into bankruptcy or lend it the necessary funds to keep going? Explain.

Table 1

Balance Sheet For Year Ended
December 31, 1992
in Thousands of Dollars

Cash/marketable securities	$ 3,906
Accounts receivable	29,357
Inventory	46,659
Current assets	$ 79,922
Land, plant, and equipment	$ 22,874
Accumulated depreciation	(6,694)
Net fixed assets	$ 16,180
Total assets	$ 96,102
Short-term bank loans	$ 18,233
Accounts payable	19,998
Accruals	7,331
Total current liabilities	$ 45,562
Long-term bank loans	$ 9,563
Mortgage	2,340
Long-term debt	$ 11,903
Total liabilities	$ 57,465
Common Stock	$ 23,269
Retained earnings	15,368
Total common equity	$ 38,637
Total liabilities & equity	$ 96,102

Table 2
Selected Case Data
in Thousands of Dollars

Liquidation Proceeds:

Cash and marketable securities	$ 3,906
Accounts receivable	22,018
Inventory	X
Land and buildings	5,000
Equipment	X
Total proceeds	$ 57,253

Distribution of Proceeds *Priority Claims:*	Claim	Payment	Percent of Claim Received	Proceeds Remaining After Claim is Paid
1. Mortgage	$ 2,340	$2,340	100.0%	$54,913
2. Trustee's fees	600	600	100.0	54,313
3. Wages due	X	X	X	X
4. Taxes due	5,000	5,000	100.0	46,982
5. Unfunded pension liability	6,000	6,000	100.0	40,982

Initial General Creditor Allocation:

General creditor claims	$ 47,794
Proceeds remaining	$ 40,982
Pro rata percentage	85.7%

	Claim	Payment	Percent of Claim Received	Proceeds Remaining After Claim is Paid
6. Accounts payable	$19,998	$17,148	85.7%	$23,834
7. ST bank loans	X	X	X	X
8. Priority LT bank loans	5,000	4,287	85.7	3,913
9. Sub LT bank loans	4,563	3,913	85.7	0
10. Remaining mortgage	0	0	N.A.	0

General Creditor Allocation After Subordination Adjustment:

	Claim	Payment	Percent of Claim Received	Proceeds Remaining After Claim is Paid
6. Accounts payable	$19,998	$17,148	85.7%	$23,834
7. ST bank loans	18,233	15,634	85.7	8,200
8. Priority LT bank loans	5,000	5,000	100.0	3,200
9. Sub LT bank loans	X	3,200	X	X
10. Remaining mortgage	0	0	N.A.	0

Shareholders' Distribution:

	Claim	Payment	Percent of Claim Received	Proceeds Remaining After Claim is Paid
11. Common stockholders	$38,637	$0	0.0%	$0

40

Merger Analysis

Nina's Fashions, Inc.

Nina's Fashions, Inc., operates a chain of retail clothing stores in Michigan, Wisconsin, and Illinois. The company has been in business since 1953, and until about 15 years ago, all of its stores were in older, downtown locations. However, in the late 1970s, the chain opened its first suburban store which differed significantly from the older stores. The new store was much larger, stocking many more items than the old stores. Many new stores followed, which were primarily located in shopping malls and shopping centers.

The new stores were a resounding success, and over the past ten years, Nina's has been aggressively selling its older locations and opening suburban stores. The downtown areas in many of Nina's locations have been revitalized and are now filled with high-rise office buildings and upscale retail outlets, so downtown property values have skyrocketed. Thus, the sale of its old store properties resulted in large cash inflows to Nina's. Since the company's strategic plans call for it to lease the new suburban stores rather than to purchase them, the firm now has a "war chest" of excess cash.

Many alternative uses have been discussed for the excess cash, ranging from repurchases of stock or debt to higher dividend payments. However, management has decided to use the cash to make one or more acquisitions, since they believe an expansion would contribute the most to stockholders' wealth. One of the acquisition candidates is Chic, a chain of eleven stores which operates in northern Illinois. The issues now facing the company are (1) how to approach Chic's management and (2) how much to offer for Chic's stock.

Executives at Nina's are good at running retail clothing stores, but they are not finance experts and have no experience with acquisitions.

Bob Sharpe, the treasurer, has an accounting background, but he did attend a three-day workshop on mergers at Harvard University last year specifically to learn something about the subject. Nina's had no acquisition plans at that time; Sharpe just felt that it would be useful to become familiar with the subject.

Table 1 contains some basic data that Sharpe developed relating to the cash flows Nina's could expect if it acquired Chic. The interest expense listed in the table includes (1) the interest on Chic's existing debt, (2) the interest on new debt that Nina's would issue to help finance the acquisition, and (3) the interest on new debt that Nina's would issue over time to help finance expansion within the new division. The required retentions shown in Table 1 represent earnings generated within Chic that would be earmarked for reinvestment within the acquired company to help finance growth. Note too that all the estimates in Table 1 are the incremental flows Chic is expected to produce and to make available to Nina's if it is acquired. Although specific estimates were only made for 1993 through 1996, the acquired company would be expected to grow at a 5 percent rate in 1997 and beyond.

Table 1

Incremental Cash Flows to Nina's if Chic is Acquired

	1993	1994	1995	1996
Net sales	$4,000,000	$6,000,000	$7,500,000	$8,500,000
Cost of goods sold (50% of sales)	2,000,000	3,000,000	3,750,000	4,250,000
Depreciation	400,000	450,000	500,000	550,000
Selling/admin. expense	300,000	400,000	500,000	600,000
Interest expense	200,000	300,000	300,000	400,000
Retentions	0	500,000	400,000	300,000

Chic currently finances with 40 percent debt; it pays taxes at a 30 percent federal-plus-state tax rate; and its beta is 1.2. If the acquisition takes place, Nina's would increase Chic's debt ratio to 50 percent, and consolidation, coupled with expected earnings improvements, would move Chic's federal-plus-state tax rate up to that of Nina's, 40 percent.

One part of the analysis involves determining a discount rate to apply to the estimated cash flows. Bob Sharpe remembers from the Harvard workshop that Professor Robert Hamada had developed some equations that can be used to unlever and then relever betas, and Sharpe believes that these equations may be helpful in the analysis:

Formula to unlever beta: $\quad b_U = \dfrac{b_L}{1 + (1 - T)(D/S)}$.

Formula to relever beta: $\quad b_L = b_U[1 + (1 - T)(D/S)]$.

Here, b_U is the beta that Chic would have if it used no debt financing, T is the applicable corporate tax rate, and D/S is the applicable market value debt-to-equity ratio. Sharpe notes that the T-bond rate is 10 percent, and a call to the company's investment bankers produced an estimate of 6 percent for the market risk premium.

Assume that you were recently hired as Bob Sharpe's assistant, and he has asked you to answer some basic questions about mergers as well as to do some calculations pertaining to the proposed Chic acquisition. Then, you and Sharpe will meet with the board of directors, and it will decide whether or not to proceed with the acquisition, how to start the negotiations, and the maximum price to offer. As you go through the questions, recognize that either Sharpe or anyone on the board could ask you follow-up questions, so you should thoroughly understand the implications of each question and answer. Your predecessor was fired for "being too mechanical and superficial," and you don't want to suffer the same fate.

Questions

1. Several factors have been proposed as providing a rationale for mergers. Among the more prominent ones are (1) tax considerations, (2) diversification, (3) control, (4) purchase of assets below replacement cost, and (5) synergy. From the standpoint of society, which of these reasons are justifiable? Which are not? Why is such a question relevant to a company like Nina's, which is considering a specific acquisition? Explain your answers.

2. Briefly describe the differences between a hostile merger and a friendly merger. Is there any reason to think that acquiring companies would, on average, pay a greater premium over target companies' pre-announcement prices in hostile mergers than in friendly mergers?

3. Use the data contained in Table 1 to construct Chic's cash flow statements for 1993 through 1996. Why is interest expense typically deducted in merger cash flow statements, whereas it is not normally deducted in capital budgeting cash flow analysis? Why are retentions deducted in the cash flow statement?

4. Conceptually, what is the appropriate discount rate to apply to the cash flows developed in Question 3? What is the numerical value? How much confidence can one place in this estimate; that is, is the estimated discount rate likely to be in error by a small amount such as 1 percentage point or a large amount such as 4 or 5 percentage points?

5. What is the terminal value of Chic; that is, what is the 1996 value of the cash flows Chic is expected to generate beyond 1996? What is Chic's value to Nina's at the beginning of 1993? Suppose another firm was evaluating Chic as a potential acquisition candidate. Would they obtain the same value? Explain.

6. a. Suppose Chic's management has a substantial ownership interest in the company, but not enough to block a merger. If Chic's managers want to keep the firm independent, what are some actions they could take to discourage potential suitors?

   b. If Chic's managers conclude that they cannot remain independent, what are some actions they might take to help their stockholders (and themselves) get the maximum price for their stock?

   c. If Chic's managers conclude that the maximum price they can get anyone to bid for the company is less than its "true value," is there any other action they might take that would benefit both outside stockholders and the managers themselves? Explain.

   d. Do Chic's managers face any potential conflicts of interest in any of the situations presented in a through c? Explain and suggest what might be done to reduce the damage from conflicts of interest.

7. Chic has 5 million shares of common stock outstanding. The shares are traded infrequently and in small blocks, but the last trade, of 500 shares, was at a price of $1.50 per share. Based on this information, and on your answers to Questions 5 and 6, how

much should Nina's offer, per share, for Chic, and how should it go about making the offer?

8. Do you agree that synergistic effects create value in the average merger? If so, how is this value generally shared between the stockholders of the acquiring and acquired companies; that is, does more of the value go to the acquired or to the acquiring firm? Explain.

9. A major concern in the analysis is the accuracy of the cash flow growth rate—how would the maximum price vary if this rate were greater or less than the expected 5 percent? If you are using the *Lotus* model, do a sensitivity analysis designed to determine the importance of the growth rate and determine the minimum growth rate that would justify a price of $2 per share. If you do not have access to the *Lotus* model, simply discuss the issue and explain why managers would be interested in such a sensitivity analysis.

10. Another major concern is the discount rate used in the analysis. What would Chic's value to Nina's be if Chic's beta were higher or lower than the 1.2 originally estimated or if the market risk premium were above or below the estimated 6 percent? Discuss the effects of these factors on the acquisition and on how much Nina's should offer. If you are using the *Lotus* model, quantify your results; otherwise, just discuss the situation.

11. Would the response of Chic's stockholders be affected by whether the offer was for cash or for stock in Nina's? Explain.

12. What are your final conclusions regarding how much Nina's should offer and the form of the offer?

41

*Entrepreneurship:
Financing and Valuing
a New Venture*

Advanced Fuels Corporation

Advanced Fuels Corporation (AFC) was founded five years ago by Dr. Zachary Aplin, who left his faculty position at Texas A&M to work full time developing a process to convert waste products into fuel. He used a government grant, personal funds, and loans from friends and relatives as seed money to finance his new company, and he was the sole stockholder.

Dr. Aplin and his two-member staff worked feverishly for three years, and at the beginning of the fourth year, they made a major breakthrough that led to the development of an efficient process for converting waste products into ethanol, a compound that can be blended with gasoline to produce a cleaner automobile fuel. Ethanol–gasoline blends have been around for some time, and over a billion gallons of ethanol a year are currently being produced in the United States. However, most ethanol is currently produced from feed corn, and the ethanol is more expensive than the gasoline to which it is added. Only a federal subsidy makes the ethanol–gasoline mixture economically feasible. However, producing ethanol from waste products would lower its cost dramatically, hence greatly increase the market potential of the blended fuel.

AFC has received a patent from the U.S. Patent Office for Dr. Aplin's unique ethanol production process. After considering licensing the process to major oil companies, Aplin decided that AFC itself should produce the ethanol. However, this would require a substantial amount of capital, and Dr. Aplin had exhausted his personal financial resources. Therefore, he began a series of discussions with AFC's accountants and bankers. Both sets of advisors stated that the first step toward attaining outside capital is to develop a business plan.

The Business Plan

A business plan is a document that describes in detail the key aspects of a proposed business venture. Everything from raw material sources to a description of how a product will meet the specific needs of future customers is contained in the plan. Business plans range from 10 to over 100 pages in length, but most are about 50 pages. The 10 key segments of a business plan for a typical manufacturing venture are listed below:

1. *Summary.* A summary of no more than three pages should (a) provide a clear and concise overview of the business and (b) capture the reader's interest.

2. *Business Description.* The business description should explain in detail what the new company will do, the markets it will serve, and how it will operate. This section should also provide industry background information. Additionally, any competitive advantages or disadvantages which the new venture will have should be discussed.

3. *Marketing.* Sales projections, supported by market research data, should be delineated in the marketing segment. This segment is a critical component of the plan for two main reasons. First, potential capital providers must be convinced that there is a well-defined customer base for the venture's product. Unless they have a clear understanding of the target market, potential investors will be reluctant to provide the necessary capital. Second, the projected sales volume will affect the size of the enterprise, hence the amount of capital it will require.

4. *Research, Design, and Development.* This section should provide a description of all research performed to date and give the extent and cost of future research required for the venture. Also, all technical processes and equipment should be explained in detail.

5. *Manufacturing.* The manufacturing segment should first define plant location(s) and the strategic reasoning behind location choices. Labor cost and availability, proximity to suppliers and customers, and community support should all be discussed.

Additionally, detailed cost data for the manufacturing process should be spelled out.

6. *Management.* The management section presents the organizational, ownership, and compensation structures of the company. All key personnel should be identified, and brief resumés for these individuals should be provided.

7. *Critical Risks Segment.* In this section, existing and potential problems, including the company's major competition and any negative industry trends, should be discussed. Alternative solutions and their costs should be offered for all current and potential obstacles.

8. *Financial Segment.* The financial segment documents the projected profitability of the venture and is absolutely crucial to the capital acquisition process. Projected income statements, balance sheets, cash flow statements, and cash budgets are included. The most important element is probably the cash flow statement. Potential lenders can use it to gain insights into the amounts and timing of external capital requirements and repayments, while potential equity investors use it to estimate future equity cash flows, which form the primary basis for estimating the value of the enterprise.

9. *Milestone Schedule.* The milestone schedule gives projected dates for future significant events in the life of the business. This schedule might include the dates that plant construction will begin and end, equipment installation dates, hiring dates, and dates of first product shipments.

10. *Critical Assumptions.* In a well-developed business plan, most of the key assumptions behind the projected financial statements are spelled out in detail throughout the document. Still, it is useful to include a summary section which lists the most important assumptions. For example, if getting final approval for pending patents is vital to moving forward, this fact should be noted here.

Generally, a start-up firm's final business plan is developed jointly by its managers and an investment banking firm that specializes in start-up financing. The investment banker must be familiar both with sources of capital and the legal requirements associated with security offerings. Often though, companies develop preliminary plans with the help of commercial bankers and CPAs; Dr. Aplin and his staff followed this route. Working on the preliminary plan is generally a useful exercise, and in this case it forced Aplin to think about issues that he had not previously considered. For example, he knew that his production process offered a cost advantage over the competition, but he was amazed to discover that his projected production costs would be only 70 percent of those of his closest competitor. On the other hand, the capital-intensive nature of the production process was revealed by the business plan, and it was sobering to learn just how much capital his fledgling firm would need to actually produce ethanol on a commercial scale.

The cost of building one production facility was determined to be $10 million. Since Aplin's manufacturing strategy called for building plants in five major cities in the United States, and since $1 million in working capital is needed to start up each plant, AFC's total capital requirement is $55 million. This was a lot more than Dr. Aplin had anticipated, so he decided to hire an investment banking firm to help him finalize AFC's business plan and to identify and approach potential capital providers.

Venture Capital Sources

The investment bankers identified four main sources of start-up capital: venture capital funds, banks, individuals, and public offerings.

Venture Capital Funds. Some financial institutions such as insurance companies and pension funds, and wealthy individuals, often allocate a certain portion of their capital to high-risk investments. Much of this risk capital is placed into venture capital funds managed by experienced professionals called "venture capitalists." Venture capital fund managers generally purchase either the common stock or convertible debentures of new businesses with the potential for rapid growth. Because of the very high risk associated with such investments, venture capitalists require a high expected rate of return, typically in the 20–40 percent range.

Banks. In the 1980s, banks would lend money to start-up companies if assets such as real estate, plant, and equipment were available for collateral. However, since 1989, when Congress approved new rules governing bank capital requirements, banks have not been active in the start-up financing market. The banks entered the 1990s with many bad real estate loans, and, after the savings-and-loan debacle, bank examiners are quick to force banks to write down problem loans, which puts additional pressure on bank capital. As a result, start-up companies now find it very difficult to obtain bank financing. Further, if bank loans are available at all, the terms are normally short-term (less than one year), hence not suitable for funding long-term investments or permanent working capital.

Individuals. Sometimes entrepreneurs are able to convince friends, relatives, or wealthy individuals to provide the capital needed to start a company. Capital provided by these individuals is termed "informal risk capital," and a wealthy individual who invests directly in a start-up venture is called an "angel." If significant amounts of money are to be obtained, it may be necessary to obtain it only from "informed, sophisticated" individuals who are in a position to understand the risks they are taking and to afford a loss should the venture fail. This qualification is generally met by having the individual sign an affidavit that his or her net worth is in excess of $1 million.

Public Offerings. A public offering involves raising capital by selling equity or debt securities to the public at large. An investment banking firm is vital to a public offering, both to assist in determining the value of the securities to be sold and to market the securities to investors. While public offerings are a valuable source of capital for companies once they get beyond the start-up stage and have established a track record, they are virtually impossible for most start-ups.

Commonly Used Terms

Venture capital financing has a "lingo" of its own. Here are some of the more commonly used terms:

Bridge Loan. It often takes some time to line up permanent investors for a start-up venture. Often, a business will obtain short-term loans from individuals or, possibly, its investment bank, to get operations started, with the intention of paying this loan off when permanent financing is obtained. Such a loan "bridges the gap from here to permanent financing," hence it is called a "bridge loan."

Equity Kicker. With start-ups, there is generally a high probability of failure, but also a small probability of success and rich rewards. For example, suppose three out of four new companies fail within a year and cause investors to lose their entire stake, but one out of four succeeds and has a payoff of 400 percent. If a fund invested equal amounts in the four companies, then it would have a 25 percent rate of return.

Now suppose a bank or other lender (as opposed to an equity investor) formed a portfolio consisting of loans to the four companies, charging a high 25 percent on each loan (in most states, usury laws would limit the rate to 16–18 percent on this type of loan). The lender would lose 100 percent on three loans, make 25 percent on the fourth, and end up with large losses on the entire operation. The moral of the story is that portfolio theory works well only if investors can share fully in upside results.

Now consider the situation when the founder of a start-up firm, such as Dr. Aplin, exhausts his personal funds and is forced to seek outside capital. Outsiders think (correctly) that the founder has better information about the firm's prospects than they do. Accordingly, they want the most secure position they can get in an admittedly risky venture. That often means that outsiders will insist on supplying their capital in the form of debt, so that they will have first claims on assets and income in the event that the founder's projections fail to materialize. However, as we have seen, lenders cannot achieve their desired results by forming portfolios of risky debt securities, because they do not share in upside gains beyond the stated interest rate.

How can lenders share in upside gains? The answer is to use convertibles or warrants, which are called "equity kickers" and which have no upside limitation. Note also that U.S. banks are prohibited from taking equity kickers; this helps explain why their participation in venture financing is limited.

Mezzanine Capital. As companies progress beyond the start-up phase, their capital often includes two or more layers of debt: senior debt, which is secured by assets, and subordinated debt, which is unsecured but which often includes an equity kicker. This second level of debt is called "mezzanine capital."

Private Placement. A private placement is any debt or equity issue that is not offered to the general public.

Seed Money. The initial capital required to start an entrepreneurial project is called "seed money." In AFC's case, this is the capital supplied by Dr. Aplin and his friends and relatives.

Venture Capital Networks. Computerized databases have been developed that contain profiles of ventures needing capital and profiles of private investors who are interested in providing venture capital. A computer program periodically compares all profiles of both types to determine if there are matches. If a match exists, the entrepreneur and the potential investor are introduced to see if a funding agreement can be reached.

Valuing Start-Up Firms

After explaining the different sources of start-up capital and some key terms, the investment banker stated that the next step should be to determine AFC's value, as this will be of interest to all potential investors. Five methods are commonly used to value the equity of a start-up firm.

Discounted Cash Flow Approach. The discounted cash flow approach recognizes that the value of a business is a function of the timing, riskiness, and amounts of cash flow that the business generates. Three steps are involved: (1) Historical financial data and current trends are used to forecast the firm's future cash flows to equityholders. In a start-up situation, the forecasting problem is complicated by a lack of historical data, which makes good judgment and market research very important. (2) A discount rate based on the riskiness of the cash flows must be determined. (3) The present value of the cash flows must be calculated to arrive at the equity value.

The discounted cash flow approach is the most comprehensive valuation technique, but for a start-up firm it has obvious weaknesses. Anyone with *Lotus 1-2-3* or some other spreadsheet can make forecasts and determine a firm's "value," but that value is no better than the forecasts. Therefore, investors also like to consider less refined, but possibly less subjective, valuation approaches.

Liquidation Value. This method determines the value if the business ceases operations and is liquidated. Liquidation value is calculated by first summing the estimated net selling prices that would be realized if each asset were sold individually. From this sum we subtract all existing liabilities, and the result is the liquidation value of the business to its equity investors. Included in liabilities are costs associated with liquidation, such as severance pay for terminated employees. The liquidation value method generally establishes the minimum worth of a business's equity. Additionally, lending institutions sometimes use the liquidation value of an individual asset to determine the amount that can be loaned using that asset as collateral.

Adjusted Tangible Book Value. This valuation method starts with the latest balance sheet. The book value of each account is adjusted upwards or downwards in order to arrive at its fair-market value. Adjustments are made to account for land appreciation, uncollectible accounts receivable, and obsolete inventories. Additionally, the values of intangible assets such as patents or goodwill and other assets or liabilities that are not on the books must be added. Once the adjusted book values have been established, total liabilities are subtracted from total assets to arrive at the business's adjusted tangible book value. This method is similar to the liquidation value method except that fair-market values are determined within the context of a continuing business.

Earnings Multiple Method. If historical income statements are available, if the past is likely to be indicative of the future, and if recent earnings are "normal" in the sense of not being relatively high or low because of temporary conditions, then one can use the earnings multiple method. First, find the price-to-earnings ratios (P/E ratios) of a group of public companies in the same industry and similar in size to the firm being valued. Data on companies that recently went public are especially useful for this purpose if such data are available. Based on comparisons of the company being valued and the public companies, judgment is used to establish a P/E ratio to apply to the company's earnings. For example, suppose a company is relatively stable and has averaged $200,000 in net income for the past three years, and a P/E of 5 is deemed appropriate. The value of the company's equity would be 5($200,000) = $1,000,000.

Replacement Value. This method requires a determination of the total cost that would be incurred if the business were to be reconstructed from scratch. The cost must include items such as land, buildings, and equipment, as well as marketing and advertising expenses associated with building a customer base. This method is most often used to value firms by companies seeking merger partners as an alternative to *de novo* expansion and by insurance companies to determine policy premiums. The firm's liabilities could be subtracted from the total replacement value to obtain the value of the equity.

Combination of Methods. Generally, more than one method is used to value a company. For example, an analyst might use the discounted cash flow and earnings multiple methods together with the replacement value method. These three values might be averaged, or greater weight might be placed on one method because of the circumstances. If it were known that a larger company wanted to make an acquisition in the industry, and the replacement valuation produced a relatively high value, then the analyst might assume that the company could be sold at close to its replacement value. Clearly, a great deal of judgment is required, and different experts will reach very different conclusions.[1]

At times, it is appropriate to analyze different groups of a firm's assets differently. For example, a steel company may have diversified outside of its core business (steel) into several different industries such as oil and chemicals. Analysts may conclude that the company's "break-up value" exceeds its value as a conglomerate corporation, and they might use the replacement value method to evaluate the chemical and oil divisions and the discounted cash flow method to evaluate the core steel business.

---

[1]For example, when Howard Hughes' Hughes Tool Company was about to go public, several investment banking firms bid on the job of making the public offering. The low bid was reported to have been about $18, while the winning bid was about $30. When sophisticated investment bankers evaluate stable, established companies in stable industries, the evaluations are generally close together. However, valuations of unique, specialized companies such as Hughes Tool or Microsoft, before their values have been established in the marketplace, are subject to wide variations.

Questions

A meeting has been scheduled next week wherein Dr. Aplin and AFC's accountant will discuss the company's plans with several bank commercial loan officers and venture capital fund representatives. He hopes to finalize AFC's financing arrangements at that time. In preparation for the meeting, Tables 1 and 2 were extracted from the business plan.

For Questions 1 through 3, assume you are a commercial-loan officer with a large regional bank.

1. What type of financing might your bank be willing to provide to AFC?

2. How would you as a banker go about preparing for your meeting with Dr. Aplin and his consultants?

3. Assume that you view AFC's venture positively and have decided to make a financing proposal for the equipment, land, and facilities. What valuation method would you use to decide how much to lend to AFC? Explain.

For Questions 4 through 9, assume that you are the manager of a venture capital fund, and that a bank is willing to lend $20 million of the $55 million financing requirement. The debt service requirements are $5, $5, $5, $5, and $10 million in Years 1 through 5, respectively. You are considering providing an equity investment for the remaining $35 million required by AFC.

4. List three question which you might ask Dr. Aplin in your meeting with him.

5. You have decided to use the discounted cash flow approach to value AFC. Based on the riskiness of the new business, you believe a 30 percent discount rate is appropriate, along with a 10 percent growth rate in equity cash flow in Year 6 and beyond. What is the forecasted value of AFC to its equity holders? (Hint: Use the cash flows in Table 2 as a starting point.)

6. What percentage of the common stock would you require in exchange for the needed $35 million? How likely is it that Dr. Aplin would be willing to offer you this percentage ownership of AFC?

7. Now assume that the estimated terminal growth rate is only 5 percent, and the bank is only willing to lend AFC $10 million?

Under these conditions, what is the smallest percentage of common stock you would require for your $45 million? Is it likely that Dr. Aplin be willing to give up this percentage ownership of AFC?

8. Use the earnings multiple method to estimate the value of AFC's equity. As a first pass, use the average projected earnings over the first five years as the best estimate of AFC's normalized earnings. Then assume the stocks of publicly traded firms with somewhat similar technologies sell at an average of 8 times earnings.

9. If you used the adjusted tangible book value method to value AFC, how would you determine the market value of the patent?

General questions.

10. In your opinion, what are the two most important segments of a business plan. Why?

11. If you had a promising idea for a business venture and wanted to acquire start-up capital, what steps would you take to attain the needed financial resources?

Table 1

Current Balance Sheet and New Capital Requirement

Current Balance Sheet			Capital Required (in Millions)
Cash	$ 1,000	Purchase of equipment	$10
Patent	400,000	Purchase of land	5
Total assets	$401,000	Construction	35
		Working capital	5
Accounts payable	$ 1,000	Total requirement	$55
Loans from friends			
and relatives	$250,000		
Total liabilities	$251,000		
Common stock	100		
Additional paid-in			
capital	149,900		
Total liabilities			
and equity	$401,000		

Table 2

Projected Cash Flow Statements
(In Millions of Dollars)

	Year 1	Year 2	Year 3	Year 4	Year 5
Sales	$ 20	$ 53	$102	$117	$129
Cost of goods sold	10	26	51	59	65
Gross margin	$ 10	$ 27	$ 51	$ 58	$ 64
General/administra-					
tive expenses	5	10	19	23	25
Debt service	5	5	5	5	10
Pre-tax income	$ 0	$ 12	$ 27	$ 30	$ 29
Taxes	0	5	12	13	14
Net income	$ 0	$ 7	$ 15	$ 17	$ 15
Depreciation/					
amortization	2	6	6	6	6
Terminal value					116
Net cash flow	$ 2	$ 13	$ 21	$ 23	$137

Notes:

(a) Depreciation/amortization expense is included in the cost of goods sold, yet it is a noncash charge. Thus, it must be added back to net income to obtain the net cash flow in each year.

(b) The terminal value is the present value, as of the end of Year 5, of the equity cash flows that are expected to occur after Year 5. This value was obtained by assuming 10 percent annual growth in equity cash flows after Year 5 and a cost of equity of 30 percent:

$$\text{Terminal value} = \frac{\$21(1.10)}{0.30 - 0.10} = \$116.$$